PLANNING GUIDE

Houghton Mifflin Harcourt

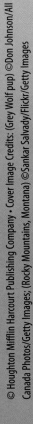

GO MATH!

Printed in the U.S.A.

ISBN 978-0-544-29331-1

8 9 10 11 12 13 14 0029 23 22 21 20 19 18 17 16
4500602322 C D E F G

Table of Contents

PROGRAM OVERVIEW

About *GO Math!*

Planning Resources

END-OF-YEAR RESOURCES

Review Projects

Getting Ready for Grade 2

These lessons review prerequisite skills and prepare for next year's content.

CORRELATIONS

It's Common Core Math

GO Math! for Kindergarten-Grade 6 combines powerful teaching strategies with never-before-seen components to offer everything needed to successfully teach and learn the Common Core State Standards.

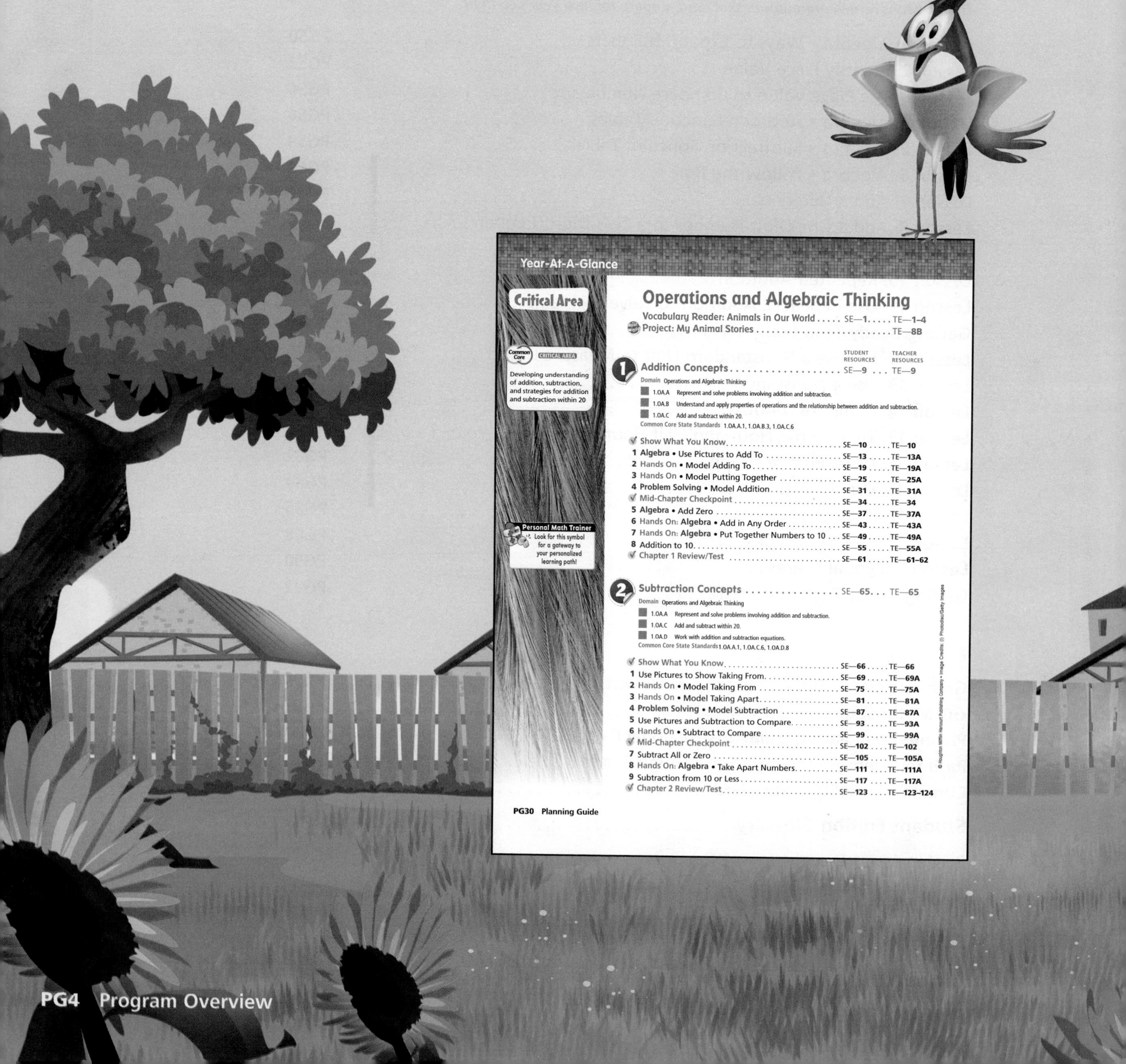

Year-At-A-Glance

Critical Area

Common Core CRITICAL AREA

Developing understanding of addition, subtraction, and strategies for addition and subtraction within 20

Operations and Algebraic Thinking

Vocabulary Reader: Animals in Our World ..... SE—**1**..... TE—**1–4**
Project: My Animal Stories ..... TE—**8B**

	STUDENT RESOURCES	TEACHER RESOURCES
1 Addition Concepts	SE—**9**	TE—**9**

Domain Operations and Algebraic Thinking
- 1.OA.A Represent and solve problems involving addition and subtraction.
- 1.OA.B Understand and apply properties of operations and the relationship between addition and subtraction.
- 1.OA.C Add and subtract within 20.

Common Core State Standards 1.OA.A.1, 1.OA.B.3, 1.OA.C.6

Show What You Know	SE—**10**	TE—**10**
1 Algebra • Use Pictures to Add To	SE—**13**	TE—**13A**
2 Hands On • Model Adding To	SE—**19**	TE—**19A**
3 Hands On • Model Putting Together	SE—**25**	TE—**25A**
4 Problem Solving • Model Addition	SE—**31**	TE—**31A**
Mid-Chapter Checkpoint	SE—**34**	TE—**34**
5 Algebra • Add Zero	SE—**37**	TE—**37A**
6 Hands On: Algebra • Add in Any Order	SE—**43**	TE—**43A**
7 Hands On: Algebra • Put Together Numbers to 10	SE—**49**	TE—**49A**
8 Addition to 10	SE—**55**	TE—**55A**
Chapter 1 Review/Test	SE—**61**	TE—**61–62**

Personal Math Trainer
Look for this symbol for a gateway to your personalized learning path!

2 Subtraction Concepts	SE—**65**	TE—**65**

Domain Operations and Algebraic Thinking
- 1.OA.A Represent and solve problems involving addition and subtraction.
- 1.OA.C Add and subtract within 20.
- 1.OA.D Work with addition and subtraction equations.

Common Core State Standards 1.OA.A.1, 1.OA.C.6, 1.OA.D.8

Show What You Know	SE—**66**	TE—**66**
1 Use Pictures to Show Taking From	SE—**69**	TE—**69A**
2 Hands On • Model Taking From	SE—**75**	TE—**75A**
3 Hands On • Model Taking Apart	SE—**81**	TE—**81A**
4 Problem Solving • Model Subtraction	SE—**87**	TE—**87A**
5 Use Pictures and Subtraction to Compare	SE—**93**	TE—**93A**
6 Hands On • Subtract to Compare	SE—**99**	TE—**99A**
Mid-Chapter Checkpoint	SE—**102**	TE—**102**
7 Subtract All or Zero	SE—**105**	TE—**105A**
8 Hands On: Algebra • Take Apart Numbers	SE—**111**	TE—**111A**
9 Subtraction from 10 or Less	SE—**117**	TE—**117A**
Chapter 2 Review/Test	SE—**123**	TE—**123–124**

PG30 Planning Guide

that's perfect for 21st century students.

In the ***GO Math!*** classroom, teachers and students can choose a print-based approach, an online approach, or a blended learning approach. In each case, the focus is on the major work of the grade. The ***GO Math!*** team of authors carefully developed a coherent K–12 progression to help students connect concepts across and within grade levels. Whether you choose print or digital pathways, you'll find the rigor required for success with the Common Core.

Math on the Spot videos, available for every lesson in *GO Math!*, support teachers and students, within the classroom and at home.

Math on the Spot

Math on the Spot
There are 14 sheep in the flock.
5 sheep run away.
How many sheep are left?
Subtract 4 to get to 10

A way of thinking about learning

GO Math! helps students engage with the standards and practices in new ways. Lessons begin with problem-based situations and then build to more abstract problems. All along the way, students use multiple models, manipulatives, quick pictures, and symbols to build mathematical understanding. Best of all, ***GO Math!*** is write-in at every grade level, so students are completely engaged.

GO Math! reflects
what is at the heart of the
Common Core Standards,
FOCUS COHERENCE RIGOR

that truly prepares students for the Common Core Assessments.

GO Math! works! Using manipulatives, multiple models, and rich, rigorous questions, students move through a carefully-sequenced arc of learning. They develop deep conceptual understanding, and then they practice, apply, and discuss what they know with skill and confidence. The equal emphases on understanding, procedural skills and fluency, and application help turn students into problem solvers and critical thinkers.

Digital resources to help personalize learning for students . . .

The Interactive Student Edition offers an alternate way to access grade-level content with audio, video, and animation. Our unique Personal Math Trainer® Powered by Knewton™ is embedded in the Interactive Student Edition to support students as they develop understanding. The Personal Math Trainer is a state-of-the-art, adaptive assessment and intervention system. In this tablet-based, mobile, and online environment, students receive a completely-personalized learning experience, focused on in-depth understanding, fluency, and application of standards.

and the HMH Player app to help teachers with planning, instruction, and collaboration.

With the HMH Player app, teachers and students can access the Interactive Student Edition while connected to the Internet from tablets, laptops, or desktop computers. They can download Personal Math Trainer assignments and content to their devices for offline access at any time. In addition, HMH Player includes powerful presentation tools for teachers and collaboration tools that keep teachers and students connected.

Create daily lesson plans with a single search.

Works in both online and offline environments.

Organize resources quickly.

See a snapshot of recent student report data.

Grab-and-Go Resources,

GO Math! works for the busy teacher. Everything from Teacher Editions to activity centers to manipulatives are organized in a ready-made, grab-and-go way to save you time.

GO Math! Teacher Editions are color-coded by Critical Area and organized by chapter to help teachers quickly identify materials and flexibly organize their curriculum. In addition, color coding is used to identify content as major, supporting, or additional work, providing teachers with a simple system to quickly identify and emphasize the most important grade-level material. The ***GO Math!*** classroom focuses on developing in-depth understanding and fosters communication within an engaging, inclusive environment.

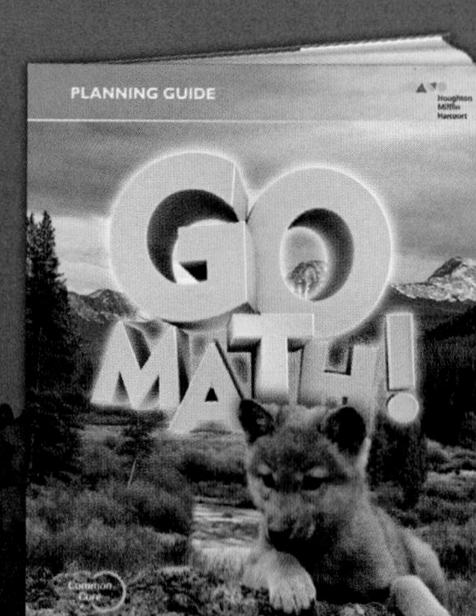

perfect for the busy teacher.

The Grab-and-Go Differentiated Centers Kits are ready-made differentiated math centers with activities, games, and literature. Resources for every lesson and special challenge materials make the Grab-and-Go Kits the perfect resource for independent practice.

GO DIGITAL Digital Resources

FOR LEARNING...

Interactive Student Edition

- Immerses students in an interactive, multi-sensory math environment
- Enhances learning with scaffolded, interactive instruction and just-in-time feedback
- Provides audio reinforcement for each lesson
- Makes learning a two-way experience, using a variety of interactive tools

FOR ASSESSMENT AND INTERVENTION...

Personal Math Trainer

- Creates a personalized learning path for each student
- Provides opportunities for practice, homework, and assessment
- Includes worked-out examples and helpful video support
- Offers targeted intervention and extra support to build proficiency and understanding

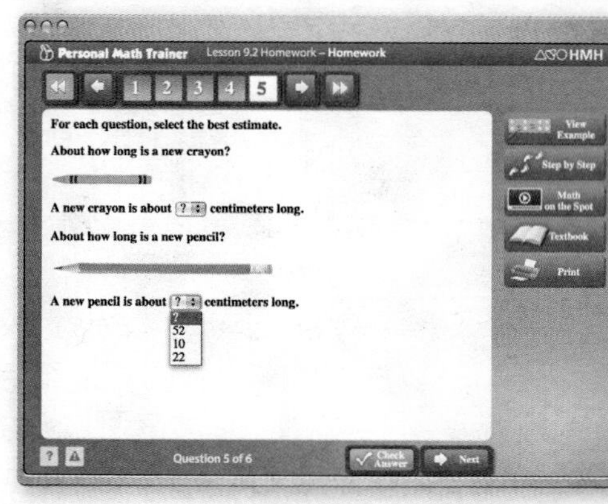

FOR DAILY MATH TUTORING...

Math on the Spot Videos

- Models good problem-solving thinking in every lesson
- Engages students through interesting animations and fun characters
- Builds student problem-solving proficiency and confidence
- Builds the skills needed for success on the Common Core Assessments

FOR SIMPLICITY...

HMH Player App

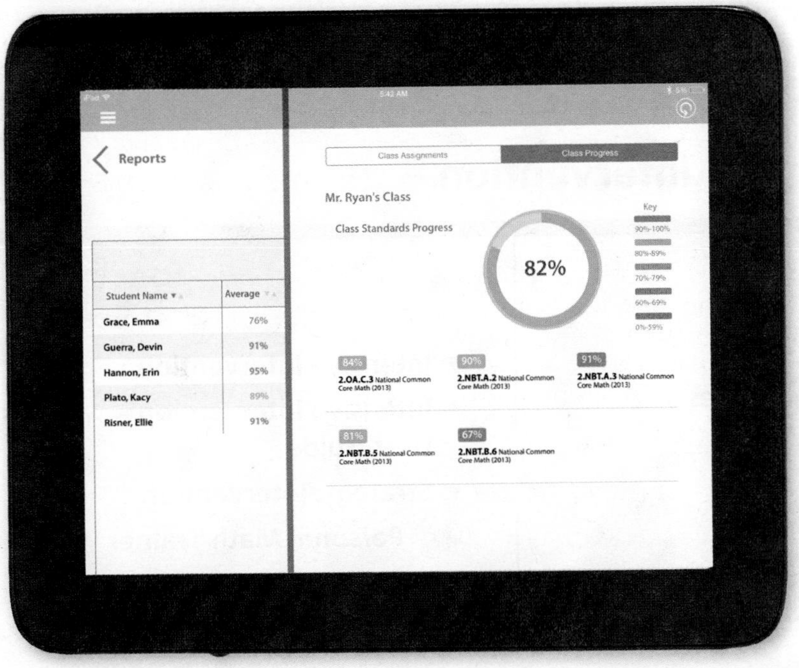

It's For Students ...

- Content is available online, offline, and on-the-go!
- Students are engaged in class, at home, and anywhere in between for uninterrupted instruction
- Raise a Hand for instant student-teacher-student communication

... And For Teachers!

- Teachers can monitor student progress in real time
- Lesson customization features allow teachers to deliver personalized learning
- Plan your lessons, make assignments, and view results from the convenience of your classroom, at home, or on-the-go
- Supports blended learning through anywhere digital instruction

FOR TEACHING...

Digital Management System

- Manage online all program content and components
- Search for and select resources based on Common Core State Standards
- Identify resources based on student ability and needs
- View and assign student lessons, practice, assessments, and more

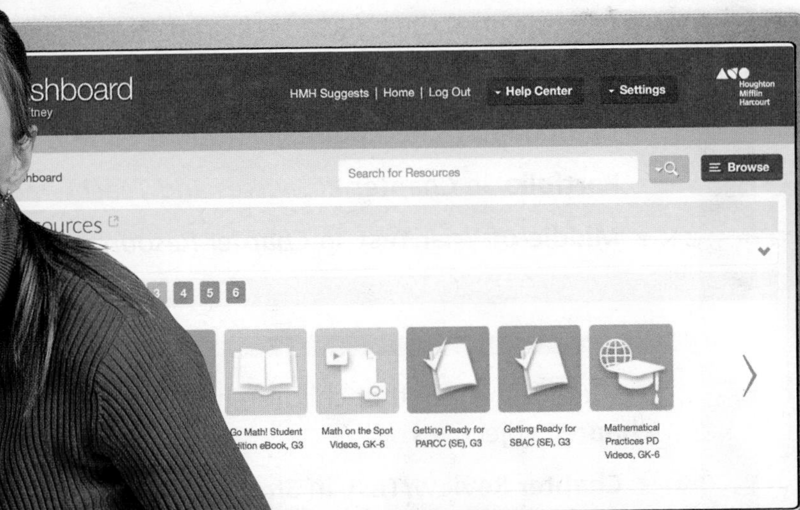

Professional Development Videos

- Learn more about the Common Core and Common Core content
- See first-hand the integration of the Mathematical Practices
- Watch students engaged in a productive struggle

Assessment ➡ Diagnosis ➡ Intervention

Data-Driven Decision Making

GO Math! allows for quick and accurate data-driven decision making so you can spend more instructional time tailored to children's needs.

Program Assessment Options with Intervention

Diagnostic

To allow children to be engaged from the beginning of the year

- **Prerequisite Skills Inventory** in *Chapter Resources*
- **Beginning-of-Year Test** in *Chapter Resources*
- **Show What You Know** in *Student Edition*

RtI

- **Intensive Intervention**
- **Intensive Intervention User Guide**
- **Strategic Intervention**
- **Personal Math Trainer**

Formative

To monitor children's understanding of lessons and to adjust instruction accordingly

- **Lesson Quick Check** in *Teacher Edition*
- **Lesson Practice** in *Student Edition*
- **Mid-Chapter Checkpoint** in *Student Edition*
- **Portfolio** in *Chapter Resources and Teacher Edition*
- **Middle-of-Year Test** in *Chapter Resources*

RtI

- **Reteach** with each lesson
- **RtI: Tier 1 and Tier 2 Activities** online
- **Personal Math Trainer**

Summative

To determine whether children have achieved the chapter objectives

- **Chapter Review/Test** in *Student Edition*
- **Chapter Test** in *Chapter Resources* (Common Core assessment format tests)
- **Performance Assessment Task** in *Chapter Resources*
- **End-of-Year Test** in *Chapter Resources*
- **Getting Ready for Grade 2 Test** in *Getting Ready Lessons and Resources*

RtI

- **Reteach** with each lesson
- **RtI: Tier 1 and Tier 2 Activities** online
- **Personal Math Trainer**

Tracking Yearly Progress

Beginning of the Year	During the Year	End of the Year
The Beginning-of-Year Test determines how many of this year's Common Core standards students already understand. Adjust lesson pacing for skills that need light coverage and allow more time for skills students find challenging.	Chapter Tests, Performance Assessments, and the Middle-of-Year Test monitor students' progress throughout the year. Plan time to reinforce skills students have not mastered.	The End-of-Year Test assesses students' mastery of this year's Common Core standards. Reinforce skills that students find challenging in order to provide the greatest possible success.

Performance Assessment

Performance Assessment helps to reveal the thinking strategies students use to solve problems. The Performance Tasks in *GO Math!* can be used to complete the picture for how students reason about mathematics.

GO Math! has a Performance Task for each Chapter and Critical Area. Each task has several parts that target specific math concepts, skills, and strategies. These tasks can help assess students' ability to use what they have learned to solve everyday problems. Teachers can plan for students to complete one task at a time or use an extended amount of time to complete the entire assessment. Projects for each Critical Area also serve to assess students' problem solving strategies and understanding of mathematical concepts they learn in the Critical Area.

Augmenting the Performance Tasks are a series of professional development videos featuring author Juli Dixon. Working with students, Juli models effective teaching and assessment practices. Additionally, each video provides insight into the dynamics of the classroom and how to use tasks not only to assess progress, but also to deepen understanding.

The Performance Tasks and Critical Area Projects offer the following features:

- They model good instruction.
- They are flexible.
- They are diagnostic.
- They use authentic instruction.
- They encourage the thinking process.
- They are scored holistically.

GO Math! Personal Math Trainer® Powered by Knewton™

- Online and adaptive homework, assessment, practice, and intervention engine
- Algorithmic, tech-enhanced items with wrong-answer feedback and learning aids
- Pre-built assignments that can generate personalized warm-ups, enrichment, or intervention

Authors

Edward B. Burger, Ph.D.
President, Southwestern University
Georgetown, Texas

Juli K. Dixon, Ph.D.
Professor, Mathematics Education
University of Central Florida
Orlando, Florida

Matthew R. Larson, Ph.D.
K-12 Curriculum Specialist for Mathematics
Lincoln Public Schools
Lincoln, Nebraska

Martha E. Sandoval-Martinez
Math Instructor
El Camino College
Torrance, California

Steven J. Leinwand
Principal Research Analyst
American Institutes for Research (AIR)
Washington, D.C.

Contributor and Consultant

Rena Petrello
Professor, Mathematics
Moorpark College
Moorpark, CA

Elizabeth Jiménez
CEO, GEMAS Consulting
Professional Expert on English Learner Education
Bilingual Education and Dual Language
Pomona, California

GO Math! Reviewers and Field Test Teachers

Janine L. Ambrose
Instructional Coach
Grades Taught: K–7
Sunset Ridge Elementary
Pendergast Elementary School District
Phoenix, Arizona

Patricia R. Barbour
Teacher: Grade 2
Sara Lindemuth Primary School
Susquehanna Township School District
Harrisburg, Pennsylvania

Pamela Bauer
Speech/Language Pathologist, M.A., CCC/SLP
Special School District of St. Louis County
Kindergarten Interventionist
Arrowpoint Elementary
Hazelwood, Missouri

James Brohn
Principal
Morning Star Lutheran School
Jackson, Wisconsin

Earl S. Brown
Teacher: Middle School Math
Susquehanna Township Middle School
Susquehanna Township School District
Harrisburg, Pennsylvania

Rebecca Centerino
Teacher: Grade 1
Zitzman Elementary
Meramec Valley RIII School District
Pacific, Missouri

Jessica Z. Jacobs
Assistant Principal
Thomas Holtzman Junior Elementary School
Susquehanna Township School District
Harrisburg, Pennsylvania

Tonya Leonard
Teacher: Grade 3
Peine Ridge Elementary
Wentzville RIV School District
Wentzville, Missouri

Jennifer Love Frier
Teacher: Grade 1
Olathe School District
Olathe, Kansas

Michelle Mieger
Teacher: Grade 3
Cedar Springs Elementary
Northwest R-1
House Springs, Missouri

Jeanne K. Selissen
Teacher: Grade 4
Tewksbury School District
Tewksbury, Massachusetts

Jo Ellen Showers
Teacher: Grade K
Sara Lindemuth Primary School
Susquehanna Township School District
Harrisburg, Pennsylvania

Judith M. Stagoski
Grades Taught: 5–8
District: Archdiocese of St. Louis
St. Louis, Missouri

Pauline Von Hoffer
Grades Taught: 4–12
Curriculum Coordinator
Wentzville School District
Wentzville, Missouri

Content Standards

PROFESSIONAL DEVELOPMENT

by Matthew R. Larson, Ph.D.
K-12 Curriculum Specialist for Mathematics
Lincoln Public Schools
Lincoln, Nebraska

Why Common Core State Standards for Mathematics?

The Common Core State Standards Initiative was a state-led process initiated by the Council of Chief State School Officers (CCSSO) and The National Governors Association (NGA). The goal was to create a set of Career and College Readiness Standards in mathematics (and English/Language Arts) so that all students graduate from high school ready for college and/or work. The K–8 standards outline a grade-by-grade roadmap to prepare students for the Career and College Readiness Standards.

Two primary concerns motivated the Common Core State Standards Initiative. First, inconsistent curricular standards, assessments, and proficiency cut scores across the 50 states raised equity issues (Reed, 2009). These different systems often led to wide disparities between student scores on state assessments in reading and math compared to student performance on the National Assessment of Educational Progress (Schneider, 2007). Second, U.S. students are not leaving school with skills necessary for success in college or the workforce. Results of international assessments, including *PISA* (Baldi, Jin, Skemer, Green, & Herget, 2007) and *TIMSS* (Gonzales, Williams, Jocelyn, Roey, Kastberg, & Brenwald, 2008) indicate that U.S. students do not achieve in mathematics at the level of students in other countries. This raises concern about U.S. economic competitiveness in an environment where U.S. students compete with students all across the globe.

Organization of the Common Core State Standards for Mathematics

The *Common Core State Standards for Mathematics* are organized into content standards and standards for mathematical practice. The content standards are addressed in this article.

The content standards have three levels of organization. The standards define what students should understand and be able to do. These standards are organized into clusters of related standards to emphasize mathematical connections. Finally, domains represent larger groups of related standards. The development and grade placement of standards considered research-based learning progressions with respect to how students' mathematical knowledge develops over time. At the elementary (K–6) level, there are ten content domains. Each grade addresses four or five domains.

Domain	Grade Level
Counting and Cardinality	K
Operations and Algebraic Thinking	K, 1, 2, 3, 4, 5
Number and Operations in Base Ten	K, 1, 2, 3, 4, 5
Measurement and Data	K, 1, 2, 3, 4, 5
Geometry	K, 1, 2, 3, 4, 5, 6
Number and Operations—Fractions	3, 4, 5
Ratios and Proportional Relationships	6
The Number System	6
Expressions and Equations	6
Statistics and Probability	6

Within each grade, each cluster (and the standards within each cluster) is considered to represent the major work of the grade, supplemental work, or additional work. Within the *Planning and Pacing Guide Instructional Path* in this *Planning Guide*, each lesson is color-coded to indicate whether the lesson is addressing the major work, the content that is supplemental, or the content that is additional.

While the total number of standards in the *Common Core* is generally less than the number of standards in many current state standard documents (NCTM, 2005; Reys, Chval, Dingman, McNaught, Regis, & Togashi, 2007), the emphasis in the *Common Core* is not simply on a list with fewer standards, but on a list that is also more specific and clear.

Critical Areas

The *Common Core* also specifies critical areas for instructional emphasis at each grade level. These areas are shown below.

Grade	Critical Areas
K	• Representing, relating, and operating on whole numbers initially with sets of objects • Describing shapes and space
1	• Developing understanding of addition, subtraction, and strategies for addition and subtraction within 20 • Developing understanding of whole number relationships and place value, including grouping in tens and ones • Developing understanding of linear measurement and measuring lengths as iterating length units • Reasoning about attributes of, and composing and decomposing geometric shapes
2	• Extending understanding of base-ten notation • Building fluency with addition and subtraction • Using standard units of measure • Describing and analyzing shapes
3	• Developing understanding of multiplication and division and strategies for multiplication and division within 100 • Developing understanding of fractions, especially unit fractions • Developing understanding of the structure of rectangular arrays and of area • Describing and analyzing two-dimensional shapes
4	• Developing understanding and fluency with multi-digit multiplication, and developing understanding of dividing to find quotients involving multi-digit dividends • Developing an understanding of fraction equivalence, addition and subtraction of fractions with like denominators, and multiplication of fractions by whole numbers • Understanding that geometric figures can be analyzed and classified based on their properties, such as having parallel sides, perpendicular sides, particular angle measures, and symmetry
5	• Developing fluency with addition and subtraction of fractions, and developing understanding of the multiplication of fractions and of division of fractions in limited cases (unit fractions divided by whole numbers and whole numbers divided by unit fractions) • Extending division to 2-digit divisors, integrating decimal fractions into the place value system and developing understanding of operations with decimals to hundredths, and developing fluency with whole number and decimal operations • Developing understanding of volume.
6	• Connecting ratio and rate to whole number multiplication and division and using concepts of ratio and rate to solve problems • Completing understanding of division of fractions and extending the notion of number to the system of rational numbers, which includes negative numbers • Writing, interpreting, and using expressions and equations • Developing understanding of statistical thinking

This design permits instruction in each grade to focus on fewer concepts and skills in greater depth, while simultaneously building a foundation for the next grade. For example, in the *Common Core,* fractions are not a significant focus of the curriculum until third grade; although, students decompose two-dimensional figures in previous grades to develop a foundation for fractions in third grade. Similarly, probability is delayed until the middle grades in the *Common Core*.

The *Common Core* states that "mathematical understanding and procedural skill are equally important," but stresses conceptual understanding of key ideas and organizing principles, to structure essential big ideas. Similar to other recent recommendations (NCTM, 2000; NMAP, 2008), this emphasis on conceptual understanding and procedural skill, along with the standards for mathematical practice calls for a balanced approach to mathematics instruction and the curriculum.

Common Core State Standards for Mathematics and *GO Math!*

Nearly all content standards today, whether articulated by a state, NCTM, or the *Common Core,* share one thing in common: they call for a more focused and coherent curriculum that treats topics in a manner that will enable students to develop deep understanding of the content. *GO Math!* espouses this emphasis on a focused and coherent curriculum that teaches for depth of understanding to help students learn.

All standards documents share one additional feature: alone they are not enough to ensure that students achieve at higher levels (Fuhrman, Resnick, & Shepard, 2009). In *GO Math!*, the *Common Core State Standards* are merely the starting point. *GO Math!* represents a comprehensive system of mathematics instruction that provides teachers the tools they need to help students succeed with more focused and rigorous mathematics standards. Research-based *GO Math!* includes multiple instructional approaches, diagnostic assessments linked to differentiated instructional resources and tiered interventions, along with technology solutions to support and motivate students.

Standards for Mathematical Practice

PROFESSIONAL DEVELOPMENT

by Juli K. Dixon, Ph.D.
Professor, Mathematics Education
University of Central Florida
Orlando, Florida

Developing Processes and Proficiencies in Mathematics Learners

There are eight mathematical practices. They are based on the National Council of Teachers of Mathematics' (NCTM) Process Standards (NCTM, 2000) and the National Research Council's (NRC) Strands of Mathematical Proficiency (NRC, 2001).

It is likely that good teachers can find evidence of each of these standards for mathematical practice in their current teaching. Regardless, it is useful to examine them and think about how each contributes to the development of mathematically proficient students.

Throughout *GO Math!*, the Mathematical Practices incorporated within a lesson are identified in the Student Edition and the Teacher Edition. In some instances, a lesson will focus on a part of a practice—this approach will break apart the standard in such a way as to support in-depth understanding of the practice and over time will aid students in attending to the full meaning of the practice.

What follows is a description of how they might look in an elementary school classroom. Each of these examples is reflective of experiences supported by *GO Math!*

GO Math! supports the Standards for Mathematical Practice through several specific features including:

- Lessons focused on depth of content knowledge
- Unlock the Problem sections to begin lessons
- Math Talk questions prompting students to use varied strategies and to explain their reasoning
- Explicit use of specific practices within a lesson, with accompanying point-of-use teacher support
- Support for manipulative use and drawings directly on the student pages
- Prompts that lead students to write their own problems or to determine if the reasoning of others is reasonable
- Real-world problems that encourage students to develop productive dispositions

Practice 1: Make sense of problems and persevere in solving them.

This practice brings to mind developing a productive disposition as described in *Adding It Up* (NRC, 2001). In order for students to develop the diligence intended with this practice, they must be provided with problems for which a pathway toward a solution is not immediately evident. If students are asked to determine how much of a cookie each person would receive if 4 cookies were shared among 5 people, a solution pathway is evident if students understand fractions. The students could simply divide each cookie into five equal pieces and give each person one fifth of each cookie or $\frac{4}{5}$ of a cookie in all. Now, consider the same problem given the constraint that the first three cookies are each broken into two equal pieces to start and each person is given half of a cookie.

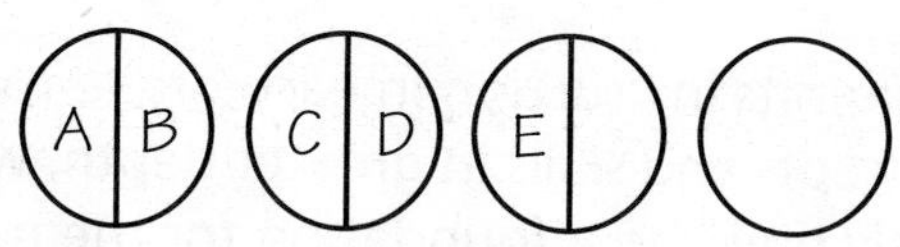

The problem is now more interesting and challenging. How will the remaining pieces of cookies be distributed among the five people? How will the students determine how much of a cookie each person has in all when all the cookies are shared? The students will likely refer back to the context of the problem to make sense of how to solve it, they will also very likely use pictures in their solution process. A solution is within reach but it will require diligence to persevere in reaching it.

Practice 2: Reason abstractly and quantitatively.

Story problems provide important opportunities for young learners to make sense of mathematics around them. Students often use strategies including acting out the problem to make sense of a solution path. Another important strategy is for students to make sense of the problem situation by determining a number sentence that could represent the problem and then solving it in a mathematically proficient way. Consider the following problem: *Jessica has 7 key chains in her collection. How many more does she need to have 15 key chains all together?*

A child is presented with this problem, but rather than focusing on key words, the child uses the story to make sense of a solution process. The child knows to start with 7 then add something to that to get 15. The child represents this story abstractly by writing $7 + \_\_\_ = 15$. Then the child reasons quantitatively by thinking $7 + 3 = 10$ and $10 + 5 = 15$ so $7 + 8$ must equal 15 (because 3 and 5 are 8). The child then returns to the problem to see if a solution of 8 key chains makes sense. In doing so, the child makes "sense of quantities and their relationships in problem situations" (NGA Center/CCSSO, 2010, p. 6).

Practice 3: Construct viable arguments and critique the reasoning of others.

Students need to explain and justify their solution strategies. They should also listen to the explanations of other students and try to make sense of them. They will then be able to incorporate the reasoning of others into their own strategies and improve upon their own solutions. An example of this follows.

A group of students explores formulas for areas of quadrilaterals. Students make sense of the formula for the area of a parallelogram as $b \times h$ by decomposing parallelograms and composing a rectangle with the same area. Following this exploration, a student conjectures that the formula for the area of the trapezoid is also $b \times h$. The student draws this picture and says that the trapezoid can be "turned into" a rectangle with the same base by "moving one triangle over to the other side."

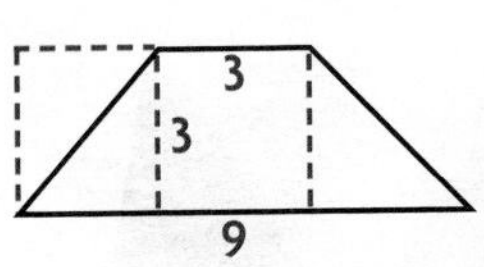

This student has constructed a viable argument based on a special type of trapezoid. Another student agrees that this formula works for an isosceles trapezoid but asks if it will also work for a general trapezoid. This second student has made sense of the reasoning of the first student and asked a question to help improve the argument.

Practice 4: Model with mathematics.

Children need opportunities to use mathematics to solve real-world problems. As students learn more mathematics, the ways they model situations with mathematics should become more efficient. Consider the problem: *Riley has 4 blue erasers, Alex has 4 yellow erasers, and Paige has 4 purple erasers. How many erasers do they have in all?* A young child would likely model this problem with $4 + 4 + 4$. However, a mathematically proficient student in third grade should model the same situation with 3×4. This demonstrates how modeling will evolve through a child's experiences in mathematics and will change as their understanding grows.

A useful strategy for making sense of mathematics is for students to develop real-life contexts to correspond to mathematical expressions. This supports the reflexive relationship that if a student can write a word problem for a given expression, then the student can model a similar word problem with mathematics. Consider $\frac{4}{5} - \frac{1}{2}$. If a student is able to create a word problem to support this fraction subtraction, then, given a word problem, the student is more likely to be able to model the word problem with mathematics and solve it.

Practice 5: Use appropriate tools strategically.

At first glance, one might think that this practice refers to technological tools exclusively, however, tools also include paper and pencil, number lines and manipulatives (or concrete models). Mathematically proficient students are able to determine which tool to use for a given task. An example to illustrate this practice involves multiplying fractions. A student might choose to use a number line for one problem and paper and pencil procedures for another. If presented the problem $\frac{1}{3} \times \frac{3}{4}$, a mathematically proficient student might draw a number line and divide the distance from 0 to 1 into 4 equal parts drawing a darker line through the first three fourths. That student would see that $\frac{1}{3}$ of the $\frac{3}{4}$ is $\frac{1}{4}$ of the whole.

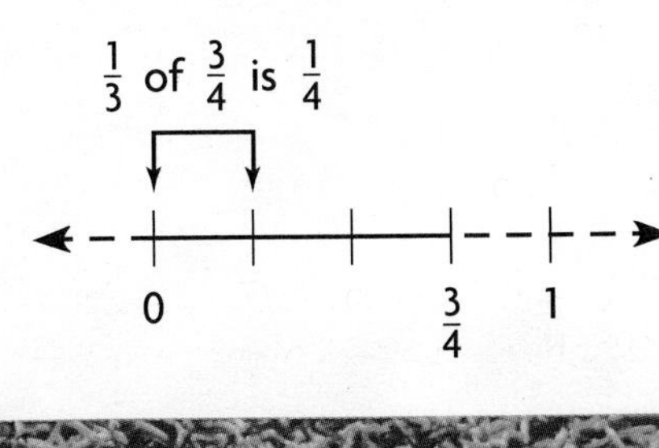

However, the same student presented with the problem $\frac{1}{3} \times \frac{4}{7}$ might not use a drawing at all but might find it more efficient to multiply the numerators and the denominators of the factors to get $\frac{4}{21}$ as the product. Both solution paths illustrate strategic use of tools for the given problems.

Practice 6: Attend to precision.

An important aspect of precision in mathematics is developed through the language used to describe it. This can be illustrated with definitions of geometric shapes. A kindergarten child is not expected to classify quadrilaterals. However, it is appropriate for a kindergarten child to name and describe shapes including squares and rectangles. Teachers seeking to support kindergarten children to attend to precision will include squares within sets of other rectangles so that these children will not use the language that all rectangles have two long sides and two short sides. These same students will be more likely to be able to correctly classify squares and rectangles in third grade because of this attention to precision when they are in kindergarten.

Practice 7: Look for and make use of structure.

Students who have made sense of strategies based on properties for finding products of single digit factors (basic facts) will be more likely to apply those properties when exploring multidigit multiplication. Consider the importance of the distributive property in looking for and making use of structure in this case. A student who has made sense of 6×7 by solving 6×5 and 6×2 has used a strategy based on the distributive property where 6×7 can be thought of as $6 \times (5 + 2)$ and then the 6 can be "distributed over" the 5 and 2. This same student can apply the distributive property to make sense of 12×24 by thinking of 24 as $20 + 4$ and solving $12 \times 20 + 12 \times 4$. A student who can make sense of multidigit multiplication in this way is on a good path to making sense of the structure of the standard algorithm for multidigit multiplication.

Practice 8: Look for and express regularity in repeated reasoning.

Whether performing simple calculations or solving complex problems, students should take advantage of the regularity of mathematics. If students who are exploring the volume of right rectangular prisms are given centimeter cubes and grid paper, they can build a prism with a given base and explore how the volume changes as the height of the prism increases. Students who look for ways to describe the change should see that the height of the prism is a factor of the volume of the prism and that if the area of the base is known, the volume of the prism is determined by multiplying the area of the base by the height of the prism. Identifying this pattern and repeated reasoning will help students build an understanding of the formula for the volume of right rectangular prisms.

As evidenced by the examples of mathematical practices in elementary school classrooms, "a lack of understanding effectively prevents a student from engaging in the mathematical practices" (NGA Center/CCSSO, 2010, p. 8). Teachers address this challenge by focusing on mathematical practices while developing an understanding of the content they support. In so doing, this process facilitates the development of mathematically proficient students.

Supporting Mathematical Practices Through Questioning

When you ask...	Students...
• What is the problem asking? • How will you use that information? • What other information do you need? • Why did you choose that operation? • What is another way to solve that problem? • What did you do first? Why? • What can you do if you don't know how to solve a problem? • Have you solved a problem similar to this one? • When did you realize your first method would not work for this problem? • How do you know your answer makes sense?	**MP1** Make sense of problems and persevere in solving them.
• What is a situation that could be represented by this equation? • What operation did you use to represent the situation? • Why does that operation represent the situation? • What properties did you use to find the answer? • How do you know your answer is reasonable?	**MP2** Reason abstractly and quantitatively.
• Will that method always work? • How do you know? • What do you think about what she said? • Who can tell us about a different method? • What do you think will happen if...? • When would that not be true? • Why do you agree/disagree with what he said? • What do you want to ask her about that method? • How does that drawing support your work?	**MP3** Construct viable arguments and critique the reasoning of others.
• Why is that a good model for this problem? • How can you use a simpler problem to help you find the answer? • What conclusions can you make from your model? • How would you change your model if...?	**MP4** Model with mathematics.
• What could you use to help you solve the problem? • What strategy could you use to make that calculation easier? • How would estimation help you solve that problem? • Why did you decide to use...?	**MP5** Use appropriate tools strategically.
• How do you know your answer is reasonable? • How can you use math vocabulary in your explanation? • How do you know those answers are equivalent? • What does that mean?	**MP6** Attend to precision.
• How did you discover that pattern? • What other patterns can you find? • What rule did you use to make this group? • Why can you use that property in this problem? • How is that like...?	**MP7** Look for and make use of structure.
• What do you remember about...? • What happens when...? • What if you... instead of...? • What might be a shortcut for...?	**MP8** Look for and express regularity in repeated reasoning.

For the full text of the Standards for Mathematical Practices, see *Mathematical Practices in GO Math!* in the *Planning Guide*.

STANDARDS FOR MATHEMATICAL PRACTICES
Mathematical Practices in *GO Math!*

Mathematical Practices	Throughout *GO Math!* Look for...	Explanation
1. **Make sense of problems and persevere in solving them.** Mathematically proficient students start by explaining to themselves the meaning of a problem and looking for entry points to its solution. They analyze givens, constraints, relationships, and goals. They make conjectures about the form and meaning of the solution and plan a solution pathway rather than simply jumping into a solution attempt. They consider analogous problems, and try special cases and simpler forms of the original problem in order to gain insight into its solution. They monitor and evaluate their progress and change course if necessary. Older students might, depending on the context of the problem, transform algebraic expressions or change the viewing window on their graphing calculator to get the information they need. Mathematically proficient students can explain correspondences between equations, verbal descriptions, tables, and graphs or draw diagrams of important features and relationships, graph data, and search for regularity or trends. Younger students might rely on using concrete objects or pictures to help conceptualize and solve a problem. Mathematically proficient students check their answers to problems using a different method, and they continually ask themselves, "Does this make sense?" They can understand the approaches of others to solving complex problems and identify correspondences between different approaches.	**Some Examples:** **Problem Solving Lessons** Grade K, Lesson 1.9 Grade 1, Lesson 8.8 Grade 2, Lesson 1.7 **Unlock the Problem** Grade K, Lesson 2.4 Grade 1, Lesson 3.12 Grade 2, Lesson 6.6	**Children learn to:** • analyze a problem. • explain what information they need to find to solve the problem. • determine what information they need to use to solve the problem. • develop a plan for solving the problem. • use concrete objects to conceptualize a problem. • draw quick pictures on MathBoards to help solve problems. • evaluate the solution for reasonableness.
	Try Another Problem Grade K, Lesson 7.6 Grade 1, Lesson 8.8 Grade 2, Lesson 2.11 **Share and Show** Grade 1, Lesson 4.6 Grade 2, Lesson 9.4 **On Your Own** Grade K, Lesson 4.5 Grade 1, Lesson 6.8 Grade 2, Lesson 6.6	**Children learn to:** • look at similar problems and apply techniques used in the original problem to gain insight into the solution of a new problem. • draw quick pictures on MathBoards to help solve problems. • evaluate the solution for reasonableness. • persevere in solving a problem, determining what methods and strategies they have learned that they can apply to solve the problem.

Teacher Edition **Student Edition**

Mathematical Practices	Throughout *GO Math!* Look for...	Explanation
2. Reason abstractly and quantitatively. Mathematically proficient students make sense of quantities and their relationships in problem situations. They bring two complementary abilities to bear on problems involving quantitative relationships: the ability to *decontextualize*—to abstract a given situation and represent it symbolically and manipulate the representing symbols as if they have a life of their own, without necessarily attending to their referents—and the ability to *contextualize*, to pause as needed during the manipulation process in order to probe into the referents for the symbols involved. Quantitative reasoning entails habits of creating a coherent representation of the problem at hand; considering the units involved; attending to the meaning of quantities, not just how to compute them; and knowing and flexibly using different properties of operations and objects.	**Some Examples:** **Model and Draw** Grade K, Lesson 5.4 Grade 1, Lesson 2.3 Grade 2, Lesson 3.9	**Children learn to:** • abstract a real-world situation and represent it symbolically as a number sentence as a way of solving a problem. • put the numbers and symbols in a number sentence back into the context of the real-world situation for the solution.
	Measurement and Geometry Lessons Grade K, Lesson 9.4 Grade 1, Lesson 11.2 Grade 2, Lesson 8.1	**Children learn to:** • focus on the meaning of quantities in measurement and geometry problems. • choose the most appropriate kind of unit to use to solve a problem.
	Lessons on the properties of operations Grade K, Lesson 5.8 Grade 1, Lesson 3.10 Grade 2, Lesson 3.2	**Children learn to use these properties of operations:** • changing the way addends are grouped in an addition problem does not change the sum. • changing the order of the addends in an addition problem does not change the sum.
	Lessons on modeling with manipulatives and drawings Grade K, Lesson 5.4 Grade 1, Lesson 5.1 Grade 2, Lesson 3.8	**Children learn to:** • represent real-world situations with concrete and pictorial models. • use bar models as one way to visualize addition and subtraction problems symbolically.

Teacher Edition **Student Edition**

Mathematical Practices	Throughout *GO Math!* Look for...	Explanation
3. **Construct viable arguments and critique the reasoning of others.** Mathematically proficient students understand and use stated assumptions, definitions, and previously established results in constructing arguments. They make conjectures and build a logical progression of statements to explore the truth of their conjectures. They are able to analyze situations by breaking them into cases, and can recognize and use counterexamples. They justify their conclusions, communicate them to others, and respond to the arguments of others. They reason inductively about data, making plausible arguments that take into account the context from which the data arose. Mathematically proficient students are also able to compare the effectiveness of two plausible arguments, distinguish correct logic or reasoning from that which is flawed, and—if there is a flaw in an argument—explain what it is. Elementary students can construct arguments using concrete referents such as objects, drawings, diagrams, and actions. Such arguments can make sense and be correct, even though they are not generalized or made formal until later grades. Later, students learn to determine domains to which an argument applies. Students at all grades can listen or read the arguments of others, decide whether they make sense, and ask useful questions to clarify or improve the arguments.	**Some Examples:** **Math Talk** Grade 1, Lesson 8.1 Grade 2, Lesson 10.5	**Children learn to:** • use mathematical language. • explain mathematical concepts. • defend, justify, or disprove a mathematical conjecture. • use deductive reasoning, definitions, and previously proven conclusions.
	Vocabulary Builder Grade K Grade 1 Grade 2 **Developing Math Language** Grade K Grade 1 Grade 2 **Vocabulary Preview** Grade 1 Grade 2	**Children learn to:** • develop, build, and reinforce mathematics vocabulary. • discuss mathematical definitions. • strengthen their abilities to communicate ideas about mathematics.
	Think Smarter Problems Grade K, Lesson 5.5 Grade 1, Lessons 2.9, 10.4 Grade 2, Lessons 6.8, 9.3 **Go Deeper** Grade K, Lesson 5.12 Grade 1, Lesson 6.3 Grade 2, Lessons 4.6, 5.2	**Children learn to:** • extend their thinking. • discuss their explanations. • give concrete examples to justify their explanations. • explain and describe mathematical understanding.

Teacher Edition **Student Edition**

Mathematical Practices	Throughout *GO Math!* Look for...	Explanation
4. **Model with mathematics.** Mathematically proficient students can apply the mathematics they know to solve problems arising in everyday life, society, and the workplace. In early grades, this might be as simple as writing an addition equation to describe a situation. In middle grades, a student might apply proportional reasoning to plan a school event or analyze a problem in the community. By high school, a student might use geometry to solve a design problem or use a function to describe how one quantity of interest depends on another. Mathematically proficient students who can apply what they know are comfortable making assumptions and approximations to simplify a complicated situation, realizing that these may need revision later. They are able to identify important quantities in a practical situation and map their relationships using such tools as diagrams, two-way tables, graphs, flowcharts and formulas. They can analyze those relationships mathematically to draw conclusions. They routinely interpret their mathematical results in the context of the situation and reflect on whether the results make sense, possibly improving the model if it has not served its purpose.	**Some Examples:** **Unlock the Problem • Real World** Grade K, Lesson 6.3 Grade 1, Lessons 3.12, 10.7 Grade 2, Lesson 8.5	**Children learn to:** • apply the mathematics they know to solve real-world problems. • write a number sentence to describe a situation. • use diagrams, tables, and graphs to help them see relationships and draw conclusions in problems.
	Hands On Lessons Grade K, Lesson 6.4 Grade 1, Lesson 2.8 Grade 2, Lesson 7.4	**Children learn to:** • model in a 'hands-on' approach to analyze problems.
	Connect To... Cross-Curricular Grade K Grade 1 Grade 2 **Literature** Grade K Grade 1 Grade 2	**Children learn to:** • apply the mathematics they know to solve problems in Literature, Science, Social Studies, Art, and other disciplines. • appreciate how mathematics influences their lives in ways both large and small.

Teacher Edition **Student Edition**

Mathematical Practices	Throughout *GO Math!* Look for...	Explanation
5. Use appropriate tools strategically. Mathematically proficient students consider the available tools when solving a mathematical problem. These tools might include pencil and paper, concrete models, a ruler, a protractor, a calculator, a spreadsheet, a computer algebra system, a statistical package, or dynamic geometry software. Proficient students are sufficiently familiar with tools appropriate for their grade or course to make sound decisions about when each of these tools might be helpful, recognizing both the insight to be gained and their limitations. For example, mathematically proficient high school students analyze graphs of functions and solutions generated using a graphing calculator. They detect possible errors by strategically using estimation and other mathematical knowledge. When making mathematical models, they know that technology can enable them to visualize the results of varying assumptions, explore consequences, and compare predictions with data. Mathematically proficient students at various grade levels are able to identify relevant external mathematical resources, such as digital content located on a website, and use them to pose or solve problems. They are able to use technological tools to explore and deepen their understanding of concepts.	**Some Examples:** **Hands-On Lessons** Grade K, Lesson 3.1 Grade 1, Lesson 12.3 Grade 2, Lesson 8.1	**Children learn to:** • use available tools to analyze problems through a concrete 'hands-on' approach.
	Geometry and Measurement Lessons Grade K, Lesson 10.7 Grade 1, Lesson 9.4 Grade 2, Lesson 11.7	**Children learn to use appropriate tools to:** • enhance and deepen their understanding of measurement and geometry concepts.
	Digital Path ***i*Tools** **Animated Math Models** **HMH Mega Math** All student lessons	**Children learn to use technological tools to:** • enhance and deepen their understanding of concepts. • enable them to visualize problems. • explore consequences of varying the data given.
6. Attend to precision. Mathematically proficient students try to communicate precisely to others. They try to use clear definitions in discussion with others and in their own reasoning. They state the meaning of the symbols they choose, including using the equal sign consistently and appropriately. They are careful about specifying units of measure, and labeling axes to clarify the correspondence with quantities in a problem. They calculate accurately and efficiently, express numerical answers with a degree of precision appropriate for the problem context. In the elementary grades, students give carefully formulated explanations to each other. By the time they reach high school they have learned to examine claims and make explicit use of definitions.	**Math Talk** Grade 1, Lesson 12.1 Grade 2, Lesson 5.4	**Children learn to:** • communicate precisely. • use mathematical vocabulary to communicate their ideas and explanations and to justify their thinking and solutions.
	Skill Lessons on number sentences and comparisons Grade K, Lesson 5.7 Grade 1, Lessons 7.3, 7.4 Grade 2, Lesson 2.12	**Children learn to:** • state the meaning of the symbols ($+$, $-$, $<$, $>$, $=$) they use in mathematical expressions and sentences accurately. • use the equal sign appropriately. • calculate accurately. • use comparison symbols ($<$, $>$) appropriately.
	Measurement Lessons Grade 1, Lesson 9.3 Grade 2, Lesson 8.6	**Children learn to:** • use correct measurement units for solutions.

Teacher Edition **Student Edition**

Mathematical Practices	Throughout *GO Math!* Look for...	Explanation
7. Look for and make use of structure. Mathematically proficient students look closely to discern a pattern or structure. Young students, for example, might notice that three and seven more is the same amount as seven and three more, or they may sort a collection of shapes according to how many sides the shapes have. Later, students will see 7×8 equals the well remembered $7 \times 5 + 7 \times 3$, in preparation for learning about the distributive property. In the expression $x^2 + 9x + 14$, older students can see the 14 as 2×7 and the 9 as $2 + 7$. They recognize the significance of an existing line in a geometric figure and can use the strategy of drawing an auxiliary line for solving problems. They also can step back for an overview and shift perspective. They can see complicated things, such as some algebraic expressions, as single objects or as being composed of several objects. For example, they can see $5 - 3(x - y)^2$ as 5 minus a positive number times a square and use that to realize that its value cannot be more than 5 for any real numbers *x* and *y*.	**Some Examples:** **Lessons with patterns** Grade K, Lesson 9.11 Grade 1, Lesson 6.1 Grade 2, Lesson 1.9	**Children learn to:** • sort shapes according to attributes. • use mathematical vocabulary to communicate their ideas and explanations and to justify their thinking and solutions. • use familiar patterns in our number system to extend counting sequences.
	Geometry Lessons Grade 1, Lessons 11.4, 12.1 Grade 2, Lesson 11.3	**Children learn to:** • verify that a new three-dimensional shape can be composed by combining three-dimensional shapes. • recognize and identify shapes by the number of side and vertices. • apply the structure of the base-ten number system to deeper understanding of the values of multi-digit numbers.
	Lessons with basic facts Grade 1, Lessons 3.1, 3.6 Grade 2, Lesson 3.7	**Children learn to:** • use a variety of different strategies to find the sums and differences of basic facts. • use benchmark number 10 when finding differences.
8. Look for and express regularity in repeated reasoning. Mathematically proficient students notice if calculations are repeated, and look both for general methods and for shortcuts. Upper elementary students might notice when dividing 25 by 11 that they are repeating the same calculations over and over again, and conclude they have a repeating decimal. By paying attention to the calculation of slope as they repeatedly check whether points are on the line through (1, 2) with slope 3, middle school students might abstract the equation $(y - 2)/(x - 1) = 3$. Noticing the regularity in the way terms cancel when expanding $(x - 1)(x + 1)$, $(x - 1)(x^2 + x + 1)$, and $(x - 1)(x^3 + x^2 + x + 1)$ might lead them to the general formula for the sum of a geometric series. As they work to solve a problem, mathematically proficient students maintain oversight of the process, while attending to the details. They continually evaluate the reasonableness of their intermediate results.	**Lessons with basic facts** Grade K, Lesson 6.7 Grade 1, Lessons 3.3, 5.5 Grade 2, Lesson 3.3	**Children learn to:** • find patterns in basic-fact strategies, such as the 'make a ten' 'doubles plus 1' and 'double minus 1'. • see the relationship between addition and subtraction. • recognize how structure and calculations are repeated as they build fact families. • discover shortcuts for finding sums of basic facts and for recognizing counting patterns.
	Multi-digit Computation Lessons Grade 1, Lesson 8.10 Grade 2, Lesson 6.7	**Children learn to:** • repeat the same steps for each place-value position in the standard algorithm for multi-digit computation.
	Lessons on Comparing Numbers Grade K, Lesson 4.7 Grade 1, Lesson 7.3 Grade 2, Lesson 2.12	**Children learn to:** • model and compare numbers to determine which is less or greater.

Teacher Edition   Student Edition

The Algebra Progression in *GO Math!* Grades K–8 and the GIMET-QR

PROFESSIONAL DEVELOPMENT

by Matthew R. Larson, Ph.D.
K–12 Curriculum Specialist for Mathematics
Lincoln Public Schools
Lincoln, Nebraska
NCTM President (2016–2018)

Nearly two decades ago, NCTM first articulated the need for algebra to be a significant strand across the K–8 curriculum in *Principles and Standards for School Mathematics* (NCTM, 2000). The importance of algebra in Grades K–8 was reemphasized in the final report of the National Mathematics Advisory Panel (NMAP, 2008). A coherent, rigorous, and sound learning progression in the K–8 mathematics curriculum is necessary to prepare students not only for high school mathematics courses, but also to ensure they leave high school both college and career ready.

The Grade-Level Instructional Materials Evaluation Tool—Quality Review (GIMET-QR) for Grades K–8 was developed to provide educators with a framework for evaluating the quality of instructional materials and choosing materials that are best suited to provide a coherent learning experience. This tool focuses on the clusters and standards along the progression to algebra continuum.

Using the progression documents from the University of Arizona Institute of Mathematics and the Progression to Algebra Continuum from the Common Core, the developers of GIMET-QR developed additional algebra-progression statements for each grade level. These particular statements provide additional specificity and clarity for the reviewers of instructional materials.

This article examines the Houghton Mifflin Harcourt *GO Math!* Grades K–8 program and the extent to which it reflects and embodies the GIMET-QR algebra-progression statements.

GO Math! Grades K–2

The GIMET-QR algebra-progression statements in this grade span draw from the Common Core domains Counting and Cardinality, Operations and Algebraic Thinking, Number and Operations in Base Ten, and Measurement and Data.

Based on the explanations, diagrams, pictorial representations, and assignments in the *GO Math!* instructional materials, and when considered in the context of the algebra-progression statements, *GO Math!* K–2 is exceptional in its comprehensive approach to algebra preparedness as defined by the GIMET-QR.

Kindergarten

In **Kindergarten**, students represent numbers in multiple ways, including with counters, drawings, and written numerals. Students show how to count objects arranged in lines and in more difficult arrangements. Teacher narrative ensures that students count each object only once and make single counting paths through scattered displays. The logical structure of *GO Math!* counting lessons supports students' understanding that each successive number name in a counting array refers to a quantity that is one greater. When students compare numbers, they do so in a variety of ways, including by using real objects, studying drawings, and counting. The assignments in the Student Edition support these comparisons as well. Lessons offer opportunities for students to match to compare numbers, and they show that one group might look like it has more objects, but matching or counting may yield another result.

It is significant that the Operations and Algebraic Thinking underpinnings for algebra in *GO Math!* at this grade span place notable emphasis on understanding written expressions and equations. Kindergarten students develop the mathematical language of addition and subtraction that is so integral to success with algebra. To solidify this development even more, addition and subtraction situations in *GO Math!* are action oriented, helping students to visualize and understand the change that takes place.

Finally, *GO Math!* Kindergarten is exceptional in its treatment of place value. Students have many hands-on opportunities to compose and decompose numbers as ten ones and some further ones, this concept being a critical step for understanding base-ten notation.

Grade 1

Students in **Grade 1** extend their understanding of algebra ideas in several ways. Students use comparison to represent problem situations, which requires students to conceptualize and represent an unknown. Mathematical language comes into play here as well. *More, fewer, or less* contextual problems can take many forms. *GO Math!* offers extensive opportunities to work toward mastery of the language and contextual complexities. Assignments require students to match objects with drawings and use labels to compare. Later, students use tape diagrams (bar models) as a tool to help them compare. Students represent *compare* situations in different ways, including as unknown-addend problems. Even though students do not use formal properties in their descriptions, they have many opportunities to recognize these properties in action.

In *GO Math!*, emphasis is placed through Math Talk structures on the explanation a student gives for his or her representation of a contextual situation. In *GO Math!* students gain extensive experience with more challenging problem subtypes as they begin developing an algebraic perspective on mathematical situations. *GO Math!* is exceptional in the ways it encourages students to link equations with representations, which leads to a deeper understanding of these precursors to formal algebra.

Here again, *GO Math!* excels in its teaching of place value. Instruction helps students recognize that the digit in the tens place is the critical digit when determining the size of a two-digit number. Assignments require students to explain why this is so. Students connect different strategies: for example, using the relationship between addition and subtraction to explain an unknown-addend problem.

In Grade 1, there are several GIMET-QR statements drawn from the Measurement and Data domain. These include transitive reasoning and the reasoning processes of seriation, conservation, and classification. Both the *GO Math!* recommended teacher instructional narrative and the assignments in the Student Edition emphasize these algebraic building blocks.

Grade 2

Grade 2 students extend their addition and subtraction representations to include two-step problems. *GO Math!* offers a recommended teacher narrative and assignments that engage students in representing two-step problems with equations by using easy subtypes. Students use drawings or combinations of drawings and equations to represent comparison problems or middle-difficulty subtypes. Assignments require students to solve one- and two-step problems that involve adding to, taking from, putting together/taking apart, and comparing and that have unknowns in all positions.

GO Math! offers the instruction and support students need to succeed when reading and writing equations with different placements of the unknown, explaining the different meanings of addition and subtraction, and showing the connection between addition and subtraction equations. Students develop and use mathematical language to explain their reasoning about *result unknown, change unknown,* and *start unknown* and the relationship between the three.

In Grade 2, there is further evidence of exceptional instruction and practice involving place value. Students are required to indicate the place value of three-digit numbers, determine the value of each digit, make connections between representations of three-digit numbers, and connect number words and numbers written in base-ten numerals as sums of their base-ten units, as well as to say the number aloud. *GO Math!* students successfully extend their understanding of place value to hundreds, which lays the foundation for base-ten structural work in later grades. Assignments help students understand that a hundred is a unit of 100 ones, and that both tens and hundreds can be composed or decomposed. Using mental math, *GO Math!* students develop the academic language required to use place value and properties of operations to explain why addition and subtraction strategies work.

GO Math! materials offer hands-on instruction and practice with measuring tools so that students understand that *one* represents a length beginning at the zero mark on a ruler and ending at 1, not the number 1 itself. The inverse relationship between the size of a unit of length and the number of units required to measure a length are well illustrated and explained.

GO Math! Grades 3–5

The GIMET-QR algebra-progression statements in the 3–5 elementary grade span are drawn from the Operations and Algebraic Thinking, Number and Operations in Base Ten, Number and Operations—Fractions, and Measurement and Data domains.

In the intermediate grades in *GO Math!*, the instruction, including the explanations and connections that foster the deep development of the concepts and skills that are part of the algebra progression in these grades, the Math Talk prompts that promote engagement and interaction between students and teacher as well as among students, and the assignments that cement the learning all fully support the algebra-progression statements in the GIMET-QR.

Grade 3

Grade 3 students in *GO Math!* have many meaningful opportunities to represent and solve contextual multiplication and division problems for unknown products, unknown group sizes, and unknown numbers of groups. Students illustrate equal groups and arrays/area representations, which lays the foundation for algebraic expressions. *GO Math!* emphasizes the academic language students need to explain their reasoning about unknown products, group sizes, and numbers of groups. Students understand that in equal groups, the roles of the factors differ. Assignments ensure that students are facile with columns and rows in arrays. Students manipulate rectangular arrays to visualize and more fully understand the Commutative Property of Multiplication. When solving for unknowns in problem situations, students make connections among problems, manipulate representations, and link equations to representations. Students build their algebraic perspective when making these connections. *GO Math!* assignments encourage students to model and apply the properties of multiplication and the relationship between multiplication and division by requiring them to illustrate the properties and relationship with drawings and equations; to make the connection that two factors are quotients of related division problems; and to relate the product, factors, or quotients to contextual problem situations.

GO Math! facilitates the development of fluency with multiplication and division by modeling decomposing and composing products that are known in order to find an unknown product. Assignments require students to explain the relationship between area and multiplication and addition, represent it in different ways, and then apply their understanding to problems involving multiplication and area.

GO Math! fully supports students' understanding of fractions as they move beyond the fraction language they learned in prior grades. Students partition a whole into equal parts and visualize unit fractions as the basic building blocks of fractions. Students use the number line to show that fractions are numbers and that unit fractions can be the measure of length. This extensive, hands-on work with fractions serves as a stepping stone from arithmetic to algebra and is consistent with the latest research on effective fraction instruction as outlined in the Institute of Education Sciences guide *Developing Effective Fractions Instruction for Kindergarten through 8th Grade* (Siegler et al., 2010) and NCTM's *Developing Essential Understanding of Rational Numbers for Teaching Mathematics in Grades 3–5* (Barnett-Clarke et al., 2010).

GO Math! materials help students conceptualize area as the amount of two-dimensional space in a bounded region and to measure it by choosing a unit of area. Students explain how they connect area to multiplication and addition. Assignments require students to determine the areas of rectilinear figures by composing and decomposing them into non-overlapping areas and adding the parts. This sophisticated way of finding area is applied to contextual problem situations.

Grade 4

In **Grade 4** multiplication and division, students focus on distinguishing multiplicative comparison from additive comparison. *GO Math!* instruction emphasizes that in an additive comparison, one asks what amount can be added to one quantity to result in the other; in multiplicative comparison, one asks what factor would multiply one quantity to result in another. The specificity and academic language for comparisons in *GO Math!* help prepare students for formal algebra and sophisticated courses in later years. Likewise, multistep contextual problems that require students to interpret remainders are assigned.

Just as in Grade 3, work with fractions is integral to building a solid foundation for formal algebra. In *GO Math!* Grade 4, students illustrate addition as putting together so that they understand the way fractions are built from unit fractions. Renaming a mixed number to a fraction is considered to be a case of fraction addition, whereas renaming an improper fraction as a mixed number is decomposition.

When comparing two decimals, *GO Math!* students use the meaning of decimals as fractions and make sure to compare fractions with the same denominator. This promotes a deeper understanding of rational numbers.

Grade 5

Grade 5 students in *GO Math!* explain how multiplying a number by a power of 10 "shifts" every digit to the left. They use place value to explain patterns in the number of zeroes in products of whole numbers, powers of 10 and exponents, and the location of the decimal point in products of decimals with powers of 10. Assignments require students to connect the academic language of multiples to powers in order to understand multiplication with exponentiation. Students explain patterns when multiplying whole numbers or decimals by powers of 10.

Work with fractions at this level involves multiplication and division. With *GO Math!* materials, students connect the interpretation of a fraction as division to an understanding of division as equal sharing. Students make the connection between fraction multiplication and finding the area of a rectangle.

With *GO Math!*, students interpret multiplication of fractions as scaling in several ways. Without multiplying, they compare the size of the product to the size of one factor on the basis of the size of the other factor. Students explain why multiplying a given number by a fraction greater than 1 results in a product greater than the given number. Likewise, they explain why multiplying a fraction by a fraction less than 1 results in a product less than the given number. *GO Math!* students view multiplication as an operation that "stretches or shrinks" by a scale factor, which leads them to reason multiplicatively with continuous quantities.

Grade 5 students find the volume of a solid figure composed of two non-overlapping right rectangular prisms by adding the volumes of the parts. In *GO Math!*, students use this method to complete a space architecture project and justify how their design meets the specific volume criterion.

GO Math! Grades 6–8

The GIMET-QR algebra-progression statements in the middle grades are drawn from the domains The Number System, Ratios and Proportional Relationships, and Expressions and Equations.

The *GO Math!* instructional models, materials, and assignments for this grade span make meaningful connections with the concepts and skills taught in prior years and fully prepare students for algebra courses and beyond in high school.

Grade 6

The **Grade 6** instruction and assignments in *GO Math!* provide many opportunities for students to use story contexts and visual models to develop and deepen their understanding of fraction division. These opportunities help connect the relation between multiplication and division to fraction division.

The number line is extended to include negative numbers so that students can investigate negative numbers in context when describing magnitude and direction. Students use the number line to compare numbers based on their relative positions rather than their magnitudes. To avoid confusion with distance from zero and absolute value, *GO Math!* provides students contextual problems where it makes sense to compare the relative positions of two rational numbers and to compare their absolute values, and to witness where these two comparisons run in different directions.

GO Math! instruction on the concepts of ratio and rate is focused on the proportional relationship between two quantities. *GO Math!* assignments require students to explain their solutions to ratio and rate-reasoning problems. To support their explanations, the materials provide instruction in the use of tables of equivalent ratios, tape diagrams (bar models), double-number line diagrams, and the unit rate a/b associated with a ratio $a:b$.

In Grade 6, students connect their previous understanding of arithmetic to algebraic expressions and equations. With *GO Math!*, students use mathematical terms to explain how one or more parts of an expression correspond to the quantities in a contextual problem. Students interpret the structure of an expression in terms of a context. Work with numerical expressions prepares students for work with algebraic expressions. *GO Math!* supports this transition by instructing students to leave numerical expressions unevaluated, which prepares students for constructing the algebraic equation to solve the problem.

GO Math! assignments require students to use the process of reasoning to find the number which makes an equation true. This process includes checking whether a given number is a solution. Students work toward finding a standard method for solving equations, but they begin by studying examples and looking for structure. Their study leads to understanding that every occurrence of a given variable has the same value throughout the solution procedure.

Students then show their understanding of quantitative relationships between dependent and independent variables. They analyze the relationship between the variables by using graphs and tables, and they explain how these relate to the equation. This work with two variables prepares students for later work with functions.

Grade 7

The **Grade 7** *GO Math!* materials define a proportional relationship and then use that definition to determine if a relationship is proportional. Students examine situations carefully to determine the existence of a proportional relationship. *GO Math!* emphasizes the importance of structure and language by prompting students to look for and understand the roles of the terms *for every, for each,* and *per*. Teachers are reminded of typical misconceptions involving proportional relationships and offered suggestions for how to avoid them. The program explains the correspondences between representations including tables, equations, graphs, diagrams, and verbal descriptions. Students are required to test for equivalent ratios by using a table or by graphing on a coordinate plane and to show how the unit rate appears in each representation.

GO Math! students add and subtract rational numbers and represent the addition and subtraction on a horizontal or vertical number line. *GO Math!* materials demonstrate that each directed line segment has a direction, a beginning, and an end. When these directed line segments are linked, the second line segment begins at the end of the first one. Students realize that if the second line segment is going in the opposite direction to the first, then it can backtrack over the first and essentially cancel all or part of it out. This realization effectively lays the foundation for work with vectors in high school.

Students in *GO Math!* learn to simplify general linear expressions with rational coefficients. Students extend their prior understanding of order of operations and applied properties of operations to linear expressions that have more operations and whose transformations require an understanding of the rules for multiplying negative numbers. Here again, the *GO Math!* teacher notes identify typical student misconceptions in simplifying expressions and offer suggestions for addressing them.

Grade 8

In **Grade 8**, *GO Math!* students apply the properties of integer exponents to generate equivalent numerical expressions. Requiring the rule $10^a \cdot 10^b = 10^{a+b}$ to hold when *a* and *b* are integers leads to the definition of the meaning of powers with 0 and negative exponents. Students prepare for learning the properties of exponents in high school by working systematically with the square root and cube root symbols in *GO Math!* Assignments require students to express and perform calculations with very large or very small numbers by using scientific notation.

GO Math! materials illustrate the connections between proportional relationships, lines, and linear equations. Students start to build a unified notion of the concept of function, leading them to compare two different proportional relationships represented in different ways. Students understand that the connection between the unit rate in a proportional relationship and the slope of its graph depends on a connection with the geometry of similar triangles.

Students use a function to model a linear relationship between two quantities. They determine the rate of change, which is the slope of the line that is the graph of the function. Students read, compute, or approximate the rate of change from a table or graph. To foster understanding of relationships between quantities, *GO Math!* assignments ask students to describe the relationships quantitatively and to pay attention to the general shape of the graph without concern for the numerical values.

The *GO Math!* K–8 program presents a coherent algebra learning progression as illustrated by its content alignment to the GIMET-QR. Its comprehensive representation of the algebra progressions in its materials and assignments, combined with an instructional design that engages learners in developing not only procedural fluency, but deep conceptual understanding, is clear evidence that *GO Math!* is a high-quality mathematics program that fully prepares students for high school mathematics courses and beyond.

Bibliography

Barnett-Clarke, Carne, William Fisher, Rick Marks, and Sharon Ross. *Developing Essential Understanding of Rational Numbers for Teaching Mathematics in Grades 3–5.* Reston, VA: NCTM, 2010.

Council of the Great City Schools. Grade-Level Instructional Materials Evaluation Tool-Quality Review (GIMET-QR). Washington, DC: Council of the Great City Schools. http://www.cgcs.org/page/475

National Council of Teachers of Mathematics. *Principles and Standards for School Mathematics.* Edited by NCTM. Reston, VA: NCTM, 2000.

National Mathematics Advisory Panel. *Foundations for Success: The Final Report of the National Mathematics Advisory Panel.* Washington, DC: U.S. Department of Education, 2008.

"Progress to Algebra in Grades K–8." In "K–8 Publishers' Criteria for the Common Core State Standards for Mathematics," 8. 20 July 2012. http://www.corestandards.org/assets/Math_Publishers_Criteria_K-8_Summer%202012_FINAL.pdf

Siegler, Robert, Thomas Carpenter, Francis (Skip) Fennell, David Geary, James Lewis, Yukari Okamoto, Laurie Thompson, and Jonathan Wray, J. *Developing Effective Fractions Instruction for Kindergarten Through 8th Grade* (NCEE #2010-4039). Washington, DC: National Center for Education Evaluation and Regional Assistance, Institute of Education Sciences, U.S. Department of Education, 2010. Retrieved from whatworks.ed.gov/publications/practiceguides.

Progress to Algebra in Grades K–8

K	1	2	3	4
Know number names and the count sequence Count to tell the number of objects Compare numbers Understand addition as putting together and adding to, and understand subtraction as taking apart and taking from Work with numbers 11–19 to gain foundations for place value	Represent and solve problems involving addition and subtraction Understand and apply properties of operations and the relationship between addition and subtraction Add and subtract within 20 Work with addition and subtraction equations Extend the counting sequence Understand place value Use place value understanding and properties of operations to add and subtract Measure lengths indirectly and by iterating length units	Represent and solve problems involving addition and subtraction Add and subtract within 20 Understand place value Use place value understanding and properties of operations to add and subtract Measure and estimate lengths in standard units Relate addition and subtraction to length	Represent and solve problems involving multiplication and division Understand properties of multiplication and the relationship between multiplication and division Multiply and divide within 100 Solve problems involving the four operations, and identify and explain patterns in arithmetic Develop understanding of fractions as numbers Solve problems involving measurement and estimation of intervals of time, liquid volumes, and masses of objects Geometric measurement: understand concepts of area and relate area to multiplication and to addition	Use the four operations with whole numbers to solve problems Generalize place value understanding for multi-digit whole numbers Use place value understanding and properties of operations to perform multi-digit arithmetic Extend understanding of fraction equivalence and ordering Build fractions from unit fractions by applying and extending previous understandings of operations Understand decimal notation for fractions, and compare decimal fractions

5	6	7	8
Understand the place value system	Apply and extend previous understandings of multiplication and division to divide fractions by fractions	Apply and extend previous understanding of operations with fractions to add, subtract, multiply, and divide rational numbers	Work with radical and integer exponents
Perform operations with multi-digit whole numbers and decimals to hundredths	Apply and extend previous understandings of numbers to the system of rational numbers	Analyze proportional relationships and use them to solve real-world and mathematical problems	Understand the connections between proportional relationships, lines, and linear equations
Use equivalent fractions as a strategy to add and subtract fractions	Understand ratio concepts and use ratio reasoning to solve problems	Use properties of operations to generate equivalent expressions	Analyze and solve linear equations and pairs of simultaneous linear equations
Apply and extend previous understandings of multiplication and division to multiply and divide fractions	Apply and extend previous understandings of arithmetic to algebraic expressions	Solve real-life and mathematical problems using numerical and algebraic expressions and equations	Define, evaluate, and compare functions
Geometric measurement: understand concepts of volume and relate volume to multiplication and to addition	Reason about and solve one-variable equations and inequalities		Use functions to model relationships between quantities
Graph points in the coordinate plane to solve real-world and mathematical problems*	Represent and analyze quantitative relationships between dependent and independent variables		

*Indicates a cluster that is well thought of as part of a student's progress to algebra, but that is currently not designated as Major by one or both of the assessment consortia in their draft materials. Apart from the asterisked exception, the clusters listed here are a subset of those designated as Major in both of the assessment consortia's draft documents.

Problem Types

Addition and Subtraction Problem Types

	Result Unknown	Change Unknown	Start Unknown
Add To	Six children are playing tag in the yard. Three more children come to play. How many children are playing in the yard now? *Situation and Solution Equation*[1]*:* 6 + 3 = □	Six children are playing tag in the yard. Some more children come to play. Now there are 9 children in the yard. How many children came to play? *Situation Equation:* 6 + □ = 9 *Solution Equation:* 9 − 6 = □	Some children are playing tag in the yard. Three more children come to play. Now there are 9 children in the yard. How many children were in the yard at first? *Situation Equation:* □ + 3 = 9 *Solution Equation:* 9 − 3 = □
Take From	Jake has 10 trading cards. He gives 3 to his brother. How many trading cards does he have left? *Situation and Solution Equation:* 10 − 3 = □	Jake has 10 trading cards. He gives some to his brother. Now Jake has 7 trading cards left. How many cards does he give to his brother? *Situation Equation:* 10 − □ = 7 *Solution Equation:* 10 − 7 = □	Jake has some trading cards. He gives 3 to his brother. Now Jake has 7 trading cards left. How many cards does he start with? *Situation Equation:* □ − 3 = 7 *Solution Equation:* 7 + 3 = □

	Total Unknown	Addend Unknown	Both Addends Unknown
Put Together/ Take Apart	There are 9 red roses and 4 yellow roses in a vase. How many roses are in the vase? [9 | 4] ____ *Situation and Solution Equation:* 9 + 4 = □	Thirteen roses are in the vase. 9 are red and the rest are yellow. How many roses are yellow? [9 | ____] 13 *Situation Equation:* 13 = 9 + □ *Solution Equation:* 13 − 9 = □	Ana has 13 roses. How many can she put in her red vase and how many in her blue vase? [____ | ____] 13 *Situation Equation:* 13 = □ + □

[1]A situation equation represents the structure (action) in the problem situation. A solution equation shows the operation used to find the answer.

	Difference Unknown	Bigger Unknown	Smaller Unknown
Compare[2]	Aki has 8 apples. Sofia has 14 apples. How many **more** apples does **Sofia** have than Aki? Aki has 8 apples. Sofia has 14 apples. How many **fewer** apples does **Aki** have than Sofia? 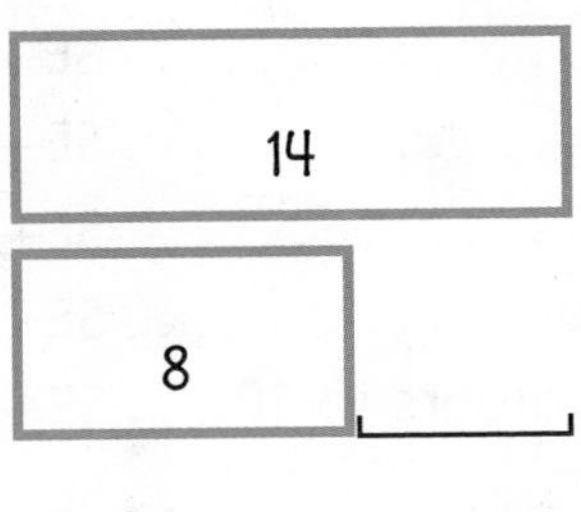 *Situation Equation:* 8 + □ = 14 *Solution Equation:* 14 − 8 = □	***"MORE"* VERSION SUGGESTS OPERATION.** Aki has 8 apples. **Sofia** has **6 more** apples than Aki. How many apples does Sofia have? ***"FEWER"* VERSION SUGGESTS WRONG OPERATION.** Aki has 8 apples. **Aki** has **6 fewer** apples than Sofia. How many apples does Sofia have? 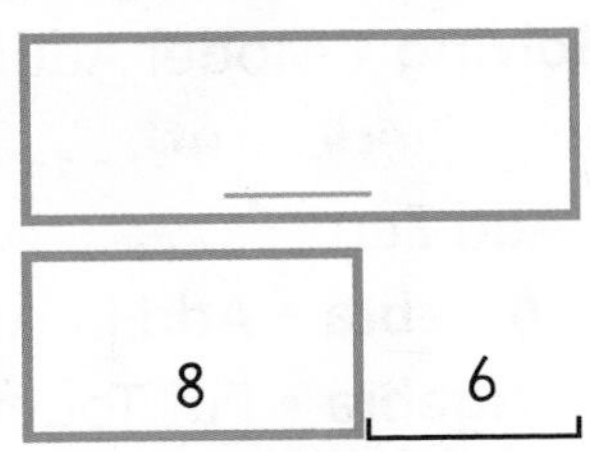 *Situation and Solution Equation:* 8 + 6 = □	***"FEWER"* VERSION SUGGESTS OPERATION.** Sofia has 14 apples. **Aki** has **6 fewer** apples than Sofia. How many apples does Aki have? ***"MORE"* VERSION SUGGESTS WRONG OPERATION.** Sofia has 14 apples. **Sofia** has **6 more** apples than Aki. How many apples does Aki have? 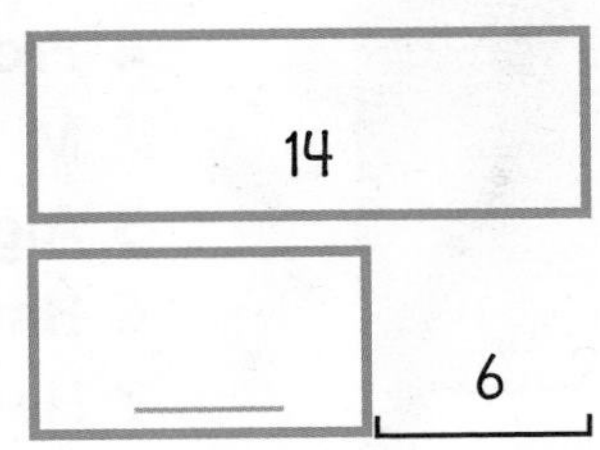 *Situation Equation:* □ + 6 = 14 *Solution Equation:* 14 − 6 = □

[2] A comparison sentence can always be said in two ways. One way uses *more*, and the other uses *fewer* or *less*.

Critical Area

Operations and Algebraic Thinking

Common Core CRITICAL AREA

Developing understanding of addition, subtraction, and strategies for addition and subtraction within 20

STUDENT RESOURCES | TEACHER RESOURCES

1 Addition Concepts ..... SE—9 ... TE—9

Domain Operations and Algebraic Thinking

- 1.OA.A Represent and solve problems involving addition and subtraction.
- 1.OA.B Understand and apply properties of operations and the relationship between addition and subtraction.
- 1.OA.C Add and subtract within 20.

Common Core State Standards 1.OA.A.1, 1.OA.B.3, 1.OA.C.6

Personal Math Trainer

Look for this symbol for a gateway to your personalized learning path!

2 Subtraction Concepts ..... SE—65 ... TE—65

Domain Operations and Algebraic Thinking

- 1.OA.A Represent and solve problems involving addition and subtraction.
- 1.OA.C Add and subtract within 20.
- 1.OA.D Work with addition and subtraction equations.

Common Core State Standards 1.OA.A.1, 1.OA.C.6, 1.OA.D.8

	STUDENT RESOURCES	TEACHER RESOURCES

3 Addition Strategies . . . . SE—127. . TE—127

Domain Operations and Algebraic Thinking

- 1.OA.A Represent and solve problems involving addition and subtraction.
- 1.OA.B Understand and apply properties of operations and the relationship between addition and subtraction.
- 1.OA.C Add and subtract within 20.

Common Core State Standards 1.OA.A.2, 1.OA.B.3, 1.OA.C.5, 1.OA.C.6

4 Subtraction Strategies . . . . SE—207. . TE—207

Domain Operations and Algebraic Thinking

- 1.OA.A Represent and solve problems involving addition and subtraction.
- 1.OA.B Understand and apply properties of operations and the relationship between addition and subtraction.
- 1.OA.C Add and subtract within 20.

Common Core State Standards 1.OA.A.1, 1.OA.B.4, 1.OA.C.5, 1.OA.C.6

Key: SE—Student Edition; **TE**—Teacher Edition

Practice and Homework

Lesson Check and Spiral Review in every lesson

Common Core MATHEMATICAL PRACTICES

1. Make sense of problems and persevere in solving them.
2. Reason abstractly and quantitatively.
3. Construct viable arguments and critique the reasoning of others.
4. Model with mathematics.
5. Use appropriate tools strategically.
6. Attend to precision.
7. Look for and make use of structure.
8. Look for and express regularity in repeated reasoning.

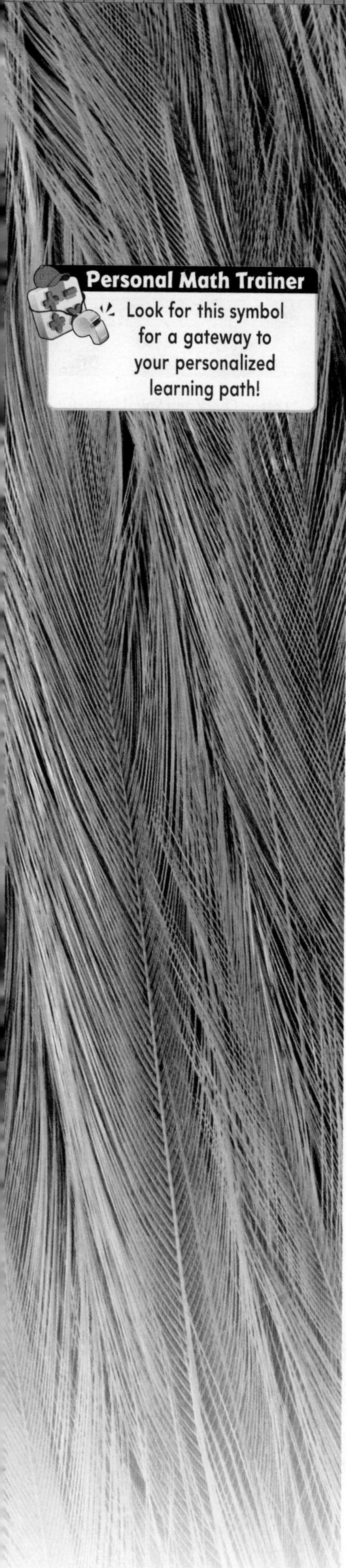

Personal Math Trainer

Look for this symbol for a gateway to your personalized learning path!

STUDENT RESOURCES | TEACHER RESOURCES

Number and Operations in Base Ten

STUDENT RESOURCES | TEACHER RESOURCES

Domain Number and Operations in Base Ten

- 1.NBT.A Extending the counting sequence.
- 1.NBT.B Understand place value.

Common Core State Standards 1.NBT.A.1, 1.NBT.B.2, 1.NBT.B.2a, 1.NBT.B.2b, 1.NBT.B.2c, 1.NBT.B.3

Domain Number and Operations in Base Ten

- 1.NBT.B Understand place value.
- 1.NBT.C Use place value understanding and properties of operations to add and subtract.

Common Core State Standards 1.NBT.B.3, 1.NBT.C.5

Key: SE—Student Edition; **TE**—Teacher Edition

Critical Area

Common Core CRITICAL AREA

Developing understanding of whole number relationships and place value, including grouping in tens and ones

Practice and Homework

Lesson Check and Spiral Review in every lesson

Common Core MATHEMATICAL PRACTICES

1. Make sense of problems and persevere in solving them.
2. Reason abstractly and quantitatively.
3. Construct viable arguments and critique the reasoning of others.
4. Model with mathematics.
5. Use appropriate tools strategically.
6. Attend to precision.
7. Look for and make use of structure.
8. Look for and express regularity in repeated reasoning.

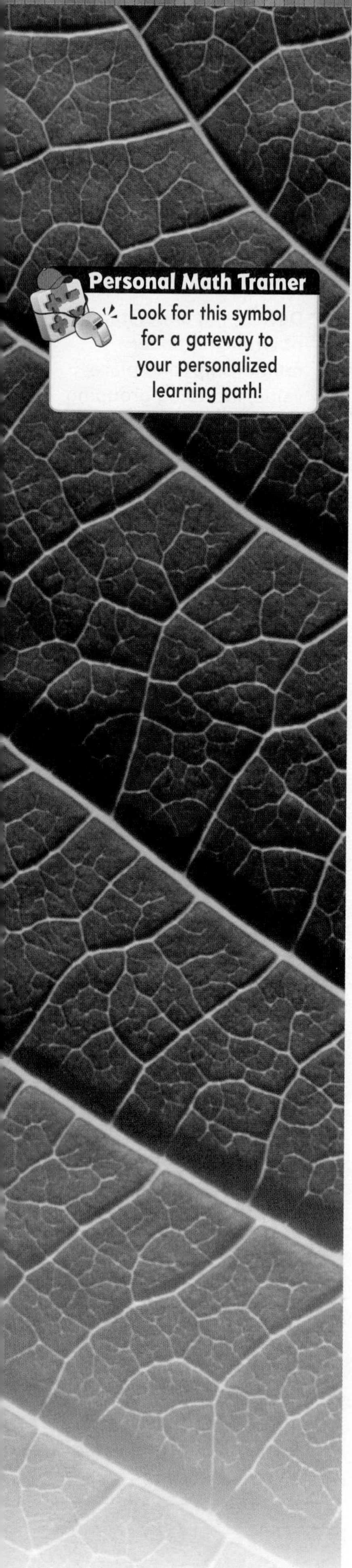

Personal Math Trainer
Look for this symbol for a gateway to your personalized learning path!

	STUDENT RESOURCES	TEACHER RESOURCES
8 Two-Digit Addition and Subtraction	SE—**433**	TE—433

Domains Operations and Algebraic Thinking, Number and Operations in Base Ten

- 1.OA.C Add and subtract within 20.
- 1.NBT.C Use place value understanding and properties of operations to add and subtract.

Common Core State Standards 1.OA.C.6, 1.NBT.C.4, 1.NBT.C.6

Measurement and Data

STUDENT RESOURCES | TEACHER RESOURCES

9 Measurement .... SE—509.. TE—509

Domain Measurement and Data

- 1.MD.A Measure lengths indirectly and by iterating length units.
- 1.MD.B Tell and write time.

Common Core State Standards 1.MD.A.1, 1.MD.A.2, 1.MD.B.3

10 Represent Data .... SE—571.. TE—571

Domain Measurement and Data

- 1.MD.C Represent and interpret data.

Common Core State Standards 1.MD.C.4

Key: SE—Student Edition; **TE**—Teacher Edition

Critical Area

Common Core CRITICAL AREA

Developing understanding of linear measurement and measuring lengths as iterating length units

Practice and Homework

Lesson Check and Spiral Review in every lesson

Common Core MATHEMATICAL PRACTICES

1. Make sense of problems and persevere in solving them.
2. Reason abstractly and quantitatively.
3. Construct viable arguments and critique the reasoning of others.
4. Model with mathematics.
5. Use appropriate tools strategically.
6. Attend to precision.
7. Look for and make use of structure.
8. Look for and express regularity in repeated reasoning.

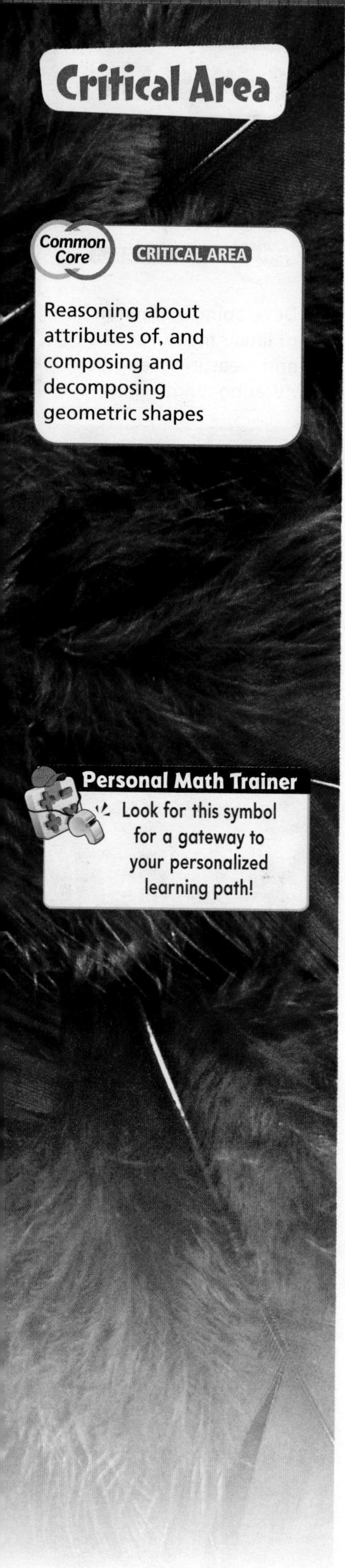

Critical Area

Common Core CRITICAL AREA

Reasoning about attributes of, and composing and decomposing geometric shapes

Personal Math Trainer

Look for this symbol for a gateway to your personalized learning path!

Geometry

12 Two-Dimensional Geometry

Domain Geometry

1.G.A Reason with shapes and their attributes.

Common Core State Standards 1.G.A.1, 1.G.A.2, 1.G.A.3

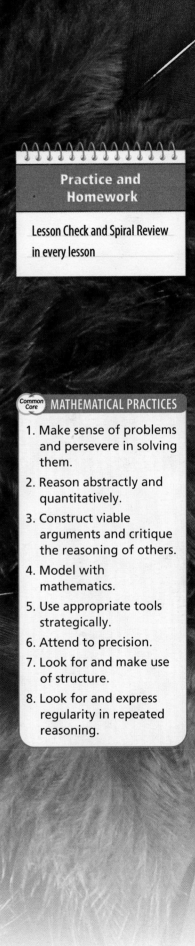

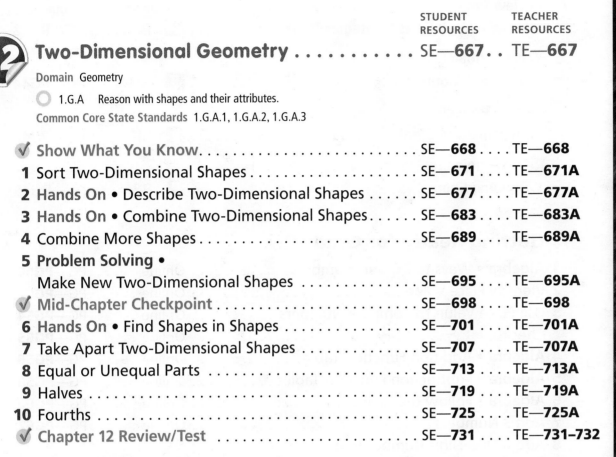

Practice and Homework

Lesson Check and Spiral Review in every lesson

Common Core MATHEMATICAL PRACTICES

1. Make sense of problems and persevere in solving them.
2. Reason abstractly and quantitatively.
3. Construct viable arguments and critique the reasoning of others.
4. Model with mathematics.
5. Use appropriate tools strategically.
6. Attend to precision.
7. Look for and make use of structure.
8. Look for and express regularity in repeated reasoning.

Key: SE—Student Edition; **TE**—Teacher Edition

End-of-Year Resources

Projects

	STUDENT RESOURCES	TEACHER RESOURCES
Review Project: Make a Math Facts Strategies Book	P—B9	PG—PG42
Review Project: Numbers Around Us	P—B13	PG—PG44
Review Project: Measure and Graph	P—B16	PG—PG46
Review Project: Building Shapes	P—B20	PG—PG48

Getting Ready for Grade 2

Key: P—Online Projects; **PG**—Planning Guide

Teacher Notes

Online Projects P

Review Project:
Make a Math Facts Strategies Book

CRITICAL AREA Developing understanding of addition, subtraction, and strategies for addition and subtraction within 20

Resources
- Planning Guide, p. PG42

Review Project:
Numbers Around Us

CRITICAL AREA Developing understanding of whole number relationships and place value, including grouping in tens and ones

Resources
- Planning Guide, p. PG44

Review Project:
Measure and Graph

CRITICAL AREA Developing understanding of linear measurement and measuring lengths as iterating length units

Resources
- Planning Guide, p. PG46

Review Project:
Building Shapes

CRITICAL AREA Reasoning about attributes of, and composing and decomposing geometric shapes

Resources
- Planning Guide, p. PG48

Common Core

Getting Ready Lessons build on Grade 1 content and prepare students for Grade 2 content.

Daily Pacing Chart

Review Projects	Lessons	Assessment	Total
4 days	20 days	2 days	26 days

LESSON 1 ALGEBRA • Ways to Expand Numbers
COMMON CORE 1.NBT.B.2, 2.NBT.A.3

Resources
- Student Lesson Pages, Online
- Planning Guide, p. PG50

GO DIGITAL

LESSON 5 ALGEBRA • Subtraction Function Tables
COMMON CORE 1.OA.C.6, 2.OA.B.2

Resources
- Student Lesson Pages, Online
- Planning Guide, p. PG58

GO DIGITAL

LESSON 6 ALGEBRA • Follow the Rule
COMMON CORE 1.OA.C.6, 2.OA.B.2

Resources
- Student Lesson Pages, Online
- Planning Guide, p. PG60

GO DIGITAL

LESSON 10 Repeated Addition
COMMON CORE 1.OA.C.6, 2.OA.C.4

Resources
- Student Lesson Pages, Online
- Planning Guide, p. PG68

GO DIGITAL

LESSON 11 Use Repeated Addition to Solve Problems
COMMON CORE 1.OA.C.6, 2.OA.C.4

Resources
- Student Lesson Pages, Online
- Planning Guide, p. PG70

GO DIGITAL

LESSON 15 Time to the Hour and Half Hour
COMMON CORE 1.MD.B.3, 2.MD.C.7

Resources
- Student Lesson Pages, Online
- Planning Guide, p. PG80

GO DIGITAL

LESSON 16 Use a Picture Graph
COMMON CORE 1.MD.C.4, 2.MD.D.10

Resources
- Student Lesson Pages, Online
- Planning Guide, p. PG82

GO DIGITAL

LESSON 20 Equal Shares
COMMON CORE 1.G.A.3, 2.G.A.3

Resources
- Student Lesson Pages, Online
- Planning Guide, p. PG90

GO DIGITAL

GO DIGITAL
- Animated Math Models
- Assessment
- HMH Mega Math
- *i*Tools
- Projects
- Multimedia *e*Glossary

LESSON 2 **Identify Place Value**

COMMON CORE **1.NBT.B.2, 2.NBT.A.3**

Resources
- Student Lesson Pages, Online
- Planning Guide, p. PG52

LESSON 3 **Use Place Value to Compare Numbers** ✓

COMMON CORE **1.NBT.B.3, 2.NBT.A.4**

Resources
- Student Lesson Pages, Online
- Planning Guide, p. PG54

LESSON 4 ALGEBRA • **Addition Function Tables**

COMMON CORE **1.OA.C.6, 2.OA.B.2**

Resources
- Student Lesson Pages, Online
- Planning Guide, p. PG56

LESSON 7 **Add 3 Numbers**

COMMON CORE **1.OA.B.3, 2.OA.B.2**

Resources
- Student Lesson Pages, Online
- Planning Guide, p. PG62

LESSON 8 **Add a One-Digit Number to a Two-Digit Number**

COMMON CORE **1.NBT.C.4, 2.NBT.B.5**

Resources
- Student Lesson Pages, Online
- Planning Guide, p. PG64

LESSON 9 **Add Two-Digit Numbers**

COMMON CORE **1.NBT.C.4, 2.NBT.B.5**

Resources
- Student Lesson Pages, Online
- Planning Guide, p. PG66

LESSON 12 **Choose a Nonstandard Unit to Measure Length**

COMMON CORE **1.MD.A.2, 2.MD.A.1**

Resources
- Student Lesson Pages, Online
- Planning Guide, p. PG74

LESSON 13 **Use a Nonstandard Ruler**

COMMON CORE **1.MD.A.2, 2.MD.A.1**

Resources
- Student Lesson Pages, Online
- Planning Guide, p. PG76

LESSON 14 **Compare Lengths**

COMMON CORE **1.MD.A.1, 2.MD.A.4**

Resources
- Student Lesson Pages, Online
- Planning Guide, p. PG78

LESSON 17 **Use a Bar Graph**

COMMON CORE **1.MD.C.4, 2.MD.D.10**

Resources
- Student Lesson Pages, Online
- Planning Guide, p. PG84

LESSON 18 **Take a Survey**

COMMON CORE **1.MD.C.4, 2.MD.D.10**

Resources
- Student Lesson Pages, Online
- Planning Guide, p. PG86

LESSON 19 **Identify Shapes**

COMMON CORE **1.G.A.1, 2.G.A.1**

Resources
- Student Lesson Pages, Online
- Planning Guide, p. PG88

✓ Assessment

An Assessment Check Mark following a lesson title indicates that a Checkpoint or Getting Ready Test is available for assessment after completing the lesson.

Checkpoints and Getting Ready Tests can be found in the online Getting Ready Lessons and Resources.

Developing understanding of addition, subtraction, and strategies for addition and subtraction within 20

Make a Math Facts Strategies Book

Objective
Apply addition and subtraction strategies to complete basic facts practice.

Materials
Online Project pp. B9–B12, connecting cubes

1 INTRODUCE

Explain that for this project children will think about the strategies they use to solve addition and subtraction sentences and then review the facts that they find the hardest. Write the following number sentences on the board.

$4 + 4 =$ ___ $\quad 4 + 5 =$ ___
$8 + 7 =$ ___ $\quad 9 + 2 =$ ___
$7 + 3 =$ ___

- **What strategies have you learned that can help you remember the sum for 4 + 4?** doubles; 4 + 4 = 8
- **What other doubles facts do you know?** Make a list of children's responses.
- **What strategies have you learned that can help you remember the sum for 4 + 5?** doubles plus 1; 4 + 5 = 9 **8 + 7?** doubles minus 1; 8 + 7 = 15 **9 + 2?** make a ten or count on; 9 + 2 = 11 **7 + 3?** make a ten or count on; 7 + 3 = 10

▶ Plan

Call attention to the exercises on page B9. Have children work independently to circle the facts they find difficult to solve. Have children solve the circled facts and then share their strategies.

2 DO THE PROJECT

▶ Put It Together

On page B10, discuss as a class how addition and subtraction are related. Then have children summarize the relationship using pictures, numbers, or words.

Have them apply their understanding to write related facts for two facts that they personally find difficult to remember. Encourage children to use connecting cubes to check that their number sentences are correct.

Name ______________________ CRITICAL AREA Developing understanding of addition, subtraction, and strategies for addition and subtraction within 20

Review Project
Make a Math Facts Strategies Book

See Planning Guide • End-of-Year Resources for Lesson Plans.

Project
Make a class book about strategies that can help you remember your math facts.

▶ Plan
Look at the facts. Which facts are hard for you? Circle them.
Then find each sum and difference.
Children's circling will vary.

9 +5 14	8 +6 14	4 +7 11	7 +8 15	5 +6 11
7 +6 13	8 +5 13	8 +8 16	4 +8 12	5 +7 12
14 −5 9	14 −7 7	11 −7 4	15 −8 7	11 −6 5
12 −5 7	13 −6 7	16 −7 9	17 −8 9	15 −6 9

▶ Put It Together
How are addition and subtraction related?
Use pictures, numbers, or words.

Check children's work.

Answers will vary for the following questions. Possible answers are given.

Write two facts that are hard for you.

8 (+) 5 = 13 $\qquad$ 17 (−) 9 = 8

Write the related facts for each hard fact.

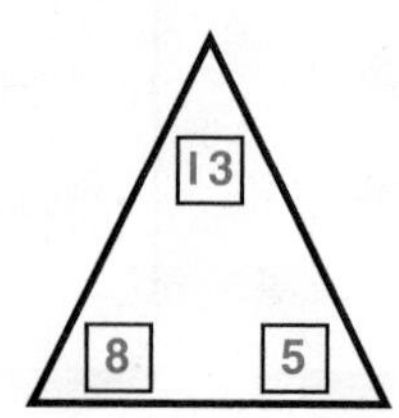

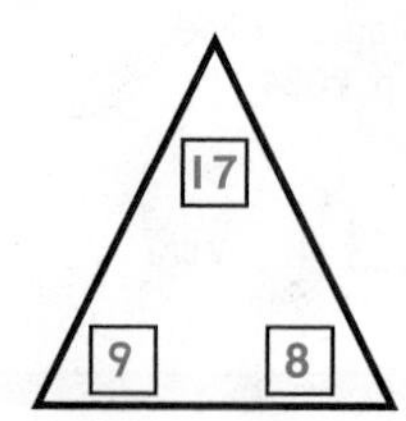

8 + 5 = 13 $\qquad$ 8 + 9 = 17
5 + 8 = 13 $\qquad$ 9 + 8 = 17
13 − 8 = 5 $\qquad$ 17 − 9 = 8
13 − 5 = 8 $\qquad$ 17 − 8 = 9

Name ______________________

Some Fact Strategies
- Doubles
- Doubles plus or minus 1
- Count on or count back
- Make a ten
- Think addition to subtract

Reflect
Find each missing number. What strategy did you use? Explain.

Strategies will vary. Possible answers are given.

1.	12 − 3 = 9	Count back. Think 12. Count back 3 numbers. Say 11, 10, 9. So, 12 − 3 = 9.
2.	8 + 9 = 17	Use doubles plus 1. Think 8 + 8 = 16. So, 8 + 8 + 1 = 17.
3.	15 − 8 = 7	Think addition to subtract. 7 plus what number is equal to 15? 7 + 8 = 15, so 15 − 8 = 7.
4.	3 + 9 = 12	Count on. Start with 9 because it is the greater number. Count on 3. Think 9. Say 10, 11, 12. So, 9 + 3 = 12.

Review Project B11

Go Beyond
Write a number from 9 to 14 to use as the whole. Use parts and wholes to complete related number sentences.

Answers will vary. Possible answers are given.

Number: 14

	part		part		whole	whole		part		part
1.	9	+	5	=	14	14	−	5	=	9
2.	8	+	6	=	14	14	−	6	=	8
3.	7	+	7	=	14	14	−	7	=	7
4.	6	+	8	=	14	14	−	8	=	6
5.	5	+	9	=	14	14	−	9	=	5

6. Choose one of the number sentences above. What strategy helps you remember how to find the sum or difference?

Answers will vary.

B12

Online Projects, pp. B11–B12

▶ Reflect

On page B11, have children explain a strategy that they can use to find each missing number.

▶ Go Beyond

On page B12, have children choose a number from 9 to 14 to use as the whole. Then have them use relationships among the parts and the whole to write pairs of related addition and subtraction sentences.

3 EXTEND THE PROJECT

- Have children choose a math fact that they used a strategy to solve. Have them draw a picture to show how the strategy helped them solve the fact.
- Combine children's pages into a class Math Facts Strategies Book.

Performance Assessment: You can use this project as a means of assessing a child's understanding of the concepts and skills found in this critical area.

Project Scoring Rubric

Performance Assessment

3	Demonstrates full understanding of the project. Correctly recalls addition and subtraction facts and uses strategies correctly.
2	Demonstrates a thorough understanding of the project. Recalls addition and subtraction facts, that may contain minor errors.
1	Demonstrates a partial understanding of the project. Recalls most of the facts and uses some of the strategies correctly.
0	Demonstrates little understanding of addition and subtraction strategies.

Developing understanding of whole number relationships and place value, including grouping in tens and ones

Numbers Around Us

Objective
Use tens and ones to show whole number relationships.

Materials
Online Project pp. B13–B15, connecting cubes

1 INTRODUCE

Use the question below to introduce the project.

- **How can you use numbers to tell about somebody or something?**

Show children a number that describes you and ask them to guess what it represents. After several guesses, share the answer.

Next, have children write a number that tells something about themselves. Ask for volunteers to share and explain their answers.

▶ Plan

Tell children that they will make a number show by gathering numbers that tell about them and their classmates.

2 DO THE PROJECT

▶ Put It Together

Have children use connecting cubes to show how many pets live in their homes. Ask children to hold up their connected cubes. Children without any pets can assist in collecting and counting the groups of cubes.

- **How can you use connecting cubes to show and count the number of pets there are in our class?** Put our cubes together. Make groups of tens.
- **How many groups of ten? How many ones? How many pets do the children in our class have?**

For Exercise 1 on page B13, have children write the class number of pets and then record the tens and ones by drawing a quick picture. For Exercise 2, have them tell how many children live in their home and show the number with connecting cubes. Have children help count all the cubes by making tens and ones and record by drawing a quick picture.

In Exercise 3 on page B14, have children choose, model, and record their favorite number from 10 to 100. Have children count crayons they have in their desk to complete Exercise 4.

Name ____________________

CRITICAL AREA Developing understanding of whole number relationships and place value, including grouping in tens and ones

Review Project
Numbers Around Us

See Planning Guide • End-of-Year Resources for Lesson Plans.

Project
Make a number show!

▶ Plan and Put It Together
Write the number. Show it with a quick picture.

Check children's work.

1. We have ____ pets.

Tens	Ones

____ tens + ____ ones = ____

2. We have ____ children in our class families.

Tens	Ones

____ tens + ____ ones = ____

3. ____ is my favorite number. Answers will vary.

Tens	Ones

____ tens + ____ ones = ____

4. I have ____ crayons in my desk. Answers will vary.

Tens	Ones

____ tens + ____ ones = ____

Online Projects, pp. B13–B14

Name ____________________

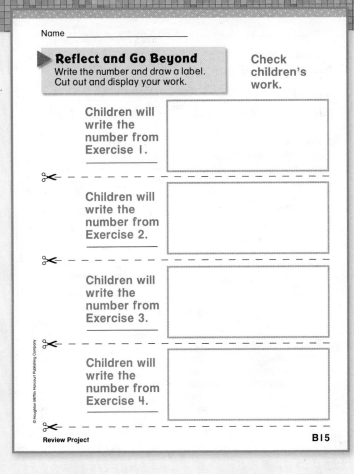

Reflect and Go Beyond
Write the number and draw a label.
Cut out and display your work.

Check children's work.

Children will write the number from Exercise 1.

Children will write the number from Exercise 2.

Children will write the number from Exercise 3.

Children will write the number from Exercise 4.

Review Project B15

Online Projects, p. B15

▶ Reflect

On page B15, have children write each of the four numbers they modeled in Exercises 1–4 on the lines provided. In the box beside each number, have them draw a picture. For example, children may draw a picture of a cat next to the number that tells how many pets the children in the class have.

▶ Go Beyond

Ask children to cut out each number and accompanying picture from the page. Have children glue these numbers and their pictures onto a large piece of paper in numerical order. Children can title this project "Numbers Around Us."

3 EXTEND THE PROJECT

Provide a variety of fun facts that involve numbers from 1 to 100. Here are some examples:

- a female alligator can lay about 60 eggs
- the giant tortoise can live over 100 years
- number of teeth an adult has: 32 teeth
- number of bones in a human hand: 26 bones

Ask children to illustrate their chosen fact on a separate sheet of paper and show the number that describes the fact in words and pictures.

Portfolio You can use this project as a means of assessing a child's understanding of the concepts and skills found in this critical area.

Project Scoring Rubric

Performance Assessment

3	Demonstrates a full understanding of the project. Is able to represent each number correctly. Is able to order the numbers appropriately.
2	Demonstrates a thorough understanding of the project. Is able to represent most numbers correctly. Is able to order most numbers appropriately.
1	Demonstrates a partial understanding of the project. Is able to represent some numbers correctly. Is able to order some numbers appropriately.
0	Demonstrates little understanding of the project.

Developing understanding of linear measurement and measuring lengths as iterating length units

Measure and Graph

Objective
Measure lengths and display the data in a tally chart and a bar graph.

Materials
Online Project pp. B16–B19, classroom objects, paper clip measuring tool, crayons

1 INTRODUCE

Explain that for this project children will measure objects using their paper clip measuring tool, record the lengths, and use a tally chart and a bar graph to display their data.

- **How do you record information in a tally chart?** Possible answer: I draw a tally mark for each object I count. If I count a group of 5, I draw 4 tally marks and a slash across them.
- **How do you record information in a bar graph?** Possible answer: I count the number of objects and color a bar so that it lines up with that number.

▶ Plan

Review with children how to measure the length of an object by lining up the end of their measuring tool with the end of the object. Children count how many paper clips long the object is from one end to the other.

2 DO THE PROJECT

▶ Put It Together

Have children find the classroom objects listed on page B16.

- **How many objects do you need to measure?** 7

Have children measure and record the length of each object using their paper clip measuring tool, making sure to measure each object's length to the nearest paper clip. Next, have children record the lengths in the top chart. Then, in the tally chart, have them draw a tally mark for each length they recorded. Make sure children understand that not every row in the tally chart will have an entry.

- **If the pencil, CD case, and marker are each about 5 paper clips long, how will you show this information in the tally chart?** Possible answer: I will draw 3 tally marks next to the number 5.

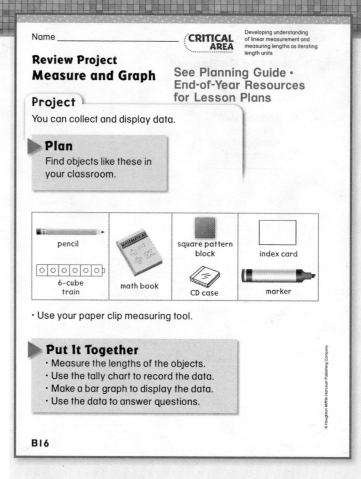

Name ______________________

CRITICAL AREA Developing understanding of linear measurement and measuring lengths as iterating length units

Review Project
Measure and Graph

See Planning Guide • End-of-Year Resources for Lesson Plans

Project
You can collect and display data.

▶ Plan
Find objects like these in your classroom.

pencil 6-cube train	math book	square pattern block CD case	index card marker

- Use your paper clip measuring tool.

▶ Put It Together
- Measure the lengths of the objects.
- Use the tally chart to record the data.
- Make a bar graph to display the data.
- Use the data to answer questions.

Measure the lengths.

Object	Length
pencil	about 5 paper clips
6-cube train	about 4 paper clips
math book	about 10 paper clips
square pattern block	about 1 paper clip
CD case	about 5 paper clips
index card	about 4 paper clips
marker	about 5 paper clips

Record in the tally chart.

Length	Number of Objects
1	|
2	
3	
4	||
5	|||
6	
7	
8	
9	
10	|

Online Projects, pp. B16–B17

Name ____________________

Make a bar graph.

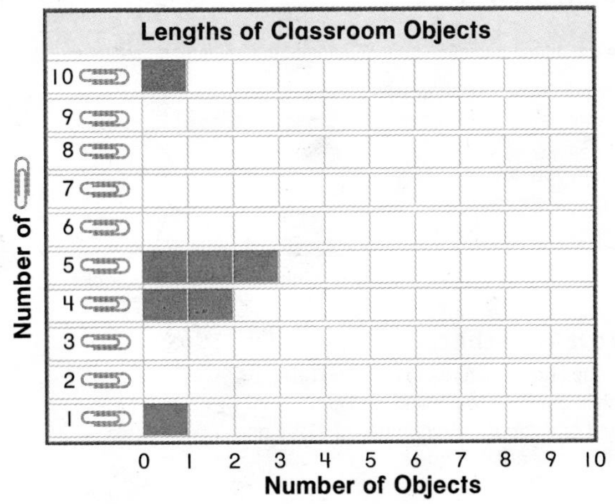

1. What length had the greatest number of objects? 5
2. What lengths had the least number of objects? 1 10
3. What is the longest length? 10
4. What is the shortest length? 1

B18

Reflect

How are the tally chart and bar graph alike?

Possible answer: They both show the same information.

How are they different?

Possible answer: The bar graph shows the information using bars. A tally chart shows the information using tally marks.

Go Beyond

Find more objects.
Measure them.
Add them to the tally chart and bar graph.
See how the tally chart and bar graph change.

Object	Length

Review Project B19

▶ Reflect

On page B18, have children use the data from their tally charts to complete the bar graph, then use the bars they colored to answer the questions.

- **How can you use the bar graph to find which length has the greatest number of objects?** Possible answer: After I color the bars for each length, I compare the bars. The longest bar is the length that has the greatest number of objects.

▶ Go Beyond

Have classroom objects readily available for children to measure using their paper clip measuring tools. Have them record their measurements on the chart on page B19. Then have children add the new measurements to the tally chart and bar graph. Discuss with children how the tally chart and bar graph change.

3 EXTEND THE PROJECT

- Distribute blank charts to children with the labels "Number of Cubes" and "Length." Have children work in groups to make 10 cube trains of different lengths. Have children record the number of cubes in each train in the chart. Then have children measure each cube train with their paper clip measuring tools and record their measurements in their chart.
- Have groups share their measurements with the class. Then create a bar graph on the board showing the class data.

Portfolio You can use this project as a means of assessing a child's understanding of the concepts and skills found in this critical area.

Project Scoring Rubric

Performance Assessment

3	Demonstrates a full understanding of the project. Accurately measures objects, records data in a tally chart, and completes a bar graph.
2	Demonstrates a thorough understanding of the project. Accurately measures objects, correctly records data in a tally chart, but does not correctly complete a bar graph.
1	Demonstrates a partial understanding of the project. Measures objects and records data in a tally chart with few errors, but does not correctly complete a bar graph.
0	Demonstrates little understanding of measuring, recording data in tally charts, and completing a bar graph.

Online Projects, pp. B18–B19

Reasoning about attributes of, and composing and decomposing geometric shapes

Building Shapes

Objective
Build two-dimensional and three-dimensional geometric shapes.

Materials
Online Project pp. B20–B23, toothpicks, clay (or mini marshmallows), pattern blocks

1 INTRODUCE

▶ Plan

Introduce the project by reviewing what children know about two-dimensional and three-dimensional shapes.

- **What shapes do you see around the classroom?**
- **How are the shapes the same? How are they different?**
- **Look out the classroom window. What shapes do you see outside?**

Point to different shapes, and have volunteers describe the attributes of each shape. Encourage children to use the number of sides and vertices in their descriptions.

Distribute the project pages and have children preview each page. Then distribute the rest of the materials.

2 DO THE PROJECT

▶ Put It Together

Guide children to use toothpicks and small balls of clay (or mini marshmallows) to make a triangle.

- **How many sides does a triangle have? How many vertices?** three sides; three vertices
- **How can you use the toothpicks and clay (or marshmallows) to build a triangle?** Use toothpicks for the sides and connect them with clay.

Point out that the picture can help them see how to place the toothpicks and the balls of clay.

Have children build a triangle and record the number of sides and vertices in the appropriate space on page B20.

Have children continue in a similar manner on page B21 to make a rectangle, trapezoid, and hexagon and record the attributes. Encourage children to recall that a square is a special kind of rectangle. Remind children that the pictures for each shape can help them build the shapes.

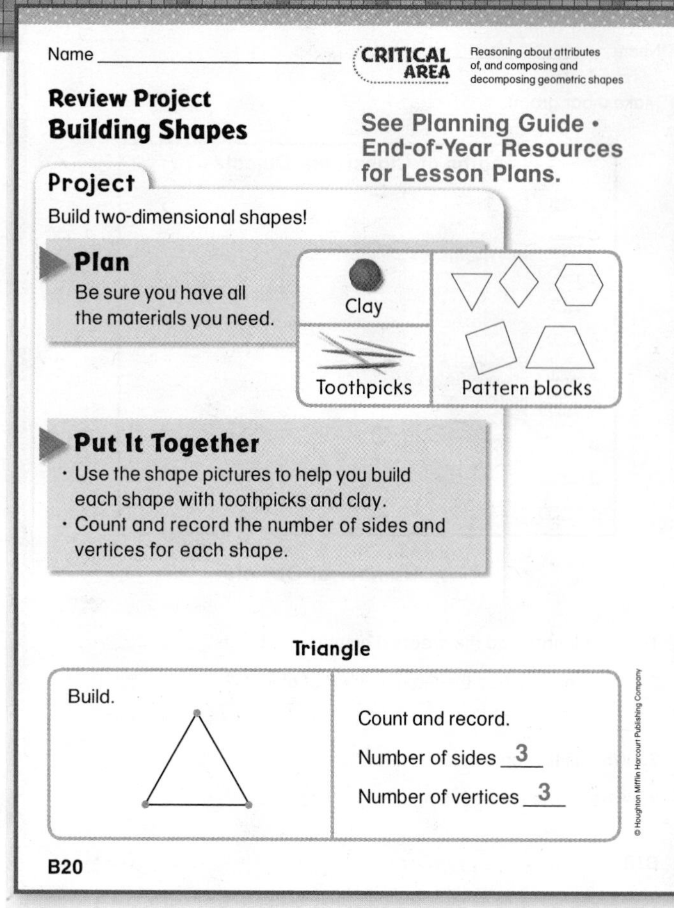
Name ____________

CRITICAL AREA Reasoning about attributes of, and composing and decomposing geometric shapes

Review Project
Building Shapes

See Planning Guide • End-of-Year Resources for Lesson Plans.

Project
Build two-dimensional shapes!

▶ Plan
Be sure you have all the materials you need.

Clay · Toothpicks · Pattern blocks

▶ Put It Together
- Use the shape pictures to help you build each shape with toothpicks and clay.
- Count and record the number of sides and vertices for each shape.

Triangle
Build.
Count and record.
Number of sides 3
Number of vertices 3

© Houghton Mifflin Harcourt Publishing Company

B20

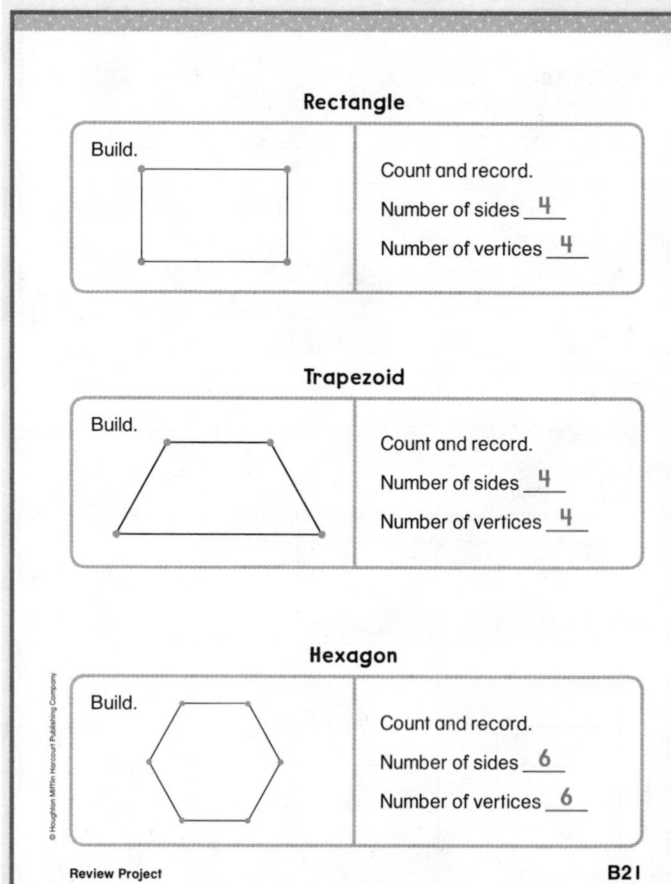
Rectangle
Build.
Count and record.
Number of sides 4
Number of vertices 4

Trapezoid
Build.
Count and record.
Number of sides 4
Number of vertices 4

Hexagon
Build.
Count and record.
Number of sides 6
Number of vertices 6

© Houghton Mifflin Harcourt Publishing Company

Review Project B21

Online Projects, pp. B20–B21

Name ______________________

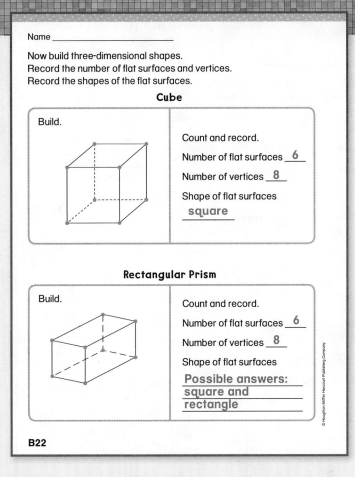

Now build three-dimensional shapes.
Record the number of flat surfaces and vertices.
Record the shapes of the flat surfaces.

Cube

Build.

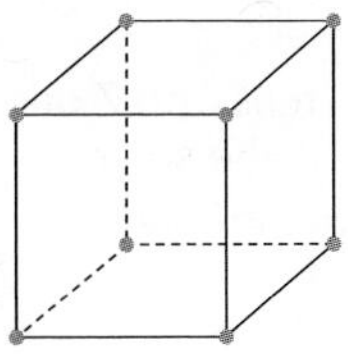

Count and record.
Number of flat surfaces 6
Number of vertices 8
Shape of flat surfaces
square

Rectangular Prism

Build.

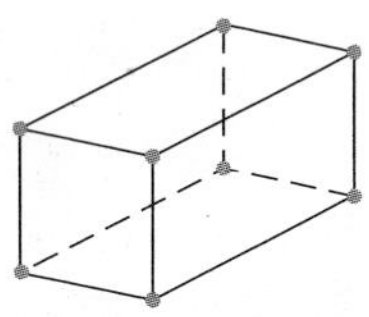

Count and record.
Number of flat surfaces 6
Number of vertices 8
Shape of flat surfaces
Possible answers:
square and
rectangle

B22

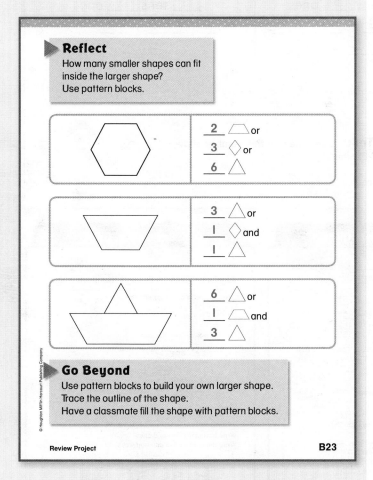

Reflect
How many smaller shapes can fit inside the larger shape?
Use pattern blocks.

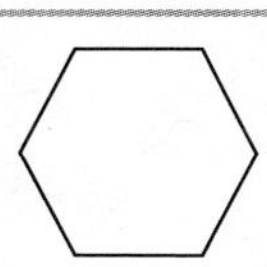

2 (trapezoid) or
3 (rhombus) or
6 (triangle)

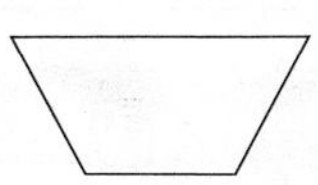

3 (triangle) or
1 (rhombus) and
1 (triangle)

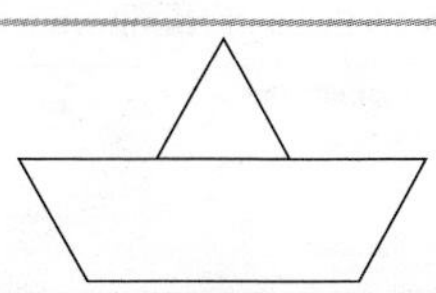

6 (triangle) or
1 (trapezoid) and
3 (triangle)

Go Beyond
Use pattern blocks to build your own larger shape.
Trace the outline of the shape.
Have a classmate fill the shape with pattern blocks.

Review Project B23

On page B22 discuss the attributes of the shapes, having children record the number of flat surfaces and vertices each shape has as well as the two-dimensional shape(s) of the flat surfaces.

▶ Reflect

For page B23, tell children they can use pattern blocks to build the shape with blocks and then trace the blocks.

▶ Go Beyond

At the bottom of the page, have children use pattern blocks to build their own shape, trace the outside of the shape, then challenge a classmate to build the shape with pattern blocks.

3 EXTEND THE PROJECT

- Ask children to design a border by laying pattern block trapezoids along a drawn 6-inch line. Have children trace and record the number of shapes used.
- Next, ask children to create the same kind of border using only triangles. Have children record the number of triangles they used. Discuss why they needed more triangles than trapezoids.

Portfolio You can use this project as a means of assessing a child's understanding of the concepts and skills found in this critical area.

Project Scoring Rubric

Performance Assessment

3	Demonstrates a full understanding of the project. Is able to compose and decompose geometric shapes and identify attributes and properties.
2	Demonstrates a thorough understanding of the project. Is able to compose and decompose most geometric shapes and identify most attributes and properties.
1	Demonstrates a partial understanding of the project. Is able to compose and decompose some geometric shapes and identify some attributes and properties.
0	Demonstrates little understanding of the project. Fails to compose and decompose shapes and identify attributes and properties.

Online Projects, pp. B22–B23

LESSON 1

Algebra • Ways to Expand Numbers

LESSON AT A GLANCE

Common Core Standards

Understand place value.
1.NBT.B.2 Understand that the two digits of a two-digit number represent amounts of tens and ones.

Understand place value.
2.NBT.A.3 Read and write numbers to 1000 using base-ten numerals, number names, and expanded form.

Lesson Objective
Write two-digit numbers in expanded form.

Essential Question
How can you write a two-digit number in different ways?

Materials
MathBoard

GO DIGITAL
- Animated Math Models
- *i*Tools: Base-Ten Blocks
- HMH Mega Math

1 TEACH and TALK

GO DIGITAL • Animated Math Models

▶ Model and Draw

MATHEMATICAL PRACTICES

Have children count the first set of base-ten models.

- **How many tens are there?** 8 **How many ones?** 7
- **What number does 8 tens stand for?** 80 **What number does 7 ones stand for?** 7
- **What number is 80 plus 7?** 87

2 PRACTICE

MATH BOARD

▶ Share and Show • Guided Practice

- **Look at Exercise 1. Explain how you will write the number in different ways.** First, I will write how many tens (3) and how many ones (5). Then, I will write 3 tens as 30 and 5 ones as 5, or 30 + 5. I will write the number with the 3 as the tens digit and the 5 as the ones digit, or 35.

This lesson builds on place value presented in Chapter 6 and prepares children for expanded notation taught in Grade 2.

Name ____________________

Algebra • Ways to Expand Numbers

Essential Question How can you write a two-digit number in different ways?

See Planning Guide • End-of-Year Resources for Lesson Plans.

Model and Draw

There are different ways to think about a number.

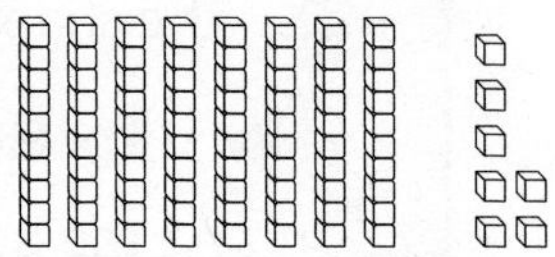

8 tens 7 ones
80 + 7
87

8 tens and 7 ones is the same as 80 plus 7.

Share and Show MATH BOARD

Write how many tens and ones.
Write the number in two different ways.

1.

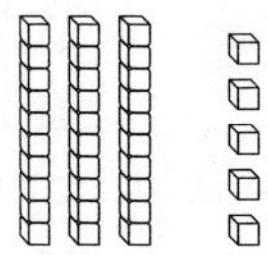

3 tens 5 ones
30 + 5
35

2.

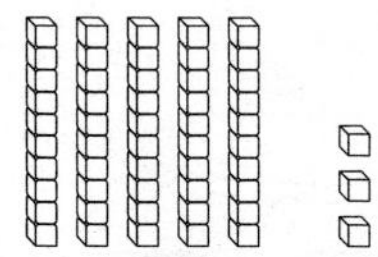

5 tens 3 ones
50 + 3
53

The 7 represents 70 because the number 72 is made up of 7 tens and 2 ones.

Math Talk Does the 7 in this number show 7 or 70? Explain.

Getting Ready for Grade 2 — one GR1

GR: Practice, p. GRP1

Name ____________ Lesson 1

Algebra • Ways to Expand Numbers

Write how many tens and ones.
Write the number in two different ways.

1. 5 tens 8 ones; 50 + 8; 58

2. 6 tens 4 ones; 60 + 4; 64

Problem Solving

3. Draw the same number using only tens.
Write how many tens and ones.
Write the number in two different ways.

5 tens 10 ones; 50 + 10; 60

6 tens 0 ones; 60 + 0; 60

Getting Ready for Grade 2 — one GRP1

GR: Reteach, p. GRR1

Name ____________ Lesson 1 Reteach

Algebra • Ways to Expand Numbers

You can write a number different ways.

Count the tens. Count the ones.
4 tens 5 ones

4 tens is the same as 40.
5 ones is the same as 5.
40 + 5 is the same as 45.

Write how many tens and ones.
Write the number two different ways.

1. 2 tens 6 ones; 20 + 6; 26

2. 6 tens 3 ones; 60 + 3; 63

Reteach — GRR1 — Grade 1

*GR – Getting Ready Lessons and Resources (*www.thinkcentral.com*)

On Your Own

Write how many tens and ones.
Write the number in two different ways.

3.

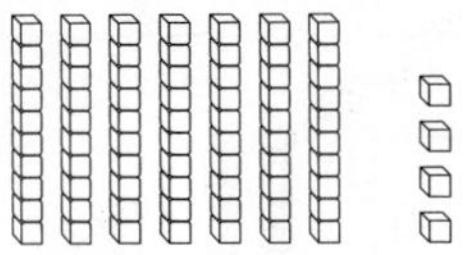

7 tens 4 ones

70 + 4

74

4.

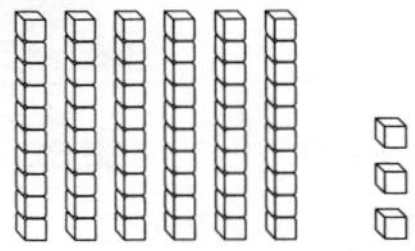

6 tens 3 ones

60 + 3

63

Problem Solving Real World

5. Draw the same number using only tens.
Write how many tens and ones.
Write the number in two different ways.

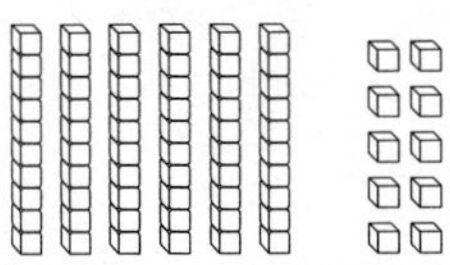

6 tens 10 ones

60 + 10

70

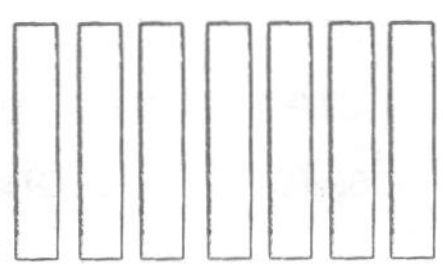

7 tens 0 ones

70 + 0

70

TAKE HOME ACTIVITY • Write a two-digit number to 99. Ask your child to write how many tens and ones and then write the number a different way.

Have children complete Exercise 2.

Use **Math Talk** to ensure that children understand that the 7 in the number 72 represents 7 tens or 70.

On Your Own

If children answered Exercises 1–2 correctly, assign Exercises 3–4. It is important that children understand the difference in value between the tens and ones digits.

- **In Exercise 3, what number does the 7 stand for in 74?** 70 **How do you know?** Possible answer: 7 is the digit in the tens place, so it stands for 7 tens. 7 tens is 70.

Problem Solving

UNLOCK THE PROBLEM Exercise 5 requires children to use higher order thinking skills. They need to understand that 10 ones is equivalent to 1 ten. It may be helpful to have children use models and match 10 ones next to 1 ten to show they are equivalent. Be sure children understand that they must replace the 10 ones with 1 ten and not just eliminate the ones.

- **Why can you write this number using only tens?** because I can trade the 10 ones for 1 ten
- **What number did you show in two different ways?** 70

3 SUMMARIZE

Common Core MATHEMATICAL PRACTICES

Essential Question

How can you write a two-digit number in different ways? I can write a two-digit number by writing the number of tens and the number of ones, like 6 tens 7 ones. Then I can write the number of tens as a number and the number of ones as another number, like 60 + 7. Then I can write the number with 6 as the tens digit and 7 as the ones digit, like 67.

Math Journal WRITE Math

Draw quick pictures to show 9 tens 2 ones. Write the number in three different ways.

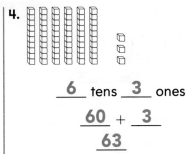

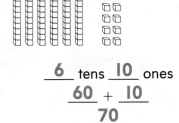

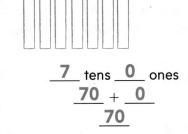

LESSON 2

Identify Place Value

LESSON AT A GLANCE

Common Core Standards
Understand place value.
1.NBT.B.2 Understand that the two digits of a two-digit number represent amounts of tens and ones.

Understand place value.
2.NBT.A.3 Read and write numbers to 1000 using base-ten numerals, number names, and expanded form.

Lesson Objective
Identify how many hundreds, tens, and ones there are in numbers to 199.

Essential Question
How can you use place value to understand the value of a number?

Materials
MathBoard, base-ten blocks

GO DIGITAL
- Animated Math Models
- *i*Tools: Base-Ten Blocks
- HMH Mega Math

1 TEACH and TALK

GO DIGITAL • Animated Math Models

Model and Draw

Common Core MATHEMATICAL PRACTICES

Work through the model with children. Point out that the chart explains what each digit stands for in the number 125.

Focus on the base-ten blocks and the quick pictures. Match them with their digits in the place value chart as you read what each digit in 125 means.

- **What does the place value chart show?** how many hundreds, tens, and ones there are in the number 125

2 PRACTICE

MATH BOARD

Share and Show • Guided Practice

- **How will you show each hundred?** I will trace to draw the square.

This lesson builds on identifying tens and ones presented in Chapter 6 and prepares children for identifying hundreds, tens, and ones taught in Grade 2.

Name ____________

Identify Place Value

Essential Question How can you use place value to understand the value of a number?

Model and Draw

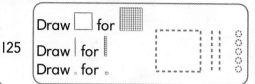

The **1** in **1**25 means 1 hundred.
The **2** in 1**2**5 means 2 tens.
The **5** in 12**5** means 5 ones.

125
Draw □ for [hundred]
Draw | for [ten]
Draw ∘ for [one]

hundreds	tens	ones
1	2	5

Share and Show MATH BOARD

Use your MathBoard and [base-ten blocks] to show the number.
Draw to complete the quick picture. Write how many hundreds, tens, and ones.

THINK
106 has no tens.

1. 106

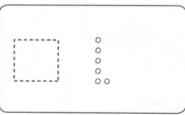

hundreds	tens	ones
1	0	6

Math Talk How is the 1 in 187 different from the 1 in 781?

The 1 in 187 means 1 hundred.
The 1 in 781 means 1 one.

Getting Ready for Grade 2 — three GR3

GR: Practice, p. GRP2

Name ____________ Lesson 2

Identify Place Value

Use your MathBoard and [base-ten blocks]. Draw to complete the quick picture. Write how many hundreds, tens, and ones. Check children's drawings.

1. 163

hundreds	tens	ones
1	6	3

2. 128

hundreds	tens	ones
1	2	8

3. 154

hundreds	tens	ones
1	5	4

Problem Solving (Real World)

Circle your answer.

4. I have 1 hundred, 2 tens, and 5 ones. What number am I?
25 100 (125)

5. I have 0 ones, 5 tens, and 1 hundred. What number am I?
103 105 (150)

Getting Ready for Grade 2 — two GRP2

GR: Reteach, p. GRR2

Name ____________ Lesson 2 Reteach

Identify Place Value

This shows the number 136.

136 has 1 hundred 3 tens 6 ones.

Write the numbers in the table.

hundreds	tens	ones
1	3	6

Draw to show 136.

Draw □ for [hundred]
Draw | for [ten]
Draw ∘ for [one]

Use your MathBoard and [base-ten blocks] to show the number. Trace to draw the quick picture. Write how many hundreds, tens, and ones.

1. 128 Check children's drawings.

hundreds	tens	ones
1	2	8

Reteach GRR2 Grade 1

***GR** – Getting Ready Lessons and Resources (*www.thinkcentral.com*)

On Your Own

Use your MathBoard and 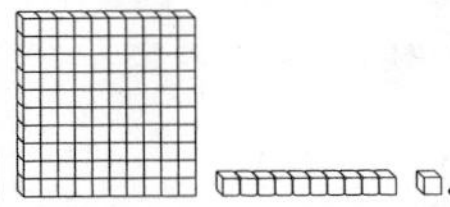.
Draw to complete the quick picture.
Write how many hundreds, tens, and ones.

2. 170

hundreds	tens	ones
1	7	0

3. 143

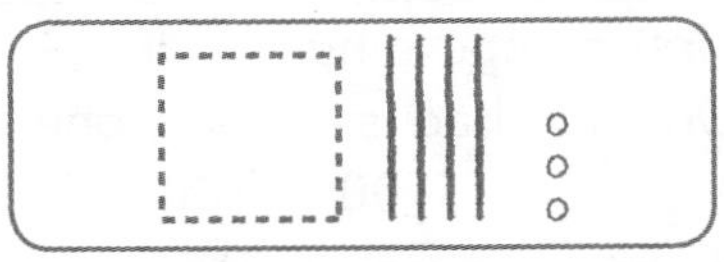

hundreds	tens	ones
1	4	3

4. 121

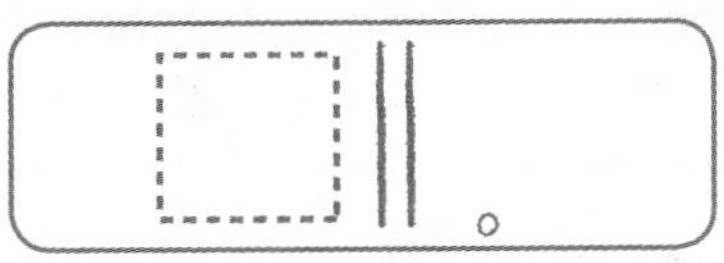

hundreds	tens	ones
1	2	1

Problem Solving Real World

Circle your answer.

5. I have 1 hundred, 9 tens, and 9 ones. What number am I?

99 100 (199)

6. I have 3 ones, 0 tens, and 1 hundred. What number am I?

107 170 (103)

TAKE HOME ACTIVITY • Write some numbers from 100 to 199. Have your child tell how many hundreds, tens, and ones are in the number.

- **How will you show tens and ones?** I will draw a line for each ten and a circle for each one.

Have children complete Exercise 1.

Use **Math Talk** to check that children understand that 1 has a different value in each number because it is in a different place.

On Your Own

If children answered Exercise 1 correctly, assign Exercises 2–4. Point out that when writing a three-digit number with either no tens or no ones, children must write 0 in the correct place.

- **How many hundreds are in the number 170?** 1
- **What does the 7 in the number 170 mean?** There are 7 tens in the number 170.
- **What does the 0 in the number 170 mean?** There are no ones in the number 170.

Problem Solving

UNLOCK THE PROBLEM Exercises 5 and 6 require children to attend to precision. Remind children that the value of a number is determined by the order of the digits.

Go Deeper

- **The numbers 103, 130, and 301 all have the same digits. Why are the numbers different?**
  Each digit has a different value because it is in a different place. The number of hundreds, tens, and ones is different in each number.

3 SUMMARIZE

MATHEMATICAL PRACTICES

Essential Question

How can you use place value to understand the value of a number? Possible answers: I can tell the value of each digit based on its place in the number. I can tell if the digit means hundreds, tens, or ones.

Math Journal WRITE Math

Tell how many hundreds, tens, and ones are in the number 154.

LESSON 3

Use Place Value to Compare Numbers

LESSON AT A GLANCE

Common Core Standards

Understand place value.
1.NBT.B.3 Compare two two-digit numbers based on meanings of the tens and ones digits, recording the results of comparisons with the symbols $>$, $=$, and $<$.

Understand place value.
2.NBT.A.4 Compare two three-digit numbers based on meanings of the hundreds, tens, and ones digits, using $>$, $=$, and $<$ symbols to record the results of comparisons.

Lesson Objective
Use $<$, $>$, and $=$ to compare numbers.

Essential Question
How can you use place value to compare two numbers?

Materials
MathBoard

GO DIGITAL
- Animated Math Models
- *i*Tools: Base-Ten Blocks
- HMH Mega Math

1 TEACH and TALK

GO DIGITAL • Animated Math Models

▶ Model and Draw

Common Core MATHEMATICAL PRACTICES

Have children tell what it means to compare two numbers.

- **What words can you use to compare two numbers?** I can say which number is greater than, less than, or equal to another number.

Point out that knowing the value of each digit is necessary to compare two numbers.

Compare 134 and 125, focusing on comparing the hundreds first and then the tens.

- **Suppose the hundreds digit and tens digit in two numbers are the same. How can you compare the numbers?** by comparing the ones

This lesson builds on comparing two-digit numbers presented in Chapter 7 and prepares children for comparing three-digit numbers taught in Grade 2.

Name ______________________

Use Place Value to Compare Numbers

Essential Question How can you use place value to compare two numbers?

Model and Draw

Use these symbols to compare numbers.

I want to eat the greater number.
45
46

$>$ is greater than
$<$ is less than
$=$ is equal to

45 < 46
45 is less than 46.

Compare 134 and 125.

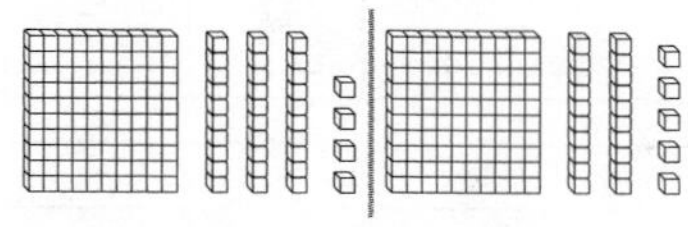

First compare hundreds.
One hundred is equal to one hundred.
100 = 100
If the hundreds are equal, compare the tens. 30 is greater than 20.
134 > 125

Share and Show MATH BOARD

Write the numbers and compare. Write $>$, $<$, or $=$.

1. 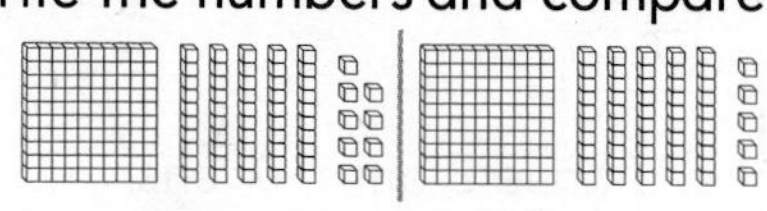
159 (>) 155

2. 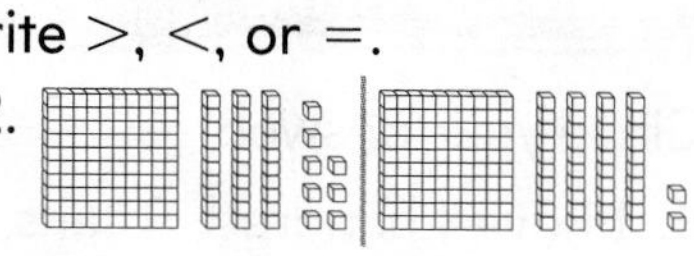
138 (<) 142

Compare the numbers using $>$, $<$, or $=$.

3. 187 (>) 168
4. 165 (>) 159
5. 127 (<) 141

Math Talk Compare 173 and 177. Did you have to compare all the digits? Why or why not?
Yes. The hundreds and tens are the same so compare the ones. 3 ones is less than 7 ones, so 173 is less than 177.

GR: Practice, p. GRP3

Name ______________________ Lesson 3

Use Place Value to Compare Numbers

Write the numbers. Compare. Write $>$, $<$, or $=$.

1. 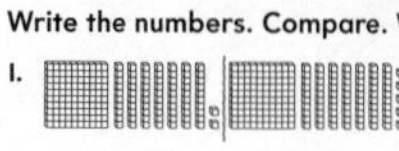
172 (<) 176

2. 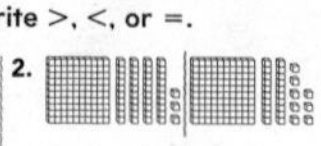
143 (>) 128

Compare the numbers using $>$, $<$, or $=$.

3. 162 (=) 162	4. 154 (>) 148	5. 195 (<) 199
6. 133 (<) 137	7. 129 (>) 126	8. 141 (=) 141
9. 119 (<) 125	10. 173 (=) 173	11. 187 (<) 192
12. 153 (=) 153	13. 191 (>) 178	14. 144 (<) 153

Problem Solving Real World

Solve.

15. Josh is thinking of a number between 100 and 199. It has 1 hundred, 4 tens, and 9 ones. Pia is thinking of a number between 100 and 199. It has 1 hundred, 8 tens, and 2 ones. Who is thinking of the greater number?

Draw or write to explain.
Check children's work.

Pia is thinking of a greater number.

GR: Reteach, p. GRR3

Name ______________________ Lesson 3 Reteach

Use Place Value to Compare Numbers

You can use models and symbols to compare numbers.

$>$ means **is greater than**
$<$ means **is less than**
$=$ means **is equal to**

Use the model to compare 142 and 147.

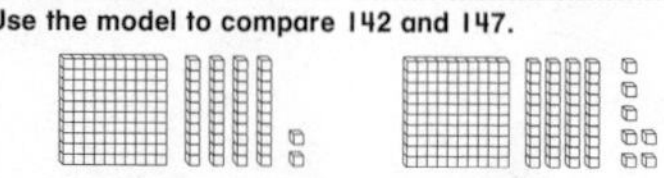

Step 1	Compare the hundreds.	1 hundred = 1 hundred
Step 2	Compare the tens.	4 tens = 4 tens
Step 3	Compare the ones.	2 ones < 7 ones

So, 142 is less than 147. 142 (<) 147

Use base-ten blocks if you need to.

Write the numbers and compare. Write $<$, $>$, or $=$.

1. 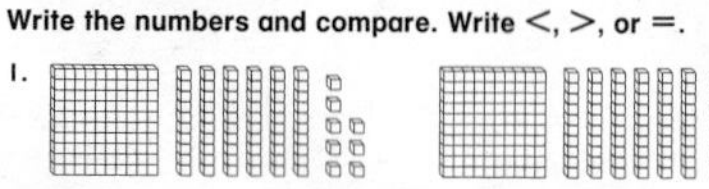
168 (>) 166

Compare the numbers using $>$, $<$, or $=$.
You may wish to make a model to check.

2. 151 (=) 151

*GR – Getting Ready Lessons and Resources (*www.thinkcentral.com*)

On Your Own

Write the numbers. Compare. Write >, <, or =.

6. 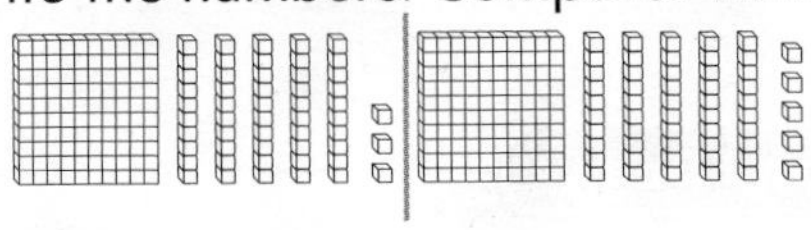

153 (<) 155

7. 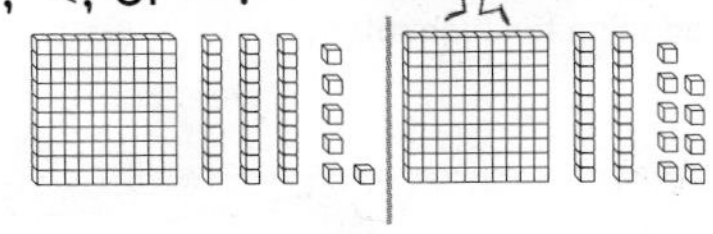

136 (>) 129

Compare the numbers using >, <, or =.

8. 143 (=) 143	**9.** 162 (>) 157	**10.** 185 (<) 188
11. 124 (<) 129	**12.** 189 (<) 195	**13.** 135 (=) 135
14. 173 (>) 164	**15.** 123 (>) 117	**16.** 118 (<) 131
17. 155 (>) 145	**18.** 181 (=) 181	**19.** 192 (>) 179
20. 122 (<) 129	**21.** 166 (<) 177	**22.** 154 (=) 154

Problem Solving Real World

23. Antonio is thinking of a number between 100 and 199. It has 1 hundred, 3 tens, and 6 ones. Kim is thinking of a number between 100 and 199. It has 1 hundred, 6 tens, and 3 ones. Who is thinking of a greater number?

Draw or write to explain.

Check children's work.

Kim is thinking of a greater number.

TAKE HOME ACTIVITY • Choose two numbers between 100 and 199 and have your child explain which number is greater.

Getting Ready Lessons and Resources, pp. GR7–GR8

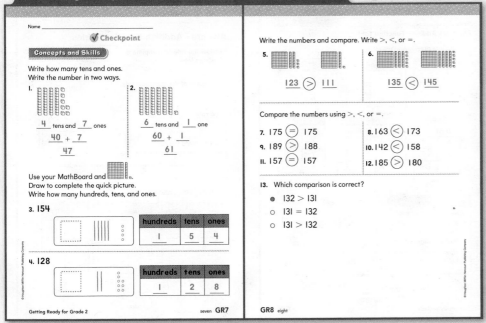

✓ Checkpoint

Name

✓ Checkpoint

Concepts and Skills

Write how many tens and ones. Write the number in two ways.

1. 4 tens and 7 ones; 40 + 7; 47

2. 6 tens and 1 one; 60 + 1; 61

Use your MathBoard and ▯. Draw to complete the quick picture. Write how many hundreds, tens, and ones.

3. 154

hundreds	tens	ones
1	5	4

4. 128

hundreds	tens	ones
1	2	8

Getting Ready for Grade 2 — seven GR7

Write the numbers and compare. Write >, <, or =.

5. 123 (>) 111

6. 135 (<) 145

Compare the numbers using >, <, or =.

7. 175 (=) 175

8. 163 (<) 173

9. 189 (>) 188

10. 142 (<) 158

11. 157 (=) 157

12. 185 (>) 180

13. Which comparison is correct?

- ● 132 > 131
- ○ 131 = 132
- ○ 131 > 132

GR8 eight

2 PRACTICE (MATH BOARD)

▶ Share and Show • Guided Practice

- **In Exercise 1, is 159 less than, greater than, or equal to 155?** greater than

Use **Math Talk** to check that children understand that to compare these numbers they must compare the ones because the hundreds and tens digits are the same.

▶ On Your Own

If children answered Exercises 1–5 correctly, assign Exercises 6–22. It is important that children understand that they must always compare the digits one place at a time.

- **What is always the first step in comparing numbers with hundreds, tens, and ones?** Compare the hundreds.

▶ Problem Solving Real World

UNLOCK THE PROBLEM Exercise 23 requires children to make sense of problems. Children will first need to compare the hundreds.

- **How can you tell how many hundreds each of the numbers will have?** Both numbers are between 100 and 199. The numbers from 100 through 199 have 1 in the hundreds place. So, both numbers have 1 in the hundreds place.
- **What will you compare next?** the tens
- **Who is thinking of the greater number?** Kim **Why?** because 6 tens is greater than 3 tens

3 SUMMARIZE

MATHEMATICAL PRACTICES

Essential Question

How can you use place value to compare two numbers? I can compare the value of each digit, one at a time, starting with the hundreds to see which number is greater than, less than, or equal to the other. If the number of hundreds is the same, I can compare the tens. If the hundreds and tens are the same, I can compare the ones.

Math Journal (WRITE Math)

Use the numbers 158 and 185. Compare the numbers using >, <, or =.

LESSON 4

Algebra: Addition Function Tables

LESSON AT A GLANCE

Common Core Standards
Add and subtract within 20.
1.OA.C.6 Add and subtract within 20, demonstrating fluency for addition and subtraction within 10. Use strategies such as counting on; making ten (e.g., 8 + 6 = 8 + 2 + 4 = 10 + 4 = 14); decomposing a number leading to a ten (e.g., 13 − 4 = 13 − 3 − 1 = 10 − 1 = 9); using the relationship between addition and subtraction (e.g., knowing that 8 + 4 = 12, one knows 12 − 8 = 4); and creating equivalent but easier or known sums (e.g., adding 6 + 7 by creating the known equivalent 6 + 6 + 1 = 12 + 1 = 13).

Add and subtract within 20.
2.OA.B.2 Fluently add and subtract within 20 using mental strategies. By end of Grade 2, know from memory all sums of two one-digit numbers.

Lesson Objective
Complete an addition function table.

Essential Question
How can you follow a rule to complete an addition function table?

Materials
MathBoard

GO DIGITAL — Animated Math Models

1 TEACH and TALK
GO DIGITAL • Animated Math Models

▶ Model and Draw
Common Core MATHEMATICAL PRACTICES

Focus on the Add 9 function table.

- **What does the rule "Add 9" tell you to do?** Add 9 to each number in the left column.
- **What addition sentences can help you complete the function table?** 7 + 9 = 16; 8 + 9 = 17; 9 + 9 = 18
- **Why do you think this is called an addition function table?** because the rule says add

Discuss how the function table works including how following the rule results in a pattern across each row.

- **What pattern do you see when you complete this table?** Each number in the right column is 9 more than the number in the same row in the left column.

This lesson builds on addition facts presented in Chapter 3 and prepares children for addition skills and strategies taught in Grade 2.

Name

Algebra • Addition Function Tables
Essential Question How can you follow a rule to complete an addition function table?

Model and Draw

The rule is Add 9. Add 9 to each number.

Add 9	
7	16
8	17
9	18

Share and Show MATH BOARD

Follow a rule to complete the table.

1.

Add 3	
7	10
8	11
9	12

2.

Add 4	
6	10
7	11
8	12

3.

Add 5	
5	10
7	12
9	14

4.

Add 8	
5	13
7	15
9	17

5.

Add 7	
6	13
8	15
9	16

6.

Add 6	
6	12
8	14
9	15

Math Talk Look at Exercise 4. How does the rule help you see a pattern? The rule is Add 8, so in each row the number on the right is 8 more than the number on the left.

GR: Practice, p. GRP4

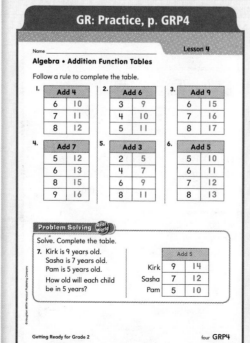

Name Lesson 4

Algebra • Addition Function Tables

Follow a rule to complete the table.

1.

Add 4	
6	10
7	11
8	12

2.

Add 6	
3	9
4	10
5	11

3.

Add 9	
6	15
7	16
8	17

4.

Add 7	
5	12
6	13
8	15
9	16

5.

Add 3	
2	5
4	7
6	9
8	11

6.

Add 5	
5	10
6	11
7	12
8	13

Problem Solving Real World

Solve. Complete the table.

7. Kirk is 9 years old. Sasha is 7 years old. Pam is 5 years old. How old will each child be in 5 years?

	Add 5	
Kirk	9	14
Sasha	7	12
Pam	5	10

Getting Ready for Grade 2 four GRP4

GR: Reteach, p. GRR4

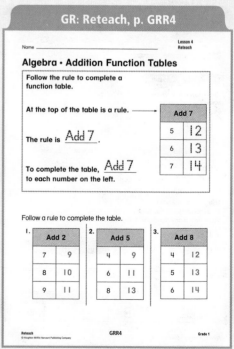

Name Lesson 4 Reteach

Algebra • Addition Function Tables

Follow the rule to complete a function table.

At the top of the table is a rule.

The rule is Add 7.

To complete the table, Add 7 to each number on the left.

Add 7	
5	12
6	13
7	14

Follow a rule to complete the table.

1.

Add 2	
7	9
8	10
9	11

2.

Add 5	
4	9
6	11
8	13

3.

Add 8	
4	12
5	13
6	14

Reteach GRR4 Grade 1

*GR – Getting Ready Lessons and Resources (*www.thinkcentral.com*)

On Your Own

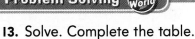

Follow a rule to complete the table.

7.

Add 7	
7	14
8	15
9	16

8.

Add 4	
7	11
8	12
9	13

9.

Add 5	
7	12
8	13
9	14

10.

Add 8	
4	12
6	14
8	16
9	17

11.

Add 3	
3	6
5	8
7	10
9	12

12.

Add 6	
6	12
7	13
8	14
9	15

Problem Solving Real World

13. Solve. Complete the table.

Tom is 8 years old.
Julie is 7 years old.
Carla is 4 years old.

How old will each child be in 4 years?

	Add 4	
Tom	8	12
Julie	7	11
Carla	4	8

TAKE HOME ACTIVITY • Copy Exercise 12 and change the numbers in the left column to 9, 7, 5, and 3. Have your child complete the table and explain how he or she used a rule to solve the problem.

2 PRACTICE

MATH BOARD

Share and Show • Guided Practice

Check that children are following the rule for each table as they complete Exercises 1–6.

- **How do you know what to do to complete each table?** I read the rule at the top and add that number to each number in left column of the table.

Use Math Talk to help children see that each number in the right column is 8 more than the number in the same row in the left column.

On Your Own

If children answered Exercises 1–6 correctly, assign Exercises 7–12.

- **How are the function tables alike?** They all have addition rules.
- **How are the function tables different?** Each rule has a different number to add.

Problem Solving Real World

UNLOCK THE PROBLEM Exercise 13 requires children to use information from the problem to establish a rule for a function table and to follow the rule to complete the table.

- **What information do you know from reading the problem?** I know how old Tom, Julie, and Carla are.
- **What did you do to solve the problem?** I added 4 to each number. **Explain why.** I wanted to know how old each child will be in 4 years and that means adding 4 to each child's age now.

3 SUMMARIZE

Common Core MATHEMATICAL PRACTICES

Essential Question

How can you follow a rule to complete an addition function table? I can add the number shown in the rule to each number in the left column of the table and then write the sum in the right column.

Math Journal

WRITE Math

What might be the rule for the addition function table if there is a 4 in the left column and an 8 in the right column?

LESSON 5

Algebra • Subtraction Function Tables

LESSON AT A GLANCE

Common Core Standards
Add and subtract within 20.
1.OA.C.6 Add and subtract within 20, demonstrating fluency for addition and subtraction within 10. Use strategies such as counting on; making ten (e.g., 8 + 6 = 8 + 2 + 4 = 10 + 4 = 14); decomposing a number leading to a ten (e.g., 13 − 4 = 13 − 3 − 1 = 10 − 1 = 9); using the relationship between addition and subtraction (e.g., knowing that 8 + 4 = 12, one knows 12 − 8 = 4); and creating equivalent but easier or known sums (e.g., adding 6 + 7 by creating the known equivalent 6 + 6 + 1 = 12 + 1 = 13).

Add and subtract within 20.
2.OA.B.2 Fluently add and subtract within 20 using mental strategies. By end of Grade 2, know from memory all sums of two one-digit numbers.

Lesson Objective
Complete a subtraction function table.

Essential Question
How can you follow a rule to complete a subtraction function table?

Materials
MathBoard

GO DIGITAL
Animated Math Models

1 TEACH and TALK
GO DIGITAL • Animated Math Models

▶ Model and Draw
Common Core MATHEMATICAL PRACTICES

Focus on the Subtract 7 function table.

- **What does the rule "Subtract 7" tell you to do?** Subtract 7 from each number in the left column.
- **What number sentences can help you complete the function table?** 14 − 7 = 7; 15 − 7 = 8; 16 − 7 = 9
- **Why do you think this is called a subtraction function table?** because the rule says subtract

Discuss how the function table works. Guide children to see that the rule makes a pattern across each row.

- **What pattern do you see when you complete this table?** Each number in the right column is 7 less than the number in the same row in the left column.

This lesson builds on subtraction facts presented in Chapter 4 and prepares children for applying subtraction skills and strategies taught in Grade 2.

Name ____________

Algebra • Subtraction Function Tables

Essential Question How can you follow a rule to complete a subtraction function table?

Model and Draw

The rule is Subtract 7. Subtract 7 from each number.

Subtract 7	
14	7
15	8
16	9

Share and Show MATH BOARD

Follow a rule to complete the table.

1.

Subtract 3	
9	6
10	7
11	8

2.

Subtract 4	
6	2
8	4
10	6

3.

Subtract 5	
6	1
8	3
10	5

4.

Subtract 8	
9	1
11	3
13	5

5.

Subtract 7	
12	5
13	6
14	7

6.

Subtract 6	
6	0
8	2
9	3

Possible answer: I subtract from the same numbers. The differences in Exercise 3 should each be 1 less, because I subtract 5 instead of 4.

Math Talk How can Exercise 2 help you solve Exercise 3?

GR: Practice, p. GRP5

Name ____________ Lesson 5

Algebra • Subtraction Function Tables

Follow a rule to complete the table.

1.

Subtract 5	
6	1
7	2
8	3

2.

Subtract 6	
9	3
10	4
11	5

3.

Subtract 4	
9	5
10	6
11	7

4.

Subtract 8	
11	3
13	5
15	7
16	8

5.

Subtract 9	
11	2
13	4
15	6
17	8

6.

Subtract 7	
9	2
12	5
13	6
15	8

Problem Solving Real World

7. Solve. Complete the table.
Layla has 6 pens.
Mark has 5 pens.
Jorge has 4 pens.
How many pens will each child have if they each give away 3 pens?

	Subtract 3	
Layla	6	3
Mark	5	2
Jorge	4	1

Getting Ready for Grade 2 five GRP5

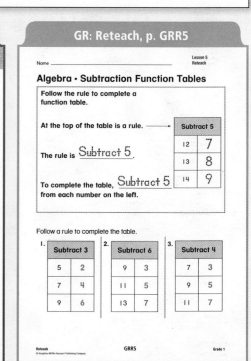

GR: Reteach, p. GRR5

Name ____________ Lesson 5 Reteach

Algebra • Subtraction Function Tables

Follow the rule to complete a function table.

At the top of the table is a rule. →

The rule is Subtract 5.

To complete the table, Subtract 5 from each number on the left.

Subtract 5	
12	7
13	8
14	9

Follow a rule to complete the table.

1.

Subtract 3	
5	2
7	4
9	6

2.

Subtract 6	
9	3
11	5
13	7

3.

Subtract 4	
7	3
9	5
11	7

Reteach GRR5 Grade 1

*GR – Getting Ready Lessons and Resources (www.thinkcentral.com)

On Your Own

Follow a rule to complete the table.

7.

Subtract 4	
11	7
12	8
13	9

8.

Subtract 6	
7	1
8	2
9	3

9.

Subtract 5	
7	2
8	3
9	4

10.

Subtract 7	
13	6
14	7
15	8
16	9

11.

Subtract 8	
12	4
14	6
16	8
17	9

12.

Subtract 9	
12	3
14	5
16	7
17	8

Problem Solving Real World

13. Solve. Complete the table.

Jane has 4 cookies.
Lucy has 3 cookies.
Seamus has 2 cookies.

How many cookies will each child have if they each eat 2 cookies?

	Subtract 2	
Jane	4	2
Lucy	3	1
Seamus	2	0

TAKE HOME ACTIVITY • Copy Exercise 12 and change the numbers in the left column to 10, 11, 12, and 13. Have your child complete the table and explain how he or she used a rule to solve the problem.

2 PRACTICE

Share and Show • Guided Practice

Check that children are following the rule for each table as they complete Exercises 1–6.

- **Which numbers would change if you changed the rule for the function table in Exercise 1?** the numbers in the right column

Use **Math Talk** to focus on similarities and differences in Exercises 2 and 3.

On Your Own

If children answered Exercises 1–6 correctly, assign Exercises 7–12.

- **Change the rule in Exercise 12. How does the table change?** Answers will vary.

Problem Solving Real World

UNLOCK THE PROBLEM To complete Exercise 13, children have to use information from the problem to establish a rule for a function table and follow the rule to complete the table.

- **What did you do to solve the problem?** I subtracted 2 from each number in the left column. **Explain why.** I wanted to know how many cookies each child will have left if he or she eats 2 cookies and that means subtracting 2 from the number of cookies each child began with.
- **How many cookies will Seamus have if he eats 2 cookies?** 0

3 SUMMARIZE

MATHEMATICAL PRACTICES

Essential Question

How can you follow a rule to complete a subtraction function table? I can subtract the number shown in the rule from each number in the left column of the table and then write how many are left in the right column.

Math Journal WRITE Math

What might be the rule for a subtraction function table if there is a 16 in the left column and a 7 in the right column?

LESSON 6

Algebra • Follow the Rule

LESSON AT A GLANCE

Common Core Standards

Add and subtract within 20.
1.OA.C.6 Add and subtract within 20, demonstrating fluency for addition and subtraction within 10. Use strategies such as counting on; making ten (e.g., 8 + 6 = 8 + 2 + 4 = 10 + 4 = 14); decomposing a number leading to a ten (e.g., 13 − 4 = 13 − 3 − 1 = 10 − 1 = 9); using the relationship between addition and subtraction (e.g., knowing that 8 + 4 = 12, one knows 12 − 8 = 4); and creating equivalent but easier or known sums (e.g., adding 6 + 7 by creating the known equivalent 6 + 6 + 1 = 12 + 1 = 13).

Add and subtract within 20.
2.OA.B.2 Fluently add and subtract within 20 using mental strategies. By end of Grade 2, know from memory all sums of two one-digit numbers.

Lesson Objective
Complete addition and subtraction function tables.

Essential Question
How can you follow a rule to complete an addition or subtraction function table?

Materials
MathBoard

GO DIGITAL — Animated Math Models

1 TEACH and TALK

GO DIGITAL • Animated Math Models

▶ Model and Draw

MATHEMATICAL PRACTICES

Compare the function tables at the top of the page.

- **What is the rule for the function table on the left?** add 1 **on the right?** subtract 1
- **How are the two function tables alike?** Both have the same numbers in the left column. **How are they different?** different rules: add 1 and subtract 1

Complete the tables together.

This lesson builds on addition and subtraction facts presented in Chapter 5 and prepares children for patterns and relationships taught in Grade 2.

Name ____________________

Algebra • Follow the Rule

Essential Question How can you follow a rule to complete an addition or subtraction function table?

Model and Draw

The rule for some tables is to add. For other tables the rule is to subtract.

Add 1	
2	3
4	5
6	7
8	9

Subtract 1	
2	1
4	3
6	5
8	7

Share and Show MATH BOARD

Follow a rule to complete the table.

1.

Add 2	
10	12
9	11
8	10
7	9

2.

Subtract 2	
10	8
9	7
8	6
7	5

3.

Subtract 1	
3	2
4	3
7	6
9	8

The rule is Add 2, so in each row the number on the right is 2 more than the number on the left.

Math Talk What is the rule for the pattern in Exercise 1?

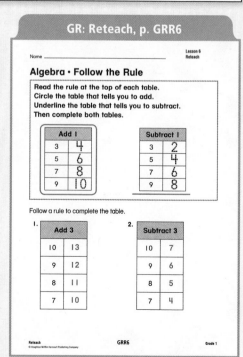

GR: Practice, p. GRP6

Name ____________________ Lesson 6

Algebra • Follow the Rule

Follow a rule to complete the table.

1.

Add 4	
6	10
7	11
8	12
9	13

2.

Subtract 2	
7	5
8	6
9	7
10	8

3.

Subtract 5	
5	0
7	2
9	4
11	6

4.

Subtract 4	
6	2
8	4
10	6
12	8

5.

Add 7	
10	17
9	16
8	15
7	14

6.

Add 3	
6	9
5	8
4	7
3	6

Problem Solving Real World

Find the rule. Complete the table.

7.

Add 2	
4	6
6	8
8	10
10	12

8.

Subtract 1	
7	6
8	7
10	9
12	11

© Houghton Mifflin Harcourt Publishing Company

Getting Ready for Grade 2 six GRP6

GR: Reteach, p. GRR6

Name ____________________ Lesson 6 Reteach

Algebra • Follow the Rule

Read the rule at the top of each table.
Circle the table that tells you to add.
Underline the table that tells you to subtract.
Then complete both tables.

Add 1	
3	4
5	6
7	8
9	10

Subtract 1	
3	2
5	4
7	6
9	8

Follow a rule to complete the table.

1.

Add 3	
10	13
9	12
8	11
7	10

2.

Subtract 3	
10	7
9	6
8	5
7	4

Reteach GRR6 Grade 1
© Houghton Mifflin Harcourt Publishing Company

***GR** – Getting Ready Lessons and Resources (*www.thinkcentral.com*)

On Your Own

Follow a rule to complete the table.

4.

Add 5	
7	12
8	13
9	14
10	15

5.

Subtract 5	
7	2
8	3
9	4
10	5

6.

Subtract 1	
8	7
9	8
11	10
13	12

7.

Subtract 3	
5	2
7	4
9	6
11	8

8.

Add 4	
6	10
7	11
8	12
9	13

9.

Add 6	
9	15
8	14
7	13
6	12

Problem Solving Real World

10. Find the rule. Complete the table.

Add 3	
3	6
5	8
7	10
9	12

TAKE HOME ACTIVITY • Copy the table for Exercise 9. Change the rule to Subtract 3. Have your child complete the table.

2 PRACTICE MATH BOARD

▶ Share and Show • Guided Practice

Check that children are following the correct rule.

- **Look at Exercises 1–3. How do you know whether to add or subtract to complete each table?** by looking at the rule at the top of the table

Have children complete Exercises 1–3.

Use **Math Talk** to have children find patterns by comparing the two columns in a function table and by comparing rows.

▶ On Your Own

If children answered Exercises 1–3 correctly, assign Exercises 4–9.

▶ Problem Solving

UNLOCK THE PROBLEM Exercise 10 requires children to look for and make use of structure in mathematics. They need to first determine the relationship between the given numbers in a function table in order to establish the rule for the function table. Then children will follow the rule to complete the table.

- **Look at the 7 and 10 in the table. Would you add or subtract to get from 7 to 10?** add **How many would you add?** 3
- **What is the rule for the table?** add 3

Have children complete the table using the rule.

3 SUMMARIZE

MATHEMATICAL PRACTICES

Essential Question

How can you follow a rule to complete an addition or subtraction function table? I can look at the rule that tells how many to add or subtract. I can follow the rule by adding or subtracting the number shown to each number in the left column of the table. I can write my answer in the right column in that row.

Math Journal WRITE Math

How do you know if the rule for a function table is to add or subtract?

LESSON 7

Add 3 Numbers

LESSON AT A GLANCE

Understand and apply properties of operations and the relationship between addition and subtraction.
1.OA.B.3 Apply properties of operations as strategies to add and subtract. *Examples: If 8 + 3 = 11 is known, then 3 + 8 = 11 is also known. (Commutative property of addition.) To add 2 + 6 + 4, the second two numbers can be added to make a ten, so 2 + 6 + 4 = 2 + 10 = 12. (Associative property of addition.)*

Add and subtract within 20.
2.OA.B.2 Fluently add and subtract within 20 using mental strategies. By the end of Grade 2, know from memory all sums of two one-digit numbers.

Lesson Objective
Choose a strategy to add 3 numbers.

Essential Question
How can you choose a strategy to help add 3 numbers?

Materials
MathBoard

GO DIGITAL
- Animated Math Models
- HMH Mega Math

1 TEACH and TALK

GO DIGITAL • Animated Math Models

▶ Model and Draw

Common Core MATHEMATICAL PRACTICES

Use the example to discuss strategies for adding 3 numbers.

- **How do you use the strategy *make a 10*?** First, I add 2 + 8 to make 10. Then I add on 6.
- **How do you use doubles?** First, I add 8 + 8. Then I add on 4.
- **How do you use the strategy *count on*?** First, I count on 3 from 6 to get 9. Then I add on 8.
- **How do you know which strategy to choose?** I look at the addends to see what is possible. If I have two numbers whose sum is 10, I can make a ten. If I have two of the same number, I can use doubles. If I have 1, 2, or 3 as an addend, I can count on.

This lesson builds on addition of 3 numbers presented in Chapter 3 and prepares children for fluent addition within 100 taught in Grade 2.

Name ______________________

Add 3 Numbers

Essential Question How can you choose a strategy to help add 3 numbers?

Model and Draw

When you add 3 numbers, you can add in any order. Using a strategy can help.

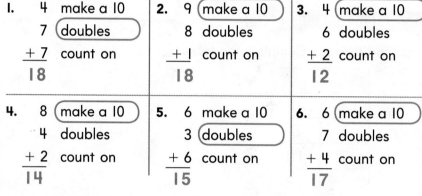

Make a 10.	Use doubles.	Use count on.
2, 6, + 8 → 10 + 6 = 16	8, 8, + 4 → 16 + 4 = 20	6, 8, + 3 → 9 + 8 = 17

Share and Show

MATH BOARD

Use strategies to find the sums. Circle any strategy you use.

Possible answers shown.

1. 4 + 7 + 7 = 18 — make a 10 / **doubles** (circled) / count on
2. 9 + 8 + 1 = 18 — **make a 10** (circled) / doubles / count on
3. 4 + 6 + 2 = 12 — **make a 10** (circled) / doubles / count on
4. 8 + 4 + 2 = 14 — **make a 10** (circled) / doubles / count on
5. 6 + 3 + 6 = 15 — make a 10 / **doubles** (circled) / count on
6. 6 + 7 + 4 = 17 — **make a 10** (circled) / doubles / count on

Possible answer: I added 6 + 4 to make a 10. Then I added 10 + 7 to find the sum, 17.

Math Talk Explain why you used the make a 10 strategy to solve Exercise 6.

GR: Practice, p. GRP7

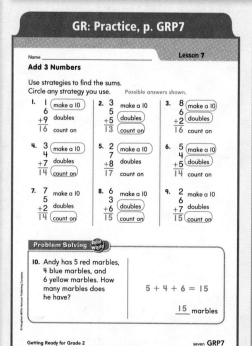

Name ______________________ Lesson 7

Add 3 Numbers

Use strategies to find the sums. Circle any strategy you use. Possible answers shown.

1. 1 + 6 + 9 = 16 — **make a 10** (circled) / doubles / count on
2. 3 + 5 + 5 = 13 — make a 10 / **doubles** (circled) / **count on** (circled)
3. 8 + 6 + 2 = 16 — **make a 10** (circled) / **doubles** (circled) / count on
4. 3 + 4 + 7 = 14 — **make a 10** (circled) / doubles / **count on** (circled)
5. 2 + 7 + 8 = 17 — **make a 10** (circled) / doubles / count on
6. 5 + 4 + 5 = 14 — **make a 10** (circled) / **doubles** (circled) / count on
7. 7 + 5 + 2 = 14 — make a 10 / doubles / **count on** (circled)
8. 6 + 3 + 6 = 15 — make a 10 / **doubles** (circled) / **count on** (circled)
9. 2 + 6 + 7 = 15 — make a 10 / doubles / **count on** (circled)

Problem Solving Real World

10. Andy has 5 red marbles, 4 blue marbles, and 6 yellow marbles. How many marbles does he have?

5 + 4 + 6 = 15

15 marbles

© Houghton Mifflin Harcourt Publishing Company

Getting Ready for Grade 2 seven GRP7

GR: Reteach, p. GRR7

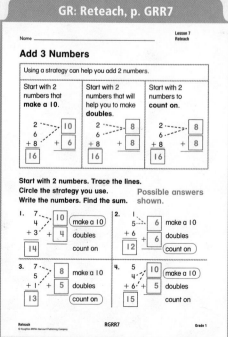

Name ______________________ Lesson 7 Reteach

Add 3 Numbers

Using a strategy can help you add 2 numbers.

Start with 2 numbers that **make a 10**.	Start with 2 numbers that will help you to make **doubles**.	Start with 2 numbers to **count on**.
2, 6, + 8 → 10 + 6; 16	2, 6, + 8 → 8 + 8; 16	2, 6, + 8 → 8 + 8; 16

Start with 2 numbers. Trace the lines. Circle the strategy you use. Write the numbers. Find the sum. Possible answers shown.

1. 7 + 4 + 3 → 10 + 4; 14 — **make a 10** (circled) / doubles / count on
2. 1 + 5 + 6 → 6 + 6; 12 — make a 10 / doubles / **count on** (circled)
3. 7 + 5 + 1 → 8 + 5; 13 — make a 10 / doubles / **count on** (circled)
4. 5 + 4 + 6 → 10 + 5; 15 — **make a 10** (circled) / doubles / count on

Reteach RGRR7 Grade 1
© Houghton Mifflin Harcourt Publishing Company

*GR – Getting Ready Lessons and Resources (*www.thinkcentral.com*)

On Your Own

Use a strategy to find the sum. Circle the strategy you choose. Possible answers shown.

7. 5 make a 10 5 (doubles) + 5 count on 15	**8.** 7 (make a 10) 3 doubles + 5 count on 15	**9.** 3 make a 10 8 doubles + 8 (count on) 19
10. 4 make a 10 2 doubles + 7 (count on) 13	**11.** 2 make a 10 9 (doubles) + 2 count on 13	**12.** 9 make a 10 9 (doubles) + 1 count on 19
13. 9 make a 10 2 doubles + 8 (count on) 19	**14.** 6 (make a 10) 3 doubles + 7 count on 16	**15.** 8 make a 10 4 doubles + 1 (count on) 13

Problem Solving Real World

16. Christine has 7 red buttons, 3 blue buttons, and 4 yellow buttons. How many buttons does she have?

$7 + 3 + 4 = 14$

14 buttons

TAKE HOME ACTIVITY • Ask your child to choose 3 numbers from 1 to 9. Have your child add to find the sum.

2 PRACTICE MATH BOARD

Share and Show • Guided Practice

- **Look at the addends in Exercise 1. What strategy could you use to find the sum? Why?** I can use doubles because there are two 7s.

Use **Math Talk** to check children's understanding of using strategies to help them add 3 numbers.

On Your Own

If children complete Exercises 1–6 correctly, assign Exercises 7–15. Children should understand they can use any strategy they choose as long as it works for the particular problem.

- **In Exercise 10, can you use doubles to help you add? Why or why not?** No. Possible answer: There are not two addends that are the same number.

Problem Solving Real World

UNLOCK THE PROBLEM Children can solve the word problem in Exercise 16 by using a strategy to add the 3 numbers.

- **Did you use a strategy to add? Explain.** Yes. I made a ten by adding 7 + 3. Then I added 10 + 4 to find the sum, 14.

3 SUMMARIZE

Common Core MATHEMATICAL PRACTICES

Essential Question

How can you choose a strategy to help add 3 numbers? I look at the addends to see which strategy will work. I might be able to make a ten, use doubles, or count on.

Math Journal WRITE Math

Use a strategy to add 1 + 8 + 9. Circle the two numbers you added first and tell what strategy you used.

LESSON 8

Add a One-Digit Number to a Two-Digit Number

LESSON AT A GLANCE

Common Core Standards
Use place value understanding and properties of operations to add and subtract.
1.NBT.C.4 Add within 100, including adding a two-digit number and a one-digit number, and adding a two-digit number and a multiple of 10, using concrete models or drawings and strategies based on place value, properties of operations, and/or the relationship between addition and subtraction; relate the strategy to a written method and explain the reasoning used. Understand that in adding two-digit numbers, one adds tens and tens, ones and ones; and sometimes it is necessary to compose a ten.

Use place value understanding and properties of operations to add and subtract.
2.NBT.B.5 Fluently add and subtract within 100 using strategies based on place value, properties of operations, and/or the relationship between addition and subtraction.

Lesson Objective
Find the sum of a 1-digit number and a 2-digit number.

Essential Question
How can you find the sum of a 1-digit number and a 2-digit number?

Materials
MathBoard

GO DIGITAL
- Animated Math Models
- HMH Mega Math

1 TEACH and TALK

GO DIGITAL • Animated Math Models

▶ Model and Draw

Common Core MATHEMATICAL PRACTICES

Have children look at the addends in the sample addition problem.

- **How many tens and ones are in the addends?** 54 is 5 tens and 4 ones. 2 is 2 ones.
- **How many ones are there in all, and how do you know?** There are 6 ones. I add 4 ones and 2 ones.
- **How many tens are there in all?** 5 tens
- **So what is the sum?** 56

This lesson builds on addition presented in Chapter 8 and prepares children for fluent addition within 100 taught in Grade 2.

Name ______

Add a One-Digit Number to a Two-Digit Number

Essential Question How can you find the sum of a I-digit number and a 2-digit number?

Model and Draw

What is 54 + 2?

To find the sum, find how many **tens** and **ones** in all.

	5 tens	4 ones	54
+		2 ones	+ 2
	5 tens	6 ones	56

Share and Show MATH BOARD

Add. Write the sum.

I. 72 + 3 = 75	2. 24 + I = 25	3. 4I + 4 = 45	4. 56 + 2 = 58
5. I4 + 4 = I8	6. 33 + 6 = 39	7. 6I + 8 = 69	8. 93 + 4 = 97
9. 3I + 6 = 37	10. II + 7 = I8	II. 40 + 4 = 44	I2. 35 + 3 = 38

Possible answer: I added 2 ones from the first addend and 3 ones from the second addend for a total of 5 ones.

Math Talk How did you find the total number of ones in Exercise I?

GR: Practice, p. GRP8

Name ______ Lesson 8

Add a One-Digit Number to a Two-Digit Number

Add. Write the sum.

I. 34 + 5 = 39	2. 44 + 3 = 47	3. 37 + I = 38
4. 37 + I = 38	5. 9I + 4 = 95	6. 84 + 2 = 86
7. 45 + 3 = 48	8. I2 + 7 = I9	9. 24 + 4 = 28
10. 32 + 5 = 37	II. 7I + 7 = 78	I2. 53 + 2 = 55

Problem Solving Real World

I3. There are 2I children in the pool. Then 5 more children join them. How many children are in the pool now?

26 children

Getting Ready for Grade 2 eight GRP8

GR: Reteach, p. GRR8

Name ______ Lesson 8 Reteach

Add a One-Digit Number to a Two-Digit Number

Add to find how many **tens** and **ones** in all.

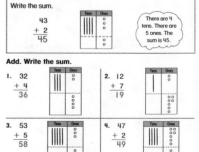

Write the sum.

43 + 2 = 45

There are 4 tens. There are 5 ones. The sum is 45.

Add. Write the sum.

I. 32 + 4 = 36	2. I2 + 7 = I9
3. 53 + 5 = 58	4. 47 + 2 = 49
5. 68 + I = 69	6. 95 + 3 = 98

Reteach GRR8 Grade 1

*GR – Getting Ready Lessons and Resources (*www.thinkcentral.com*)

On Your Own

Add. Write the sum.

13. 22 + 7 = 29	14. 53 + 3 = 56	15. 46 + 2 = 48	16. 71 + 8 = 79
17. 84 + 5 = 89	18. 93 + 4 = 97	19. 16 + 3 = 19	20. 37 + 1 = 38
21. 62 + 2 = 64	22. 23 + 5 = 28	23. 82 + 2 = 84	24. 44 + 4 = 48

Problem Solving Real World

25. There are 23 children in the first grade class. Then 3 more children join the class. How many children are there now?

26 children

TAKE HOME ACTIVITY • Tell your child you had 12 pennies and then you got 5 more. Have your child add to find how many pennies in all.

2 PRACTICE MATH BOARD

Share and Show • Guided Practice

- **Look at Exercise 2. How many tens are there in all? How many ones are there in all?** 2 tens; 5 ones

Use Math Talk to check children's understanding of how to find the total number of ones when adding a 1-digit number to a 2-digit number.

On Your Own

If children complete Exercises 1–12 correctly, assign Exercises 13–24. Have children draw a quick picture to show the numbers in Exercise 13.

- **What does your quick picture show?** 22 is 2 tens and 2 ones. 7 is 7 ones. There are 2 tens and 9 ones in all.

Problem Solving Real World

UNLOCK THE PROBLEM Read aloud the word problem in Exercise 25.

- **Will you add or subtract to find the number of children? Explain.** I will add because the class has 23 children plus 3 more.

3 SUMMARIZE

Common Core MATHEMATICAL PRACTICES

Essential Question

How can you find the sum of a 1-digit number and a 2-digit number? Possible answer: I can find how many tens and ones there are altogether in both addends.

Math Journal WRITE Math

Use words or pictures to tell how to use tens and ones to add 14 + 5.

LESSON 9

Add Two-Digit Numbers

LESSON AT A GLANCE

Common Core Standards
Use place value understanding and properties of operations to add and subtract.
1.NBT.C.4 Add within 100, including adding a two-digit number and a one-digit number, and adding a two-digit number and a multiple of 10, using concrete models or drawings and strategies based on place value, properties of operations, and/or the relationship between addition and subtraction; relate the strategy to a written method and explain the reasoning used. Understand that in adding two-digit numbers, one adds tens and tens, ones and ones; and sometimes it is necessary to compose a ten.

Use place value understanding and properties of operations to add and subtract.
2.NBT.B.5 Fluently add and subtract within 100 using strategies based on place value, properties of operations, and/or the relationship between addition and subtraction.

Lesson Objective
Find the sum of two 2-digit numbers.

Essential Question
How can you find the sum of two 2-digit numbers?

Materials
MathBoard

GO DIGITAL
- Animated Math Models
- HMH Mega Math

1 TEACH and TALK

GO DIGITAL • Animated Math Models

▶ Model and Draw

MATHEMATICAL PRACTICES

Have children look at the sample addition problem.

- **How many tens and ones are in 23?** 2 tens and 3 ones.
- **How many tens and ones are in 14?** 1 ten and 4 ones.

Discuss with children the process of adding the tens in each addend and the ones in each addend. Guide children to see that this gives them the sum.

- **How many tens and ones are there in all?** 3 tens and 7 ones
- **What is the sum?** 37

This lesson builds on addition presented in Chapter 8 and prepares children for fluent addition within 100 taught in Grade 2.

Name ______

Add Two-Digit Numbers

Essential Question How can you find the sum of two 2-digit numbers?

Model and Draw

What is 23 + 14?

You can find how many **tens** and **ones** in all.

2 tens	**3** ones	**2 3**
+ **1** ten	**4** ones	+ **1 4**
3 tens	7 ones	37

Share and Show MATH BOARD

Add. Write the sum.

1. 82 + 12 = 94	2. 25 + 43 = 68	3. 15 + 14 = 29	4. 71 + 12 = 83
5. 36 + 21 = 57	6. 43 + 41 = 84	7. 57 + 32 = 89	8. 21 + 12 = 33
9. 12 + 12 = 24	10. 41 + 21 = 62	11. 32 + 41 = 73	12. 51 + 14 = 65

Possible answer: There are 3 tens. I add the tens digits, 2 + 1.

Math Talk How many tens are in 26 + 11? How do you know?

GR: Practice, p. GRP9

Name ______ Lesson 9

Add Two-Digit Numbers

Add. Write the sum.

1. 31 + 52 = 83	2. 65 + 34 = 99	3. 21 + 32 = 53
4. 14 + 21 = 35	5. 72 + 26 = 98	6. 46 + 31 = 77
7. 53 + 12 = 65	8. 34 + 54 = 88	9. 27 + 50 = 77
10. 84 + 11 = 95	11. 32 + 53 = 85	12. 56 + 22 = 78

Problem Solving Real World

13. Evan has 15 toy cars. His brother has 13 toy cars. How many toy cars do the boys have together?

28 toy cars

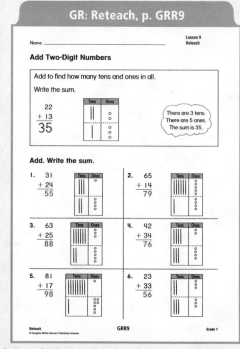

GR: Reteach, p. GRR9

Name ______ Lesson 9 Reteach

Add Two-Digit Numbers

Add to find how many tens and ones in all.

Write the sum.

22 + 13 = 35

There are 3 tens. There are 5 ones. The sum is 35.

Add. Write the sum.

1. 31 + 24 = 55	2. 65 + 14 = 79
3. 63 + 25 = 88	4. 42 + 34 = 76
5. 81 + 17 = 98	6. 23 + 33 = 56

*GR – Getting Ready Lessons and Resources (*www.thinkcentral.com*)

On Your Own

Add. Write the sum.

13. 83 + 12 = 95	14. 73 + 21 = 94	15. 16 + 51 = 67	16. 23 + 43 = 66
17. 24 + 55 = 79	18. 67 + 21 = 88	19. 64 + 23 = 87	20. 51 + 24 = 75
21. 26 + 32 = 58	22. 51 + 25 = 76	23. 46 + 22 = 68	24. 34 + 45 = 79

Problem Solving Real World

25. Emma has 21 hair clips. Her sister has 11 hair clips. How many hair clips do the girls have together?

32 hair clips

TAKE HOME ACTIVITY • Tell your child you drove 21 miles and then you drove 16 more. Have your child add to find how many miles in all.

2 PRACTICE

MATH BOARD

Share and Show • Guided Practice

- **How do you find how many ones in all?** I add the ones of both numbers together.
- **How do you find how many tens in all?** I add the tens of both numbers together.

Use Math Talk to check children's understanding of adding two 2-digit numbers.

On Your Own

If children completed Exercises 1–12 correctly, assign Exercises 13–24. Some children may benefit by drawing quick pictures to show the problems they find difficult.

- **How can drawing a quick picture help you solve?** A quick picture shows how many tens and ones there are in each addend and how many tens and ones in all.

Problem Solving Real World

UNLOCK THE PROBLEM Discuss the word problem in Exercise 25.

- **What do you know?** Emma has 21 hair clips. Her sister has 11 hair clips.
- **What do you need to find?** how many hair clips in all
- **How will you solve the problem?** I will add 21 + 11.

3 SUMMARIZE

Common Core MATHEMATICAL PRACTICES

Essential Question

How can you find the sum of two 2-digit numbers? I can add the tens of each number together and the ones of each number together to find how many tens and ones there are in all.

Math Journal

WRITE Math

Draw quick pictures to show how to use tens and ones to find 26 + 31.

LESSON 10

Repeated Addition

LESSON AT A GLANCE

Common Core Standards
Add and subtract within 20.
1.OA.C.6 Add and subtract within 20, demonstrating fluency for addition and subtraction within 10. Use strategies such as counting on; making ten (e.g., 8 + 6 = 8 + 2 + 4 = 10 + 4 = 14); decomposing a number leading to a ten (e.g., 13 − 4 = 13 − 3 − 1 = 10 − 1 = 9); using the relationship between addition and subtraction (e.g., knowing that 8 + 4 = 12, one knows 12 − 8 = 4); and creating equivalent but easier or known sums (e.g., adding 6 + 7 by creating the known equivalent 6 + 6 + 1 = 12 + 1 = 13).

Work with equal groups of objects to gain foundations for multiplication.

2.OA.C.4 Use addition to find the total number of objects arranged in rectangular arrays with up to 5 rows and up to 5 columns; write an equation to express the total as a sum of equal addends.

Lesson Objective
Use repeated addition to add equal groups.

Essential Question
How can you find how many items there are in equal groups without counting one at a time?

Materials
MathBoard, two-color counters

GO DIGITAL — Animated Math Models

1 TEACH and TALK
GO DIGITAL • Animated Math Models

▶ Model and Draw
MATHEMATICAL PRACTICES

Have children use their MathBoards and model the problem with counters.

- **How many groups are there?** 4
- **How many counters are in each group?** 2

Model how to add 2 + 2 + 2 + 2. Say and point to the numbers: **2 + 2 = 4, 4 + 2 = 6, 6 + 2 = 8.**

2 PRACTICE
MATH BOARD

▶ Share and Show • Guided Practice
Have children complete Exercises 1–3.

Check that children are recording the number in each group on the blanks and not the number of groups.

This lesson builds on addition presented in Chapter 5 and prepares children for adding equal groups taught in Grade 2.

Name ______________________

Repeated Addition

Essential Question How can you find how many items there are in equal groups without counting one at a time?

Model and Draw

When all groups have the same number they are equal groups.

Ayita is putting 2 plants on each step up to her porch. She has 4 steps. How many plants does she need?

There are 4 equal groups. There are 2 in each group. Add to find how many in all.

2 + 2 + 2 + 2 = 8

Ayita needs 8 plants.

Share and Show MATH BOARD

Use your MathBoard and ●. Make equal groups. Complete the addition sentence.

	Number of Equal Groups	Number in Each Group	How many in all?
1.	4	3	3 + 3 + 3 + 3 = 12
2.	2	5	5 + 5 = 10
3.	3	4	4 + 4 + 4 = 12

Add: 4 + 4 + 4 + 4 + 4 = 20

Math Talk How can you use addition to find 5 groups of 4?

GR: Practice, p. GRP10

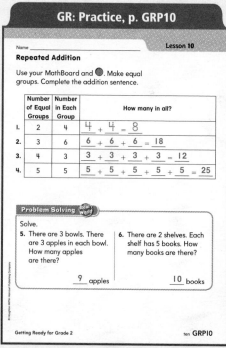

Name ______________ Lesson 10

Repeated Addition

Use your MathBoard and ●. Make equal groups. Complete the addition sentence.

	Number of Equal Groups	Number in Each Group	How many in all?
1.	2	4	4 + 4 = 8
2.	3	6	6 + 6 + 6 = 18
3.	4	3	3 + 3 + 3 + 3 = 12
4.	5	5	5 + 5 + 5 + 5 + 5 = 25

Problem Solving Real World

Solve.

5. There are 3 bowls. There are 3 apples in each bowl. How many apples are there?
9 apples

6. There are 2 shelves. Each shelf has 5 books. How many books are there?
10 books

Getting Ready for Grade 2 ten GRP10

GR: Reteach, p. GRR10

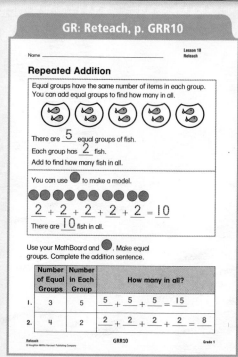

Name ______________ Lesson 10 Reteach

Repeated Addition

Equal groups have the same number of items in each group. You can add equal groups to find how many in all.

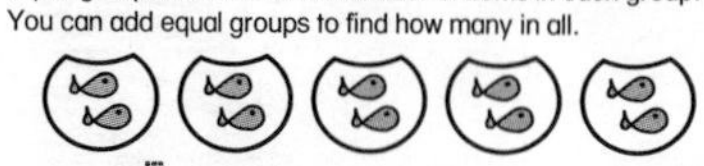

There are 5 equal groups of fish.
Each group has 2 fish.
Add to find how many fish in all.

You can use ● to make a model.

●● ●● ●● ●● ●●

2 + 2 + 2 + 2 + 2 = 10

There are 10 fish in all.

Use your MathBoard and ●. Make equal groups. Complete the addition sentence.

	Number of Equal Groups	Number in Each Group	How many in all?
1.	3	5	5 + 5 + 5 = 15
2.	4	2	2 + 2 + 2 + 2 = 8

Reteach

GRR10 Grade 1

*GR – Getting Ready Lessons and Resources (*www.thinkcentral.com*)

On Your Own

Use your MathBoard and ●. Make equal groups. Complete the addition sentence.

	Number of Equal Groups	Number in Each Group	How many in all?
4.	2	3	3 + 3 = 6
5.	3	5	5 + 5 + 5 = 15
6.	4	4	4 + 4 + 4 + 4 = 16
7.	4	5	5 + 5 + 5 + 5 = 20
8.	5	7	7 + 7 + 7 + 7 + 7 = 35

Problem Solving Real World

Solve.

9. There are 3 flower pots. There are 2 flowers in each flower pot. How many flowers are there?

6 flowers

10. There are 2 plants. There are 4 leaves on each plant. How many leaves are there?

8 leaves

TAKE HOME ACTIVITY • Use dry cereal or pasta to make 3 equal groups of 5. Ask your child to find the total number of items.

- **How did you know what numbers to add in each problem?** I repeated the number that told how many are in each group.

Use **Math Talk** to make sure children understand that to use repeated addition to find 5 groups of 4, they must add 4 five times.

On Your Own

If children answered Exercises 1–3 correctly, assign Exercises 4–8.

- **How are all the addition sentences you wrote alike?** I add the same numbers two or more times in each addition sentence.

Problem Solving Real World

UNLOCK THE PROBLEM For Exercises 9 and 10, children are asked to complete problems using repeated addition.

- **How can you find the answer to Exercise 9 by adding equal groups?** I can add three groups of 2.
- **How can you find the answer to Exercise 10 by adding equal groups?** I can add two groups of 4.

3 SUMMARIZE

Common Core MATHEMATICAL PRACTICES

Essential Question

How can you find how many items there are in equal groups without counting one at a time? I can add the number of items in each group as many times as the number of groups.

Math Journal WRITE Math

Use pictures to show 5 groups that each have 5 marbles. Then write a number sentence to show how to find how many marbles there are in all.

LESSON 11

Use Repeated Addition to Solve Problems

LESSON AT A GLANCE

Common Core Standards
Add and subtract within 20.
1.OA.C.6 Add and subtract within 20, demonstrating fluency for addition and subtraction within 10. Use strategies such as counting on; making ten (e.g., $8 + 6 = 8 + 2 + 4 = 10 + 4 = 14$); decomposing a number leading to a ten (e.g., $13 - 4 = 13 - 3 - 1 = 10 - 1 = 9$); using the relationship between addition and subtraction (e.g., knowing that $8 + 4 = 12$, one knows $12 - 8 = 4$); and creating equivalent but easier or known sums (e.g., adding $6 + 7$ by creating the known equivalent $6 + 6 + 1 = 12 + 1 = 13$).

Work with equal groups of objects to gain foundations for multiplication.

2.OA.C.4 Use addition to find the total number of objects arranged in rectangular arrays with up to 5 rows and up to 5 columns; write an equation to express the total as a sum of equal addends.

Lesson Objective
Use repeated addition to solve real world problems.

Essential Question
How can you use repeated addition to solve problems?

Materials
MathBoard, crayons

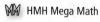

GO DIGITAL

HMH Mega Math

1 TEACH and TALK

GO DIGITAL • Animated Math Models

Model and Draw

MATHEMATICAL PRACTICES

Have children use their MathBoards to record the addition sentence and draw the 3 groups of 4 balloons.

- **How many equal groups are there?** 3
- **How many balloons are in each group?** 4
- **How can you use this information to write a repeated addition sentence?** Possible answer: I can add three 4s, and that is $4 + 4 + 4$.
- **How can you solve $4 + 4 + 4$?** Possible answer: $4 + 4 = 8$, and $8 + 4 = 12$. So, Dyanna needs 12 balloons in all.

This lesson builds on addition presented in Chapter 5 and prepares children for repeated addition taught in Grade 2.

Name ____________

Use Repeated Addition to Solve Problems

Essential Question How can you use repeated addition to solve problems?

Model and Draw

Dyanna will have 3 friends at her party.
She wants to give each friend 4 balloons.
How many balloons does Dyanna need?

12 balloons

THINK $4 + 4 + 4 = 12$

Share and Show MATH BOARD

Draw pictures to show the story.
Write the addition sentence to solve.

1. Ted plays with 2 friends. He wants to give each friend 5 cards. How many cards does Ted need?

10 cards

Children should draw 2 groups of 5 cards.

$5 + 5 = 10$

2. Aisha shops with 4 friends. She wants to buy each friend 2 roses. How many roses does Aisha need?

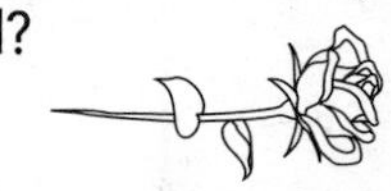

8 roses

Children should draw 4 groups of 2 roses.

$2 + 2 + 2 + 2 = 8$

Possible answer: There are 4 friends. Each gets 2 roses, so I used repeated addition and I added $2 + 2 + 2 + 2 = 8$.

Math Talk What pattern can you use to find the answer to Exercise 2?

GR: Practice, p. GRP11

Name ____________ Lesson 11

Use Repeated Addition to Solve Problems

Draw pictures to show the story.
Write the addition to solve.

1. Krista plays with 3 friends. She wants to give each friend 4 pretzels. How many pretzels does Krista need?
12 pretzels
Children should draw 3 groups of 4 pretzels.
$4 + 4 + 4 = 12$

2. Ed plants seeds with 5 friends. He wants to give each friend 5 seeds. How many seeds does Ed need?
25 seeds
Children should draw 5 groups of 5 seeds.
$5 + 5 + 5 + 5 + 5 = 25$

Problem Solving Real World

Circle the way you can model the problem.
Then solve.

3. There are 5 friends. Each friend has 4 books. How many books are there?
5 groups of 5 books
(5 groups of 4 books)
4 groups of 5 books
There are 20 books.

Getting Ready for Grade 2 eleven GRP11

GR: Reteach, p. GRR11

Name ____________ Lesson 11 Reteach

Use Repeated Addition to Solve Problems

Loren has 3 jars. She wants to put 5 flowers in each jar.
How many flowers does Loren need?

Draw a picture to show the story.

Step 1 Draw 3 jars.
Step 2 Draw 5 flowers in each jar.
Step 3 Find how many in all. 5 + 5 + 5 = 15
Loren needs 15 flowers.

Draw pictures to show the story.
Write the addition sentence to solve.

1. Matt plays with 2 friends. He wants to give each friend 4 cars. How many cars does Matt need?
8 cars
Children should draw 2 groups of 4 cars.
4 + 4 = 8

2. Liz shops with 3 friends. She wants to buy each friend 3 hair clips. How many hair clips does Liz need?
9 hair clips
Children should draw 3 groups of 3 hair clips.
3 + 3 + 3 = 9

Reteach GRR11 Grade 1

*GR – Getting Ready Lessons and Resources (*www.thinkcentral.com*)

On Your Own

Draw pictures to show the story.
Write the addition sentence to solve.

3. Lea plays with 3 friends. She wants to give each friend 5 ribbons. How many ribbons does Lea need?

15 ribbons

Children should draw 3 groups of 5 ribbons.

5 + 5 + 5 = 15

4. Harry shops with 5 friends. He wants to buy each friend 2 pens. How many pens does Harry need?

10 pens

Children should draw 5 groups of 2 pens.

2 + 2 + 2 + 2 + 2 = 10

5. Cam plays with 4 friends. She wants to give each friend 4 stickers. How many stickers does Cam need?

16 stickers

Children should draw 4 groups of 4 stickers.

4 + 4 + 4 + 4 = 16

Problem Solving Real World

Circle the way you can model the problem. Then solve.

6. There are 4 friends. Each friend has 3 apples. How many apples are there?

4 groups of 4 apples
(4 groups of 3 apples)
3 groups of 4 apples

There are 12 apples.

TAKE HOME ACTIVITY • Use small items such as cereal pieces to act out each problem. Have your child check the answers on this page.

Getting Ready Lessons and Resources, pp. GR25–GR26

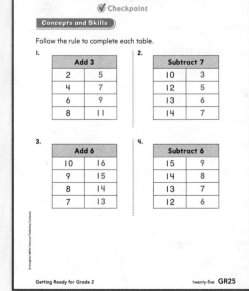

✓ Checkpoint

Name

✓ Checkpoint

Concepts and Skills

Follow the rule to complete each table.

1.

Add 3	
2	5
4	7
6	9
8	11

2.

Subtract 7	
10	3
12	5
13	6
14	7

3.

Add 6	
10	16
9	15
8	14
7	13

4.

Subtract 6	
15	9
14	8
13	7
12	6

Use strategies to find the sums. Circle any strategy you use.
Possible answers shown.

5. 4 + 3 + 4 = 11 — make a 10, (doubles), count on

6. 3 + 7 + 5 = 15 — (make a 10), doubles, count on

Add. Write the sum.

7. 32 + 14 = 46
8. 52 + 46 = 98
9. 18 + 21 = 39
10. 43 + 35 = 78

Use your MathBoard and ●. Make equal groups. Complete the addition sentence.

	Number of Equal Groups	Number in Each Group	How many in all?
11.	3	2	2 + 2 + 2 = 6
12.	2	4	4 + 4 = 8

13. Choose the way to model the problem.
James has 4 letters. He puts 2 stamps on each letter. How many stamps does he use in all?

○ 2 groups of 4 stamps
○ 4 groups of 4 stamps
○ 2 groups of 2 stamps
● 4 groups of 2 stamps

2 PRACTICE

MATH BOARD

Share and Show • Guided Practice

Have children complete Exercises 1 and 2. Check that children are drawing pictures and writing a repeated addition sentence to find each answer.

Use Math Talk to focus on children's understanding of how they can use a pattern of repeated addition to find the total when adding the same number multiple times.

On Your Own

If children answered Exercises 1–2 correctly, assign Exercises 3–5.

- **How many equal groups are there in Exercise 3? How many are in each group?** There are 3 groups. There are 5 in each group.
- **How can drawing a picture help you solve the problem?** Possible answer: I can draw 3 groups of 5 and use the picture to count how many ribbons in all.

Problem Solving Real World

UNLOCK THE PROBLEM For Exercise 6, children are asked to relate their understanding of repeated addition to add equal groups.

- **What addition sentence can help solve this problem? What is the answer?** 3 + 3 + 3 + 3 = 12; There are 12 apples in all.

3 SUMMARIZE

Common Core MATHEMATICAL PRACTICES

Essential Question

How can you use repeated addition to solve problems? Possible answer: When a problem has groups with the same number of things, I can add the same number over and over to find the total.

Math Journal

WRITE Math

5 friends each have 3 toys. Use numbers and pictures to show the number of toys in all.

Getting Ready for Grade 2 Test

LESSONS 1 TO 11

Summative Assessment

Use the **Getting Ready Test** to assess children's progress in Getting Ready for Grade 2 Lessons 1–11.

Getting Ready Tests are provided in multiple-choice and mixed-response format in the *Getting Ready Lessons and Resources*.

GO DIGITAL Getting Ready Test is available online.

Name ____________________ Getting Ready Test Lessons 1–11 Page 1

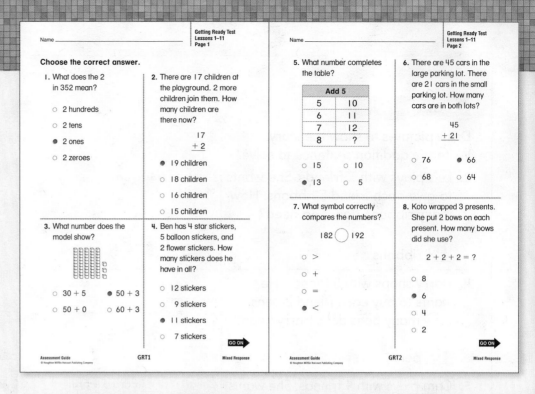

Choose the correct answer.

1. What does the 2 in 352 mean?
   - ○ 2 hundreds
   - ○ 2 tens
   - ● 2 ones
   - ○ 2 zeroes

2. There are 17 children at the playground. 2 more children join them. How many children are there now?

   $$\begin{array}{r} 17 \\ +\ 2 \\ \hline \end{array}$$

   - ● 19 children
   - ○ 18 children
   - ○ 16 children
   - ○ 15 children

3. What number does the model show?

   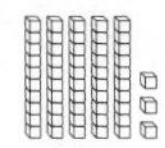

   - ○ 30 + 5
   - ● 50 + 3
   - ○ 50 + 0
   - ○ 60 + 3

4. Ben has 4 star stickers, 5 balloon stickers, and 2 flower stickers. How many stickers does he have in all?
   - ○ 12 stickers
   - ○ 9 stickers
   - ● 11 stickers
   - ○ 7 stickers

GO ON

Assessment Guide © Houghton Mifflin Harcourt Publishing Company GRT1 Mixed Response

---

Name ____________________ Getting Ready Test Lessons 1–11 Page 2

5. What number completes the table?

Add 5	
5	10
6	11
7	12
8	?

   - ○ 15
   - ○ 10
   - ● 13
   - ○ 5

6. There are 45 cars in the large parking lot. There are 21 cars in the small parking lot. How many cars are in both lots?

   $$\begin{array}{r} 45 \\ +\ 21 \\ \hline \end{array}$$

   - ○ 76
   - ● 66
   - ○ 68
   - ○ 64

7. What symbol correctly compares the numbers?

   182 ◯ 192

   - ○ >
   - ○ +
   - ○ =
   - ● <

8. Koto wrapped 3 presents. She put 2 bows on each present. How many bows did she use?

   2 + 2 + 2 = ?

   - ○ 8
   - ● 6
   - ○ 4
   - ○ 2

GO ON

Assessment Guide © Houghton Mifflin Harcourt Publishing Company GRT2 Mixed Response

---

Name ____________________ Getting Ready Test Lessons 1–11 Page 3

9. What number completes the table?

Add 6	
9	15
7	13
5	?
3	9

   - ○ 8
   - ○ 10
   - ○ 9
   - ● 11

10. Christy's address is 495 West Street. What does the 4 in 495 mean?
    - ● 4 hundreds
    - ○ 4 tens
    - ○ 4 ones
    - ○ 4 zeroes

11. Which is a way to model the problem?

    Molly has 3 sisters. She wants to give 2 books to each of her sisters. How many books does she need?
    - ○ 2 groups of 2 books
    - ○ 2 groups of 3 books
    - ● 3 groups of 2 books
    - ○ 3 groups of 3 books

12. What number completes the table?

Subtract 8	
12	4
14	6
16	?
18	10

    - ○ 5
    - ○ 7
    - ○ 6
    - ● 8

GO ON

Assessment Guide © Houghton Mifflin Harcourt Publishing Company GRT3 Mixed Response

---

Name ____________________ Getting Ready Test Lessons 1–11 Page 4

13. There are 3 children on the swings, 9 children on the monkey bars, and 1 child on the slide. How many children are there in all?
    - ○ 10
    - ○ 11
    - ○ 12
    - ● 13

14. Kassidy made a table.

Subtract 3	
9	6
10	7
?	8
12	9

    What number completes the table?
    - ○ 15
    - ○ 13
    - ● 11
    - ○ 14

15. Kara has 16 red balloons and 12 green balloons. How many balloons does she have in all?

    $$\begin{array}{r} 16 \\ +\ 12 \\ \hline \end{array}$$

    - ● 28
    - ○ 18
    - ○ 16
    - ○ 4

16. Max makes 5 gift bags. He puts 3 pencils in each bag. How many pencils does he use?

    3 + 3 + 3 + 3 + 3 = ?

    - ○ 9
    - ● 15
    - ○ 12
    - ○ 18

GO ON

Assessment Guide © Houghton Mifflin Harcourt Publishing Company GRT4 Mixed Response

---

Data-Driven Decision Making RtI

Item	Lesson	Common Error	Intervene With
1, 10	2	May confuse place value	**R**—p. GRR2
2, 22	8	May incorrectly add the ones	**R**—p. GRR8
3, 17, 21	1	May confuse tens and ones	**R**—p. GRR1
4, 13	7	May not understand how to use strategies to add three numbers	**R**—p. GRR7
5, 23	4	May not understand which numbers to add	**R**—p. GRR4
6, 15, 20	9	May incorrectly and ones or tens	**R**—p. GRR9

Key: R—Getting Ready Lessons and Resources: Reteach

Name ________ Getting Ready Test Lessons 1–11 Page 5

17. Jason uses tens and ones to show a number.

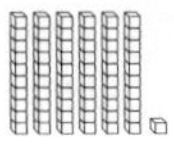

What number does Jason show?

○ 16 ● 61
○ 51 ○ 65

18. Which is a way to model the problem?

Mrs. Lee makes 4 lunches. She puts 2 plums in each lunch. How many plums does she use in all?

○ 2 groups of 4 plums
● 4 groups of 2 plums
○ 4 groups of 4 plums
○ 6 groups of 2 plums

19. What number completes the table?

Subtract 6	
7	1
9	?
11	5
13	7

● 3 ○ 6
○ 8 ○ 12

20. Mr. Lowe worked 42 hours one week. He worked 36 hours the next week. How many hours did he work in all?

$$\begin{array}{r} 42 \\ +\,36 \\ \hline \end{array}$$

● 78 hours ○ 68 hours
○ 75 hours ○ 65 hours

GO ON

Assessment Guide © Houghton Mifflin Harcourt Publishing Company GRT5 Mixed Response

Name ________ Getting Ready Test Lessons 1–11 Page 6

21. Which is a way to write the number?

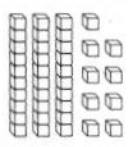

○ 20 + 5
○ 20 + 9
○ 30 + 5
● 30 + 9

22. David has 23 books about animals. He gets 4 more. How many books about animals does he have now?

○ 29
○ 28
● 27
○ 25

23. Which is a rule for the table?

?	
9	13
8	12
7	11
6	10

● Add 4
○ Add 3
○ Subtract 5
○ Subtract 3

24. Jon compares 186 and 194. Which way to compare is correct?

○ 186 > 194
○ 194 < 186
○ 194 = 186
● 194 > 186

STOP

Assessment Guide © Houghton Mifflin Harcourt Publishing Company GRT6 Mixed Response

Portfolio

Portfolio Suggestions The portfolio represents the growth, talents, achievements, and reflections of the mathematics learner. Children might spend a short time selecting work samples for their portfolios.

You may want to have children respond to the following questions:

- Which question was difficult?
- What would you like to learn more about?

For information about how to organize, share, and evaluate portfolios, see the *Chapter Resources*.

Data-Driven Decision Making RtI

Item	Lesson	Common Error	Intervene With
7, 24	3	May confuse comparison symbols	R—p. GRR3
8, 16	10	May not understand how to recognize equal groups and find the total number	R—p. GRR10
9, 14	6	May not understand whether to add or subtract, or which numbers to use	R—p. GRR6
11, 18	11	May confuse the number of equal groups and the number in each group	R—p. GRR11
12, 19	5	May subtract incorrectly	R—p. GRR5

Key: R—Getting Ready Lessons and Resources: Reteach

LESSON 12

Choose a Nonstandard Unit to Measure Length

LESSON AT A GLANCE

Common Core Standards
Measure lengths indirectly and by iterating length units.
1.MD.A.2 Express the length of an object as a whole number of length units, by laying multiple copies of a shorter object (the length unit) end to end; understand that the length measurement of an object is the number of same-size length units that span it with no gaps or overlaps. *Limit to contexts where the object being measured is spanned by a whole number of length units with no gaps or overlaps.*

Measure and estimate lengths in standard units.
2.MD.A.1 Measure the length of an object by selecting and using appropriate tools such as rulers, yardsticks, meter sticks, and measuring tapes.

Lesson Objective
Compare and choose nonstandard units to measure length.

Essential Question
How can you decide which nonstandard unit to use to measure the length of an object?

Materials
MathBoard, paper clips, pencils, connecting cubes, common objects

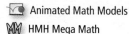

GO DIGITAL
Animated Math Models
HMH Mega Math

This lesson builds on using nonstandard units to measure length presented in Chapter 12 and prepares children for choosing the appropriate unit for measuring length taught in Grade 2.

Name ______

Choose a Nonstandard Unit to Measure Length

Essential Question How can you decide which nonstandard unit to use to measure the length of an object?

Model and Draw

Use 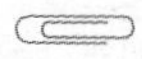 to measure short things.

Use  to measure long things.

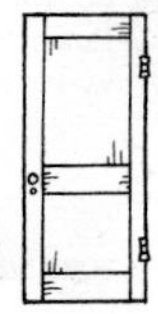

Share and Show MATH BOARD

Check children's answers.

Use real objects. Circle the unit you would use to measure. Then measure.

	Object	Unit	Measurement
1.		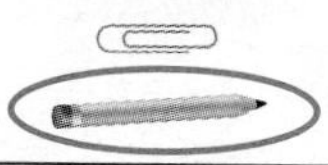	about ___
2.		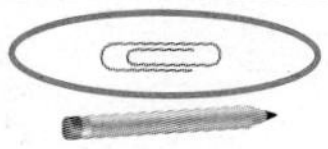	about ___
3.		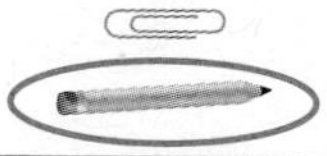	about ___
4.	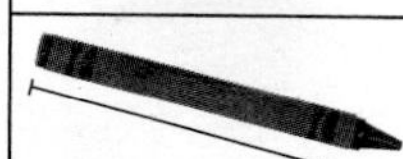	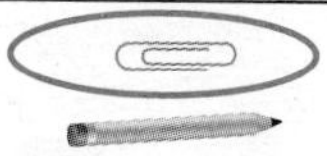	about ___

Paper clips; paper clips are shorter than the pencil.

Math Talk Alex measured a book with 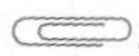. Then he measured with . Did he use more 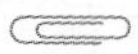 or ? Explain.

GR: Practice, p. GRP12

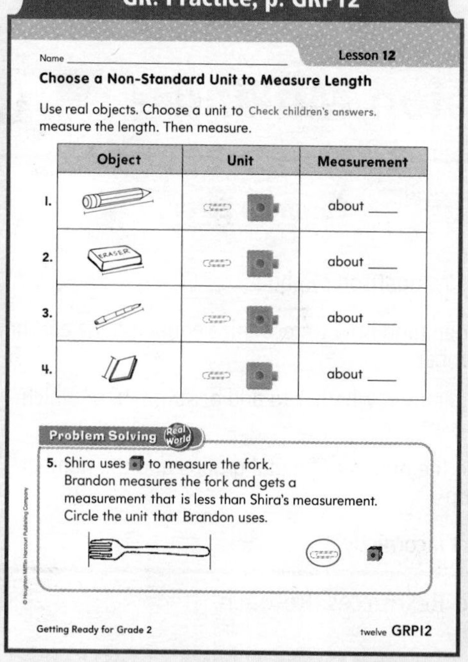

Name ______ Lesson 12

Choose a Non-Standard Unit to Measure Length

Use real objects. Choose a unit to measure the length. Then measure. Check children's answers.

	Object	Unit	Measurement
1.			about ___
2.			about ___
3.			about ___
4.			about ___

Problem Solving Real World

5. Shira uses ▪ to measure the fork. Brandon measures the fork and gets a measurement that is less than Shira's measurement. Circle the unit that Brandon uses.

Getting Ready for Grade 2 twelve GRP12

GR: Reteach, p. GRR12

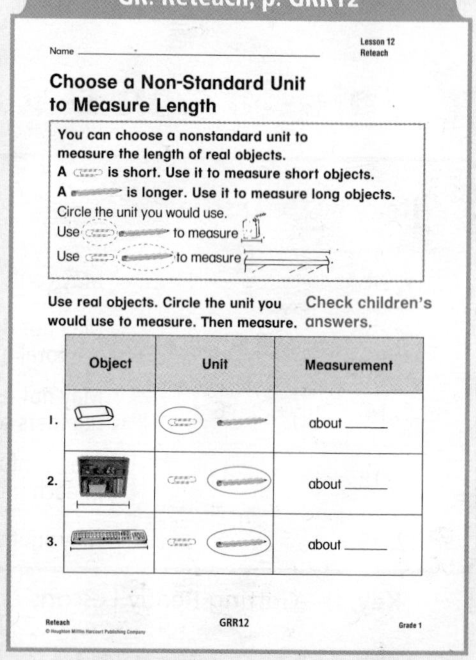

Name ______ Lesson 12 Reteach

Choose a Non-Standard Unit to Measure Length

You can choose a nonstandard unit to measure the length of real objects.
A ▭ is short. Use it to measure short objects.
A ▭ is longer. Use it to measure long objects.
Circle the unit you would use.
Use ___ to measure ___
Use ___ to measure ___

Use real objects. Circle the unit you would use to measure. Then measure. Check children's answers.

	Object	Unit	Measurement
1.			about ___
2.			about ___
3.			about ___

Reteach GRR12 Grade 1

*GR – Getting Ready Lessons and Resources (*www.thinkcentral.com*)

1 TEACH and TALK

GO DIGITAL Animated Math Models

▶ Model and Draw

Common Core MATHEMATICAL PRACTICES

Explain that length is the measure of how long an object is.

- **What are some things you would measure with a paper clip?** Possible answers: a stapler, a crayon **What are some things you would measure with a pencil?** Possible answers: a table, a desk
- **Why is it better to use a pencil than a paper clip to measure longer objects? Explain.** Possible answer: A pencil is longer than a paper clip. It would take many more paper clips than pencils to measure something long.

On Your Own

Use real objects. Choose a unit to measure the length. Circle it. Then measure.
Ask children to explain their responses.

	Object	Unit	Measurement
5.	ruler	paper clip / cube	about ____
6.	lunch box	paper clip / cube	about ____
7.	marker	paper clip / cube	about ____
8.	crayon box	paper clip / cube	about ____

Problem Solving (Real World)

9. Fred uses a cube to measure the stick.
Sue measures the stick and gets the same measurement.
Circle the unit that Sue uses.

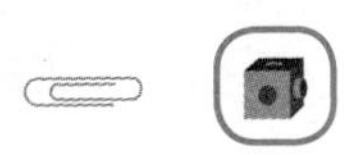

TAKE HOME ACTIVITY • Have your child measure something around the house by using small objects such as paper clips and then by using larger objects such as pencils. Discuss why the measurements differ.

2 PRACTICE (MATH BOARD)

▶ Share and Show • Guided Practice

Model how to use each nonstandard unit to measure the length of a classroom object.

- **Which unit would you use to measure the board?** a pencil **Why?** because a board is long and can be measured with a unit longer than a paper clip

Then have children complete the chart.

Use **Math Talk** to ensure that children understand that it takes more of a shorter unit than a longer unit to measure the same object.

▶ On Your Own

If children completed Exercises 1–4 correctly, assign Exercises 5–8. You may wish to have children share and compare their answers.

- **Look at Exercise 8. Explain how to use cubes to measure the length of a crayon box.** Possible answer: I would start at one end of the box and place cubes, end to end, along the box. Then I would count the cubes.

▶ Problem Solving (Real World)

UNLOCK THE PROBLEM In order to solve Exercise 9, children need to understand that Sue should use the same unit to get the same measurement.

- **Would Sue and Fred get the same measurement if Sue uses the paper clip? Why or why not?** No; Possible answer: because a paper clip and a cube are not the same length so the measurements will probably not be the same.

3 SUMMARIZE

MATHEMATICAL PRACTICES

Essential Question

How can you decide which nonstandard unit to use to measure the length of an object?
Possible answers: I can choose a unit that is shorter than the object I am measuring. I can choose shorter units to measure shorter objects and longer units to measure longer objects.

Math Journal (WRITE Math)

Which unit could you use to measure the length of a pencil box? Explain.

LESSON 13

Use a Non-Standard Ruler

LESSON AT A GLANCE

Common Core Standards
Measure lengths indirectly and by iterating length units.
1.MD.A.2 Express the length of an object as a whole number of length units, by laying multiple copies of a shorter object (the length unit) end to end; understand that the length measurement of an object is the number of same-size length units that span it with no gaps or overlaps. *Limit to contexts where the object being measured is spanned by a whole number of lengths units with no gaps or overlaps.*
Measure and estimate lengths in standard units.
2.MD.A.1 Measure the length of an object by selecting and using appropriate tools such as rulers, yardsticks, meter sticks, and measuring tapes.

Lesson Objective
Measure length with a nonstandard ruler.

Essential Question
How can you use a nonstandard measuring tool to find length?

Materials
MathBoard

GO DIGITAL
Animated Math Models
HMH Mega Math

1 TEACH and TALK

GO DIGITAL • Animated Math Models

Model and Draw

Common Core MATHEMATICAL PRACTICES

Point out the paper clip ruler at the top of the page.

- **What does the black vertical line at the end of the paper clips show?** that the paper clips and pencil are lined up correctly
- **How do you use the paper clips to find how many paper clips long the pencil is?** I count the paper clips from one end of the pencil to the other.
- **About how long is the pencil?** about 4 paper clips long

2 PRACTICE

MATH BOARD

Share and Show • Guided Practice

- **Are the paper clips in the correct position in Exercise 1? Explain.** Yes, because the left ends are lined up.

This lesson builds on non-standard length presented in Chapter 9 and prepares children for measurement taught in Grade 2.

Name ____________

Use a Non-Standard Ruler

Essential Question How can you use a non-standard measuring tool to find length?

Model and Draw

About how long is the pencil?

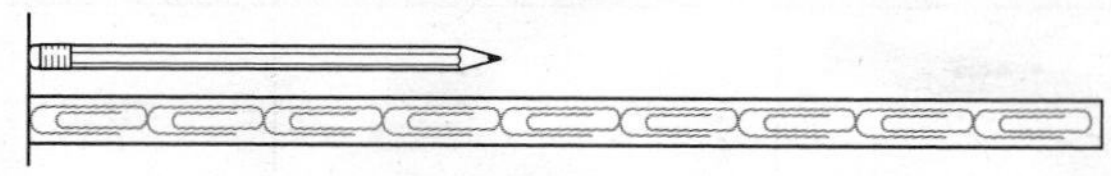

The end of the pencil and the end of the (paper clip) must line up. Count how many (paper clips) from one end of the pencil to the other.

about 4 (paper clips)

Share and Show MATH BOARD

About how long is the string?

1.

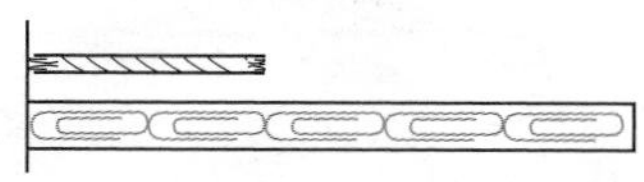

about 2 (paper clips)

2.

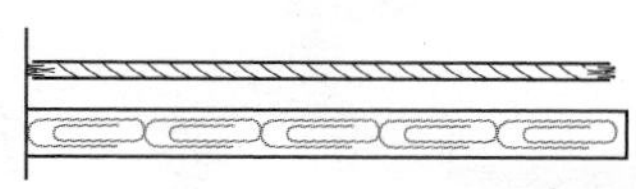

about 5 (paper clips)

Possible answer: If they do not line up, you are measuring more or less than the pencil.

Math Talk In Exercise 1, why must the end of the pencil and the end of the (paper clip) line up?

GR: Practice, p. GRP13

Name ____________ Lesson 13

Use a Non-Standard Ruler

About how long is the string?

1. about 9 (paper clips)

2. about 4 (paper clips)

3. about 6 (paper clips)

Problem Solving

4. Travis measures his marker. He says it is about 7 (paper clips) long. Is he correct? Explain.

Possible answer: Yes. The end of the ruler and the end of the marker are lined up. So the measurement is correct.

Getting Ready for Grade 2 thirteen GRP13

GR: Reteach, p. GRR13

Name ____________ Lesson 13 Reteach

Use a Non-Standard Ruler

Use the (paper clip) to measure the marker.

7 (paper clips)

The marker is about 7 (paper clips) long.

How many (paper clips) long is the string?

1. about 8 (paper clips) long

2. about 5 (paper clips) long

Reteach © Houghton Mifflin Harcourt Publishing Company GRR13 Grade 1

*GR – Getting Ready Lessons and Resources (*www.thinkcentral.com*)

On Your Own

About how long is the string?

3.

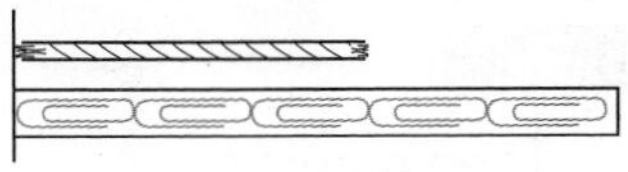

about 3 paper clips

4.

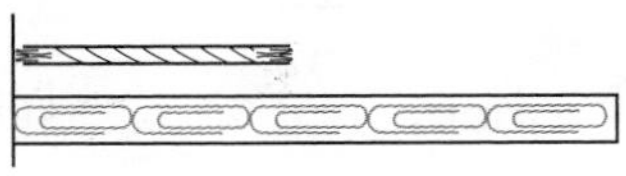

about 2 paper clips

5.

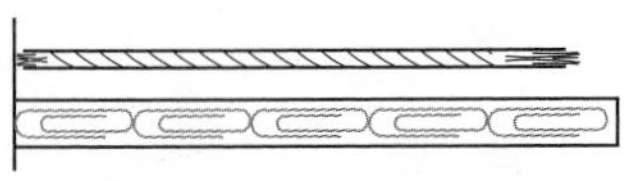

about 5 paper clips

Problem Solving Real World

6. Wendy measures her pencil. She says it is about 2 paper clips long. Is she correct? Explain.

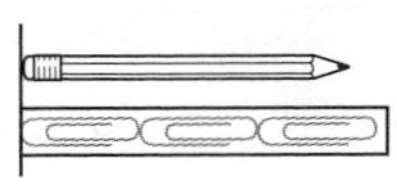

Possible answer: No. The end of the pencil is closer to 3 paper clips, not 2 paper clips.

TAKE HOME ACTIVITY • Have your child use 20 paper clips to measure different small objects in your house. Be sure the paper clips touch end to end.

Use **Math Talk** to discuss the importance of lining up the object being measured and the measuring tool.

On Your Own

If children completed Exercises 1–2 correctly, assign Exercises 3–5.

- **What do you notice about the paper clips?** The paper clips touch each other and do not overlap.

Problem Solving Real World

UNLOCK THE PROBLEM Lead a class discussion on accurate measuring techniques. Then have children check to see if Wendy measured correctly in Exercise 6.

- **How do you position a ruler when you measure an object?** I line up the left end of the ruler with the left end of the object.
- **How do you find how many units long the object is?** I count the units from one end of the object to the other.

3 SUMMARIZE

Common Core MATHEMATICAL PRACTICES

Essential Question

How can you use a non-standard ruler to measure length? I line up the end of the ruler with the object I am measuring. Then I count the number of units from one end of the object to the other.

Math Journal WRITE Math

Use paper clips. Draw a line that is 6 paper clips long. Label your line.

LESSON 14

Compare Lengths

LESSON AT A GLANCE

Common Core Standards

Measure lengths indirectly and by iterating length units.
1.MD.A.1 Order three objects by length; compare the lengths of two objects indirectly by using a third object.

Measure and estimate length in standard units.
2.MD.A.4 Measure to determine how much longer one object is than the other, expressing the length difference in terms of a standard length.

Lesson Objective
Compare and then measure lengths with nonstandard units.

Essential Question
How can you compare lengths of objects?

Materials
MathBoard, base-ten unit cubes

GO DIGITAL
- Animated Math Models
- HMH Mega Math

1 TEACH and TALK

GO DIGITAL • Animated Math Models

▶ Model and Draw

Common Core MATHEMATICAL PRACTICES

Materials base-ten unit cubes

Point out the strings at the top of the page.

- **Which string is shortest?** the top string **How can you tell?** The left ends of the strings are lined up. So I look at the right ends to find the shortest string.
- **Use base-ten unit cubes to measure the strings. What lengths are the strings, from shortest to longest?** about 4 cubes, about 6 cubes, about 8 cubes
- **Which string measures the greatest number of cubes?** the longest string

2 PRACTICE

MATH BOARD

▶ Share and Show • Guided Practice

- **In Exercise 1, what number do you write to order the shortest string?** 1 **Why does the shortest string come first?** You are ordering from shortest to longest.

Use **Math Talk** to show children that measuring with cubes can be used to determine the order of the strings from shortest to longest.

This lesson builds on ordering lengths presented in Chapter 9 and prepares children for comparing standard measurements taught in Grade 2.

Name ____________________

Compare Lengths

Essential Question How can you compare lengths of objects?

Model and Draw

First, write 1, 2, and 3 to order the strings from **shortest** to **longest**. Then measure with ▢.

Order		Length	
1	string	about 4 ▢	← Shortest
3	string	about 8 ▢	← Longest
2	string	about 6 ▢	

Share and Show MATH BOARD

Write 1, 2, and 3 to order the strings from **shortest** to **longest**. Then measure with ▢. Write the lengths.

	Order		Length
1.	2	string	about 5 ▢
	1	string	about 3 ▢
	3	string	about 9 ▢

Possible answer: The string that measures the least number of cubes is shortest. The string that measures the greatest number of cubes is longest.

Math Talk How can you measuring with cubes tell you the order of the strings?

GR: Practice, p. GRP14

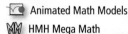

Name ____________________ Lesson 14

Compare Lengths

1. Write 1, 2, and 3 to order the ribbons **shortest** to **longest.** Then measure in ▢. Write the lengths.

Order		Length
2	ribbon	about 7 ▢
1	ribbon	about 5 ▢
3	ribbon	about 10 ▢

2. Write 1, 2, and 3 to order the ribbons from **shortest** to **longest.** Then measure in ▢. Write the lengths.

Order		Length
3	ribbon	about 8 ▢
1	ribbon	about 4 ▢
2	ribbon	about 5 ▢

Problem Solving Real World

3. Julie has these pieces of lace. Julie gives Megan the shortest one. Measure with ▢ and write the length of Megan's lace.

about 8 ▢

© Houghton Mifflin Harcourt Publishing Company

Getting Ready for Grade 2 fourteen GRP14

GR: Reteach, p. GRR14

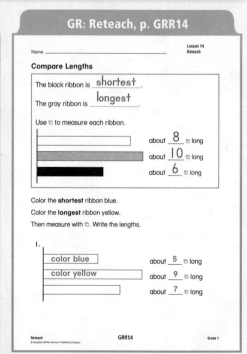

Name ____________________ Lesson 14 Reteach

Compare Lengths

The black ribbon is shortest.

The gray ribbon is longest.

Use ▢ to measure each ribbon.

about 8 ▢ long
about 10 ▢ long
about 6 ▢ long

Color the **shortest** ribbon blue.
Color the **longest** ribbon yellow.
Then measure with ▢. Write the lengths.

1.

color blue	about 5 ▢ long
color yellow	about 9 ▢ long
	about 7 ▢ long

Reteach GRR14 Grade 1
© Houghton Mifflin Harcourt Publishing Company

***GR** – Getting Ready Lessons and Resources (*www.thinkcentral.com*)

On Your Own

2. Write 1, 2, and 3 to order the strings from **shortest** to **longest**. Then measure with ▢. Write the lengths.

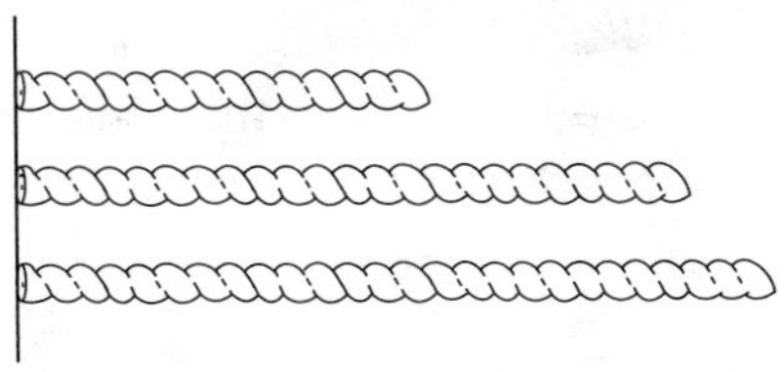

1	about 4 ▢
2	about 7 ▢
3	about 8 ▢

3. Write 1, 2, and 3 to order the strings from **shortest** to **longest**. Then measure with ▢. Write the lengths.

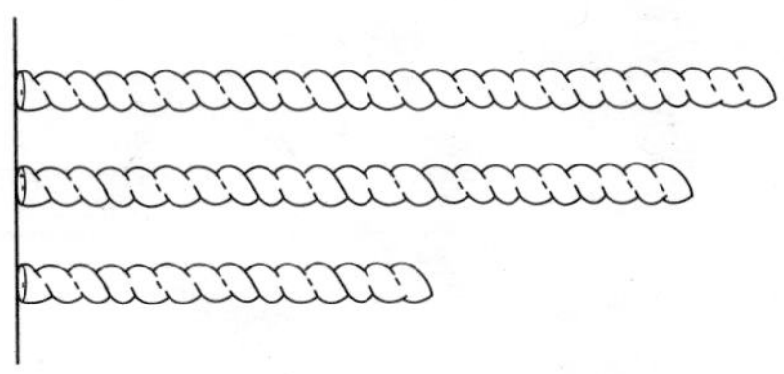

3	about 8 ▢
2	about 7 ▢
1	about 4 ▢

Problem Solving (Real World)

4. Kate has these ribbons. Kate gives Hannah the longest one. Measure with ▢ and write the length of Hannah's ribbon.

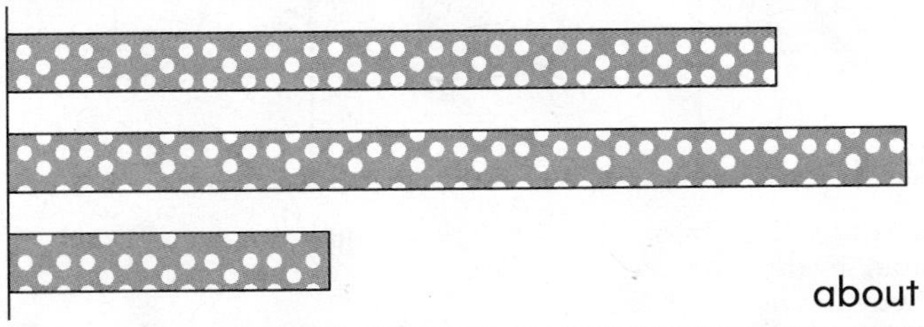

about 13 ▢

TAKE HOME ACTIVITY • Give your child three strips of paper. Have your child cut them about 4 paper clips long, about 2 paper clips long, and about 5 paper clips long. Then have your child order the paper strips from shortest to longest.

▶ On Your Own

If children complete Exercise 1 correctly, assign Exercises 2 and 3.

- **Predict which string in Exercise 2 will measure the fewest number of cubes.** Possible answer: the shortest string, the string at the top of the page

▶ Problem Solving (Real World)

UNLOCK THE PROBLEM Read aloud the problem in Exercise 4. Children can solve by visually determining which ribbon is longest and then measuring that ribbon.

- **Do you need to measure each ribbon? Explain.** No, I only need to measure the longest ribbon because the longest ribbon is Hannah's ribbon.

3 SUMMARIZE

Common Core MATHEMATICAL PRACTICES

Essential Question

How can you compare lengths of objects?

I can look at the objects to compare their lengths. Or, I can measure the lengths and compare the measurements.

Math Journal WRITE Math

Suppose there are three lines, about 2 cubes long, about 4 cubes long, and about 5 cubes long. Are the lines in order from shortest to longest? Write your prediction and then check by drawing the lines.

LESSON 15

Time to the Hour and Half Hour

LESSON AT A GLANCE

Common Core Standards

Tell and write time.
1.MD.B.3 Tell and write time in hours and half-hours using analog and digital clocks.

Work with time and money.
2.MD.C.7 Tell and write time from analog and digital clocks to the nearest five minutes, using a.m. and p.m.

Lesson Objective
Tell and write time to the hour and half hour using an analog clock.

Essential Question
How do you tell time to the hour and half hour on an analog clock?

Materials
MathBoard

GO DIGITAL
- Animated Math Models
- *i*Tools: Measurement (Clocks)
- HMH Mega Math

1 TEACH and TALK

GO DIGITAL • Animated Math Models

▶ Model and Draw

Common Core MATHEMATICAL PRACTICES

Materials *i*Tools: Measurement (Clocks)

Use the illustrations at the top of the page or the *i*Tools analog clock to review time in hours and half hours. Use clocks that show 4:00 and 4:30.

Direct children's attention to the clock showing 4:00.

- **Where does the hour hand point on this clock?** at 4 **What is the time?** 4:00

Direct children's attention to the clock showing 4:30.

- **Where does the hour hand point on this clock?** halfway between 4 and 5 **What is the time?** 4:30
- **Where does the minute hand point for time to the hour?** at 12 **Where does it point for time to the half hour?** at 6

This lesson builds on time presented in Chapter 9 and prepares children for time taught in Grade 2.

Name ______

Time to the Hour and Half Hour

Essential Question How do you tell time to the hour and half hour on an analog clock?

Model and Draw

The hour hand and the minute hand show the time.
Write the time shown on the clock.

4:00

4:30

Share and Show MATH BOARD

Read the clock. Write the time.

1. 
9:30

2. 
2:00

3. 
3:30

Possible answer: In one hour, the hour hand moves from one number to the next. So, at half past 5:00, the hour hand is halfway between the 5 and 6.

Math Talk Why does the hour hand point halfway between 5 and 6 at half past 5:00?

Getting Ready for Grade 2 thirty-three GR33

GR: Practice, p. GRP15

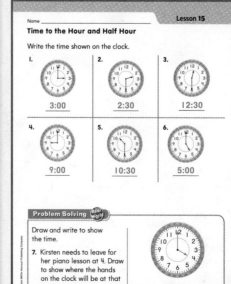

Name ______ Lesson 15

Time to the Hour and Half Hour

Write the time shown on the clock.

1. 3:00
2. 2:30
3. 12:30
4. 9:00
5. 10:30
6. 5:00

Problem Solving

Draw and write to show the time.

7. Kirsten needs to leave for her piano lesson at 4. Draw to show where the hands on the clock will be at that time. Write the time.

4:00

Getting Ready for Grade 2 fifteen GRP15

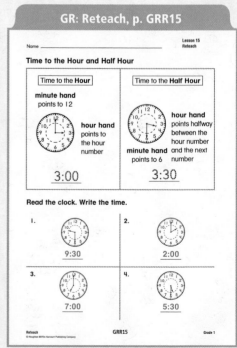

GR: Reteach, p. GRR15

Name ______ Lesson 15 Reteach

Time to the Hour and Half Hour

Time to the Hour	Time to the Half Hour
minute hand points to 12; hour hand points to the hour number; 3:00	hour hand points halfway between the hour number and the next number; minute hand points to 6; 3:30

Read the clock. Write the time.

1. 9:30
2. 2:00
3. 7:00
4. 5:30

Reteach GRR15 Grade 1

***GR** – Getting Ready Lessons and Resources (*www.thinkcentral.com*)

On Your Own

Read the clock. Write the time.

4.

2:30

5.

12:00

6.

11:30

7.

11:00

8.

6:30

9.

10:00

Problem Solving (Real World)

Draw and write to show the time.

10. Liam has soccer practice at half past 10:00.

10:30

TAKE HOME ACTIVITY • Say a time, such as half past 1:00 or 7:00. Ask your child where the clock hands will point at that time.

Getting Ready Lessons and Resources, pp. GR35–GR36 ✓ Checkpoint

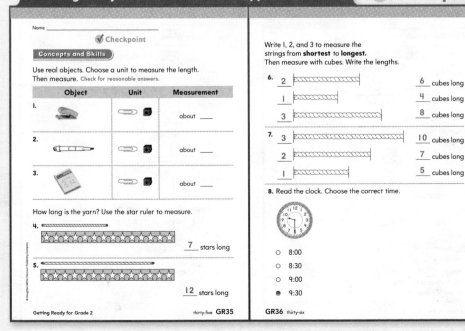

Name ____________

✓ Checkpoint

Concepts and Skills

Use real objects. Choose a unit to measure the length. Then measure. Check for reasonable answers.

Object	Unit	Measurement
1.		about ___
2.		about ___
3.		about ___

How long is the yarn? Use the star ruler to measure.

4. 7 stars long

5. 12 stars long

Write 1, 2, and 3 to measure the strings from **shortest** to **longest**. Then measure with cubes. Write the lengths.

6. 2 — 6 cubes long
1 — 4 cubes long
3 — 8 cubes long

7. 3 — 10 cubes long
2 — 7 cubes long
1 — 5 cubes long

8. Read the clock. Choose the correct time.

○ 8:00
○ 8:30
○ 9:00
● 9:30

2 PRACTICE (MATH BOARD)

Share and Show • Guided Practice

- **Where does the hour hand point for time to the hour and time to the half hour?** For time to the hour, the hour hand points to the number. At time to the half hour, the hour hand points halfway between two numbers.

Have children complete Exercises 1–3.

Use **Math Talk** to discsuss with children the placement of the hour hand at half past an hour.

On Your Own

If children complete Exercises 1–3 correctly, assign Exercises 4–9.

- **What is the time in Exercise 6?** 11:30 **What is the time in Exercise 7?** 11:00

Problem Solving (Real World)

UNLOCK THE PROBLEM For Exercise 10, children draw clock hands to show time at the half hour.

- **Is the time Liam has soccer practice a time to the hour or the half hour? How do you know?** time to the half hour; Possible answer: half past 10:00 names a time to the half hour.

3 SUMMARIZE

Common Core MATHEMATICAL PRACTICES

Essential Question

How do you tell time to the hour and half hour on an analog clock? I look at the hour hand. On the hour, it points to the hour. On the half hour, it points halfway between the hour number and the next hour number. The minute hand points to 12 on the hour and to 6 on the half hour.

Math Journal (WRITE Math)

Draw a clock with an hour hand and a minute hand. Show the time 3:00.

LESSON 16

Use a Picture Graph

LESSON AT A GLANCE

Common Core Standards
Represent and interpret data.
1.MD.C.4 Organize, represent, and interpret data with up to three categories; ask and answer questions about the total number of data points, how many in each category, and how many more or less are in one category than in another.

Represent and interpret data.
2.MD.D.10 Draw a picture graph and a bar graph (with single-unit scale) to represent a data set with up to four categories. Solve simple put-together, take-apart, and compare problems using information presented in a bar graph.

Lesson Objective
Read and interpret information displayed on a picture graph.

Essential Question
How do you read a picture graph?

Materials
MathBoard

GO DIGITAL
Animated Math Models
HMH Mega Math

1 TEACH and TALK
GO DIGITAL • Animated Math Models

Model and Draw
Common Core MATHEMATICAL PRACTICES

Read aloud the title and labels on the graph.

- **What does this picture graph show?** whether children chose mustard or ketchup
- **How many children chose mustard or ketchup?** 8 **How do you know?** Each stick person stands for 1 child, and there are 8 stick people.
- **How many children chose mustard?** 3 **How do you know?** I count the stick people in the row labeled "mustard."

2 PRACTICE
MATH BOARD

Share and Show • Guided Practice

- **What does this picture graph show?** whether children are wearing black, white, or blue socks

Have children complete Exercises 1–3.

Use **Math Talk** to ensure children understand how to read a picture graph.

This lesson builds on picture graphs presented in Chapter 10 and prepares children for using graphs taught in Grade 2.

Name ______

Use a Picture Graph
Essential Question How do you read a picture graph?

Model and Draw

Our Favorite Hot Dog Toppings					
mustard	🧍	🧍	🧍		
ketchup	🧍	🧍	🧍	🧍	🧍

Each 🧍 stands for 1 child.

__3__ children chose .

Most children chose __ketchup__.

__2__ fewer children chose than .

Share and Show MATH BOARD

Our Sock Colors						
black	🧍	🧍				
white	🧍	🧍	🧍	🧍	🧍	🧍
blue	🧍	🧍	🧍			

Each 🧍 stands for 1 child.

Use the picture graph to answer the questions.

1. How many children are wearing ? __3__
2. What color of socks are most of the children wearing? __white__
3. How many more children wear than ? __4__

Possible answer: I counted back to find the difference between 6 and 2.

Math Talk How did you find the answer to Exercise 3?

GR: Practice, p. GRP16

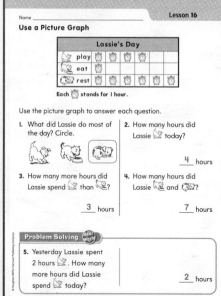

Name ______ Lesson 16

Use a Picture Graph

Lassie's Day						
play	⏰	⏰	⏰	⏰		
eat	⏰					
rest	⏰	⏰	⏰	⏰	⏰	⏰

Each ⏰ stands for 1 hour.

Use the picture graph to answer each question.

1. What did Lassie do most of the day? Circle.
2. How many hours did Lassie today? __4__ hours
3. How many more hours did Lassie spend than ? __3__ hours
4. How many hours did Lassie and ? __7__ hours

Problem Solving Real World

5. Yesterday Lassie spent 2 hours . How many more hours did Lassie spend today? __2__ hours

© Houghton Mifflin Harcourt Publishing Company

Getting Ready for Grade 2 sixteen GRP16

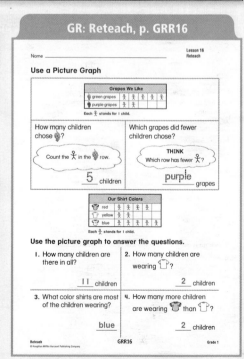

GR: Reteach, p. GRR16

Name ______ Lesson 16 Reteach

Use a Picture Graph

Grapes We Like					
green grapes	🧍	🧍	🧍	🧍	🧍
purple grapes	🧍	🧍			

Each 🧍 stands for 1 child.

How many children chose ?
Count the 🧍 in the row.
__5__ children

Which grapes did fewer children chose?
THINK Which row has fewer 🧍?
__purple__ grapes

Our Shirt Colors					
red	🧍	🧍	🧍	🧍	
yellow	🧍	🧍			
blue	🧍	🧍	🧍	🧍	🧍

Each 🧍 stands for 1 child.

Use the picture graph to answer the questions.

1. How many children are there in all? __11__ children
2. How many children are wearing ? __2__ children
3. What color shirts are most of the children wearing? __blue__
4. How many more children are wearing than ? __2__ children

Reteach © Houghton Mifflin Harcourt Publishing Company GRR16 Grade 1

*GR – Getting Ready Lessons and Resources (*www.thinkcentral.com*)

On Your Own

Our Weather						
rainy	○	○	○	○		
sunny	○	○				
cloudy	○	○	○	○	○	○

Each ○ stands for 1 day.

Use the picture graph to answer each question.

4. How many days in all are shown on the graph?

12 days

5. What was the weather for most days? Circle.

6. How many fewer days were rainy than cloudy?

2 days

7. How many sunny and cloudy days were there?

8 days

Problem Solving Real World

8. Today is sunny. Robin puts one more sunny on the graph. How many sunny days are there now?

3 days

TAKE HOME ACTIVITY • Help your child make a picture graph to show the eye color of 10 friends and family members.

GR38 thirty-eight

On Your Own

If children complete Exercises 1–3 correctly, assign Exercises 4–7. Children will need to read the picture graph, answer questions about the data, and make comparisons.

- **How do you compare three rows on a picture graph?** I look to see which row has more. I can count to see how many more or how many fewer.

Problem Solving Real World

UNLOCK THE PROBLEM In order to solve the problem in Exercise 8, children will need to refer to the graph at the top of the page.

- **What do you need to find on the picture graph in order to solve the problem?** I need to find how many sunny days are already shown on the picture graph.

3 SUMMARIZE

Common Core MATHEMATICAL PRACTICES

Essential Question

How do you read a picture graph? I can see how many pieces of data are recorded and how many are in each category. I can see which category has more or less, and I can find how many more or less.

Math Journal WRITE Math

Look at the picture graph, Our Weather. Write a different question that can be answered by reading the graph.

LESSON 17

Use a Bar Graph

LESSON AT A GLANCE

Common Core Standards
Represent and interpret data.
1.MD.C.4 Organize, represent, and interpret data with up to three categories; ask and answer questions about the total number of data points, how many in each category, and how many more or less are in one category than in another.

Represent and interpret data.
2.MD.D.10 Draw a picture graph and a bar graph (with single-unit scale) to represent a data set with up to four categories. Solve simple put-together, take-apart, and compare problems using information presented in a bar graph.

Lesson Objective
Read and interpret information displayed on a bar graph.

Essential Question
How do you read a bar graph?

Materials
MathBoard

GO DIGITAL
Animated Math Models
HMH Mega Math

1 TEACH and TALK
GO DIGITAL • Animated Math Models

Model and Draw
Common Core MATHEMATICAL PRACTICES

Read aloud the title and labels on the graph.

- **What does this bar graph show?** the number of goldfish, guppies, and angel fish in the class aquarium
- **How is a bar graph different from a picture graph?** A bar graph has numbers at the bottom, and it has bars instead of pictures.

2 PRACTICE
MATH BOARD

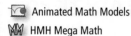

Share and Show • Guided Practice

- **How do you tell the number of fish by looking at a bar?** You read the number below the end of the bar.
- **How do you compare data on the graph?** You compare the lengths of the bars or the numbers the bars show.

Have children complete Exercises 1–4.

Use **Math Talk** to check children's understanding of how to read a bar graph.

This lesson builds on bar graphs presented in Chapter 10 and prepares children for using graphs taught in Grade 2.

Name ____________________

Use a Bar Graph
Essential Question How do you read a bar graph?

Model and Draw

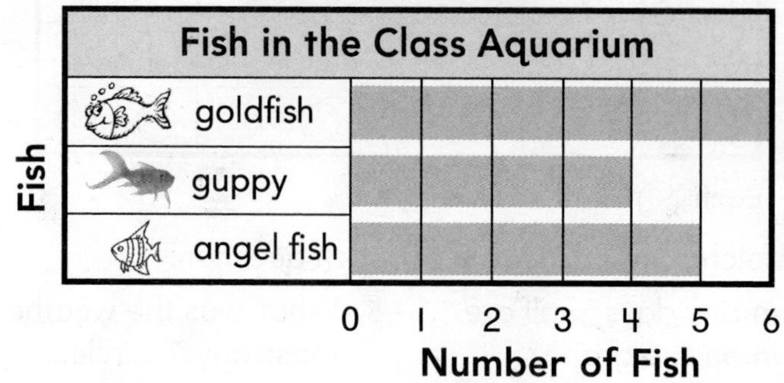

To find how many, read the number below the end of the bar.

6 fish are [goldfish].

Share and Show MATH BOARD

Use the bar graph to answer the questions.

1. How many fish are in the aquarium? 15 fish
2. How many fish in the aquarium are [angel fish]? 5 fish
3. How many fewer fish are [guppy] than [goldfish]? 2 fish
4. Are more of the fish [goldfish] or [angel fish]? goldfish

Possible answer: I added 6 + 4 + 5.

Math Talk How did you find the answer for Exercise 1?

Getting Ready for Grade 2 thirty-nine GR39

GR: Practice, p. GRP17

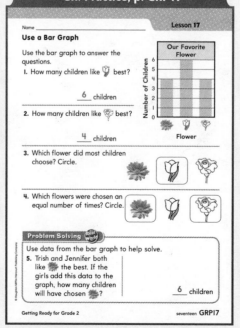

Name ____________________ Lesson 17

Use a Bar Graph

Use the bar graph to answer the questions.

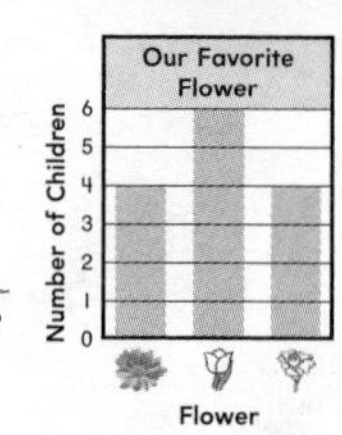

1. How many children like [tulip] best? 6 children
2. How many children like [rose] best? 4 children
3. Which flower did most children choose? Circle.
4. Which flowers were chosen an equal number of times? Circle.

Problem Solving Real World

Use data from the bar graph to help solve.

5. Trish and Jennifer both like [flower] the best. If the girls add this data to the graph, how many children will have chosen [flower]? 6 children

Getting Ready for Grade 2 seventeen GRP17

GR: Reteach, p. GRR17

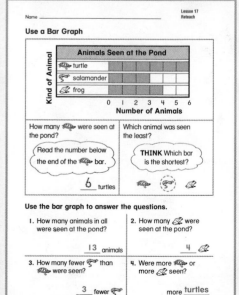

Name ____________________ Lesson 17 Reteach

Use a Bar Graph

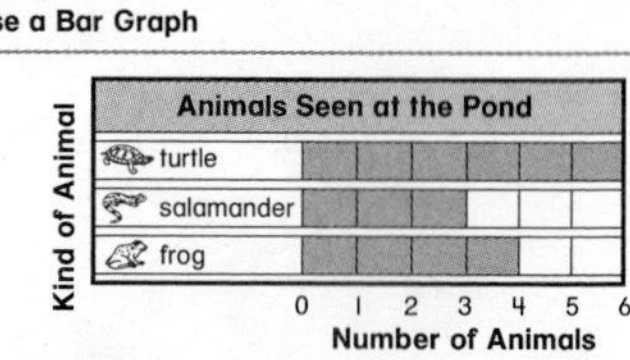

How many [turtles] were seen at the pond?
Read the number below the end of the [turtle] bar.
6 turtles

Which animal was seen the least?
THINK Which bar is the shortest?

Use the bar graph to answer the questions.

1. How many animals in all were seen at the pond? 13 animals
2. How many [frogs] were seen at the pond? 4 [frogs]
3. How many fewer [salamanders] than [turtles] were seen? 3 fewer [salamanders]
4. Were more [turtles] or more [frogs] seen? more turtles

Reteach GRR17 Grade 1

***GR** – Getting Ready Lessons and Resources (*www.thinkcentral.com*)

On Your Own

Use the bar graph to answer the questions.

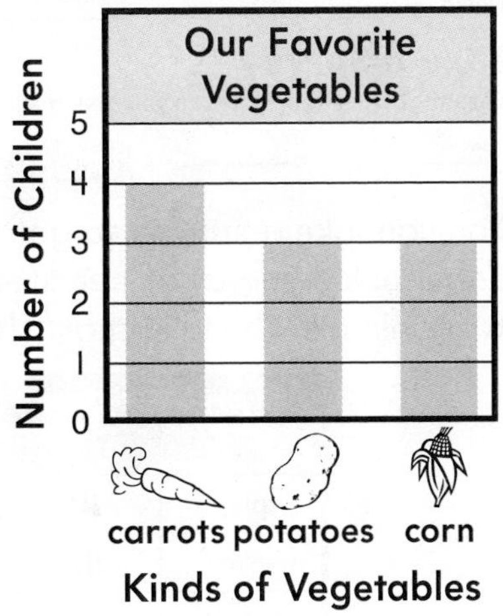

5. How many children chose ?

3 children

6. How many children chose ?

4 children

7. Which vegetable did most children choose? Circle.

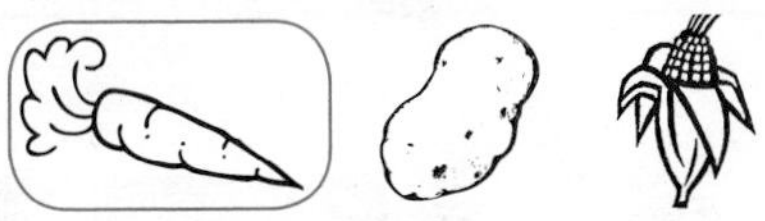

8. Which vegetables were chosen the same number of times? Circle.

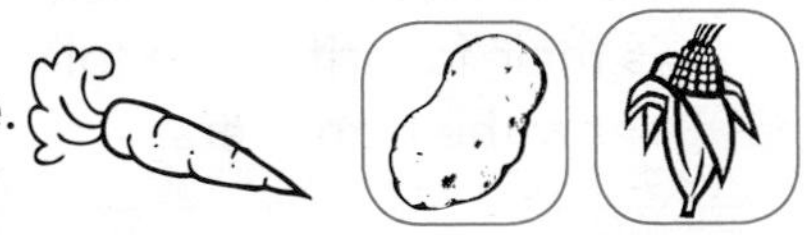

Problem Solving Real World

Use the bar graph to solve.

9. Brad and Glen both like corn the best. If the boys add this to the graph, how many children will have chosen corn?

5 children

TAKE HOME ACTIVITY • Ask your child to decide whether they prefer carrots or potatoes. Then have your child color to add their choice to the bar graph on this page.

On Your Own

If children complete Exercises 1–4 correctly, assign Exercises 5–8. To complete the exercises, children will need to use the bar graph at the top of the page.

- **What does this bar graph show?** how many children prefer carrots, potatoes, or corn

Problem Solving Real World

UNLOCK THE PROBLEM Children can solve the problem in Exercise 9 by using the bar graph.

- **What do you need to find on the bar graph in order to solve the problem?** I need to find how many children chose corn.

3 SUMMARIZE

Common Core MATHEMATICAL PRACTICES

Essential Question

How do you read a bar graph? Possible answer: I can see how many are in each category. I can see which category has more or less, and I can find how many more or less.

Math Journal WRITE Math

Look at the bar graph, Our Favorite Vegetables. Write a different question that can be answered by reading the graph.

LESSON 18

Take a Survey

LESSON AT A GLANCE

Common Core Standards
Represent and interpret data.
1.MD.C.4 Organize, represent, and interpret data with up to three categories; ask and answer questions about the total number of data points, how many in each category, and how many more or less are in one category than in another.

Represent and interpret data.
2.MD.D.10 Draw a picture graph and a bar graph (with single-unit scale) to represent a data set with up to four categories. Solve simple put-together, take-apart, and compare problems using information presented in a bar graph.

Lesson Objective
Take a survey and record the results.

Essential Question
How can you take a survey?

Vocabulary
survey

Materials
MathBoard

GO DIGITAL
Animated Math Models

This lesson builds on reading tally charts presented in Chapter 9 and prepares children for interpreting data collected from surveys taught in Grade 2.

Name ____________________

Take a Survey
Essential Question How can you take a survey?

Model and Draw

You can take a **survey** to get information. Jane took a survey of her friends' favorite wild animals. The tally chart shows the results.

REMEMBER Each tally mark stands for one friend's choice.

Favorite Wild Animal	
Animal	**Tally**
elephant	𝍸
monkey	|||
tiger	||

Share and Show MATH BOARD

1. Take a survey. Check children's work.
Ask 10 classmates which wild animal is their favorite. Use tally marks to show their answers.

Our Favorite Wild Animal	
Animal	**Tally**
elephant	
monkey	
tiger	

For 2–4, answers should reflect data represented in tally charts.

2. How many children did not choose tiger?
_________ children

3. Did more children choose elephant or tiger? _________

4. The most children chose _________ as their favorite.

Math Talk Describe a different survey that you could take. What would the choices be?
Possible answer: I could take a survey of favorite art projects with choices drawing, painting, and clay.

1 TEACH and TALK

GO DIGITAL • Animated Math Models

▶ Model and Draw

Common Core MATHEMATICAL PRACTICES

Review tally charts by having children tell what they are.

- **What does this tally chart show?** Jane's friends' favorite wild animals; 5 of Jane's friends chose elephants, 3 chose monkeys, and 2 chose tigers.
- **How do you think Jane took this survey?** Possible answer: She chose three wild animals and asked each of 10 friends to name their favorite of the three wild animals. Then Jane recorded her friends' answers in a tally chart.

2 PRACTICE

MATH BOARD

▶ Share and Show • Guided Practice

Before children take their surveys, remind them to ask 10 classmates which wild animal is their favorite. Have them record the choices in the tally chart.

- **Will any children choose lions? Why or why not?** No, because the tally chart on this page does not list lion as a choice.

GR: Practice, p. GRP18

Name ____________________ Lesson 18

Take a Survey

1. Take a survey. Ask 10 classmates which fruit is their favorite. Use tally marks to show their answers.
Check children's work.
Exercises 2–5 should reflect data recorded in the chart.

Our Favorite Fruit	
Fruit	**Tally**
apple	
banana	
orange	

2. Which fruit did the fewest classmates choose? _________

3. Which fruit did the most classmates choose? _________

4. Did more classmates choose apple or orange? _________

5. _________ classmates chose a fruit that was not apple.

Problem Solving Real World

6. Felix wants to ask 12 friends which pet is their favorite. He makes 1 tally mark for each child's answer. How many more friends does he need to ask?

Our Favorite Pets	
Pet	**Tally**
dog	𝍸
cat	|||
bird		

3 more friends

© Houghton Mifflin Harcourt Publishing Company

Getting Ready for Grade 2 eighteen GRP18

GR: Reteach, p. GRR18

Name ____________________ Lesson 18 Reteach

Take a Survey

When you take a survey, you collect information. Tally marks help you keep track of the information you collect.

Chris took a survey of his friends' favorite lunch. The tally chart shows their answers.

3 children chose sandwich.
6 children chose pizza.
1 child chose salad.

Our Favorite Lunch	
Lunch	**Tally**
sandwich	|||
pizza	𝍸	
salad		

The most children chose pizza.

Check children's work.
1. Take a survey.
Ask 10 classmates which lunch is their favorite. Use tally marks to show their answers.

Our Favorite Lunch	
Lunch	**Tally**
sandwich	
pizza	
salad	
taco	

2. Did more children choose pizza or taco? _________

3. The most children chose _________.

Reteach GRR18 Grade 1
© Houghton Mifflin Harcourt Publishing Company

*GR – Getting Ready Lessons and Resources (*www.thinkcentral.com*)

On Your Own

Our Favorite Color	
Color	Tally
red	
blue	
green	

5. Take a survey. Ask 10 classmates which color is their favorite. Use tally marks to show their answers.

Check children's work.

For 6–10, answers should reflect data recorded in the chart.

6. Which color was chosen by the fewest classmates? ________

7. Which color did the most classmates choose? ________

8. Did more classmates choose red or green? ________

9. ________ classmates chose a color that was not red.

10. Did fewer children choose blue or green? ________

Problem Solving Real World

Our Favorite Snack	
Snack	Tally
pretzels	II
apples	I
popcorn	卌

11. Jeff wants to ask 10 classmates which snack is their favorite. He makes 1 tally mark for each child's answer. How many more classmates does he need to ask?

2 more classmates

TAKE HOME ACTIVITY • Have your child survey family members about their favorite sport and make a tally chart to show the results.

Have children complete Exercises 1–4.

Use Math Talk to encourage children to suggest possible surveys, such as favorite school subjects or favorite books. Discuss possible choices for each survey.

On Your Own

If children completed Exercises 1–4 correctly, assign Exercises 5–10.

Point out the three color choices shown in the tally chart. Have a volunteer suggest a survey question to ask about favorite colors. Have children take the survey and record the data in the tally chart. Children then use the tally chart to answer Exercises 6–10.

- **How can you check to make sure that you asked 10 classmates to answer your survey question?** Possible answer: I can count the total number of tally marks to be sure there are 10 in all.

Problem Solving Real World

UNLOCK THE PROBLEM Exercise 11 requires children to model with mathematics to find the total number of tallies already in the chart and then subtract that number from 10.

- **What is the first step you will do to solve this problem?** Count the number of tally marks there are so far in the tally chart.
- **What is the next step you will do?** Subtract the number from 10 to find how many more classmates need to be surveyed to have 10 in all.

Have volunteers suggest a question that can be answered by using the information in the tally chart. Then use the chart to answer the question.

3 SUMMARIZE

Common Core MATHEMATICAL PRACTICES

Essential Question

How can you take a survey? Possible answer: I can make up a survey question with some choices. I can ask a number of people the question. Then I can record their answers next to each choice, using tally marks in a tally chart.

Math Journal WRITE Math

Make a tally chart to show that 7 children like the color green and 4 children like the color purple.

LESSON 19

Identify Shapes

LESSON AT A GLANCE

Common Core Standards
Reason with shapes and their attributes.
1.G.A.1 Distinguish between defining attributes (e.g., triangles are closed and three-sided) versus non-defining attributes (e.g., color, orientation, overall size); build and draw shapes to possess defining attributes.

Reason with shapes and their attributes.
2.G.A.1 Recognize and draw shapes having specified attributes, such as a given number of angles or a given number of equal faces. Identify triangles, quadrilaterals, pentagons, hexagons, and cubes.

Lesson Objective
Use attributes to help identify two-dimensional shapes.

Essential Question
How can attributes help you identify a shape?

Materials
MathBoard

GO DIGITAL
- Animated Math Models
- HMH Mega Math

1 TEACH and TALK

GO DIGITAL • Animated Math Models

▶ Model and Draw

MATHEMATICAL PRACTICES

Use the small diagram to review the terms *side* and *vertex*. Then discuss these attributes.

- **How can sides and vertices help you identify a hexagon?** I can count to see if there are 6 sides and 6 vertices.
- **Can you always identify the shape by counting the sides and vertices? Explain.** No. Possible answer: A shape with 4 sides and 4 vertices might be a square, rectangle, or trapezoid. It depends on how long the sides are and if they are slanted.

2 PRACTICE

MATH BOARD

▶ Share and Show • Guided Practice

- **How are the first two shapes in Exercise 1 alike?** They both have 3 sides, 3 vertices, and the same shape name.

Have children complete Exercises 1–4.

Use **Math Talk** to have children compare attributes of a square and a non-square rectangle.

This lesson builds on identifying shapes presented in Chapter 11 and prepares children for further work with attributes in Grade 2.

Name ______

Identify Shapes

Essential Question How can attributes help you identify a shape?

Model and Draw

The number of sides and vertices help you identify a shape.

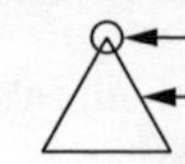

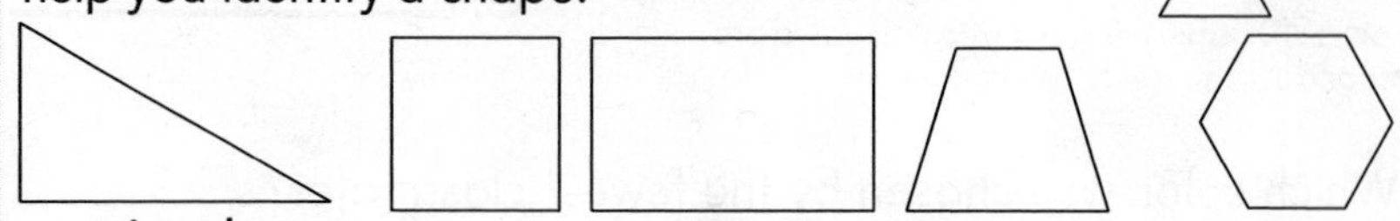

Share and Show MATH BOARD

Circle to answer the question. Write to name the shape.

1. Which shape has 4 sides?

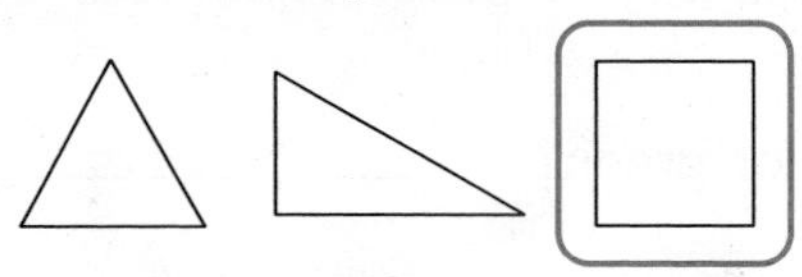

square

2. Which shape has 3 vertices?

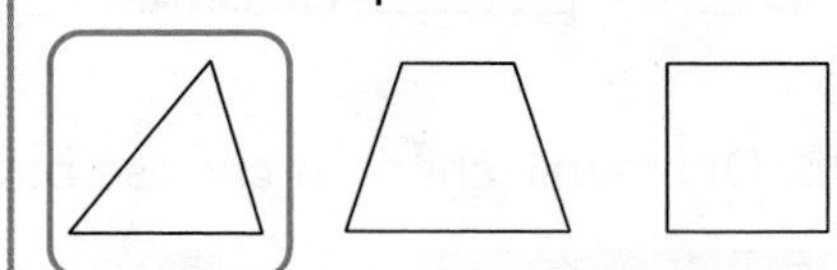

triangle

3. Which shape has 6 sides?

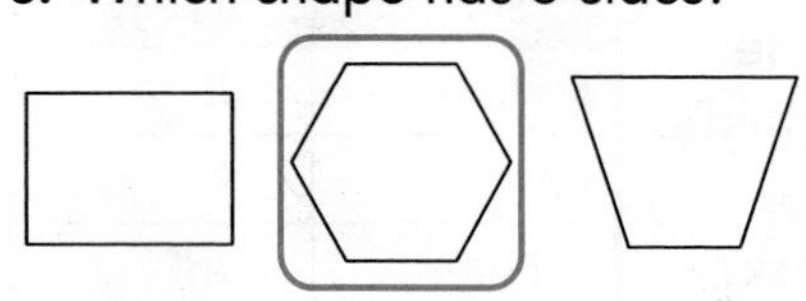

hexagon

4. Which shape has 4 vertices?

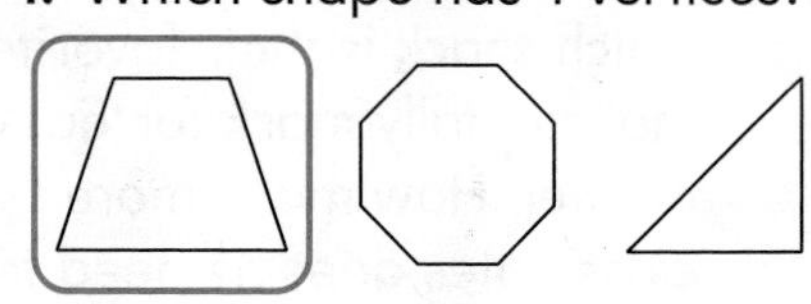

trapezoid

Possible answer: They both have 4 sides and 4 vertices.

Math Talk How are a square and a rectangle alike?

GR: Practice, p. GRP19

Name ______ Lesson 19

Identify Shapes

Circle to answer the question. Write to name.

1. Which shape has 4 vertices? triangle hexagon trapezoid — trapezoid
2. Which shape has 4 sides? rectangle hexagon triangle — rectangle
3. Which shape has 6 sides? triangle hexagon square — hexagon
4. Which shape has 3 vertices? rectangle triangle trapezoid — triangle

Problem Solving Real World

5. Mira, Liz, and Devin all draw shapes with 4 vertices. Their shapes look different and have different names. Draw 3 shapes the children might have drawn. Label each shape with its shape name.

rectangle square trapezoid

Getting Ready for Grade 2 nineteen GRP19

GR: Reteach, p. GRR19

Name ______ Lesson 19 Reteach

Identify Shapes

vertex side side vertex side vertex

triangle 3 sides, 3 vertices
hexagon 6 sides, 6 vertices
square rectangle trapezoid 4 sides, 4 vertices

Circle to answer the question. Write to name the shape.

1. Which shape has 4 vertices? rectangle
2. Which shape has 3 vertices? triangle
3. Which shape has 4 sides? trapezoid
4. Which shape has 6 sides? hexagon

Reteach GRR19 Grade 1

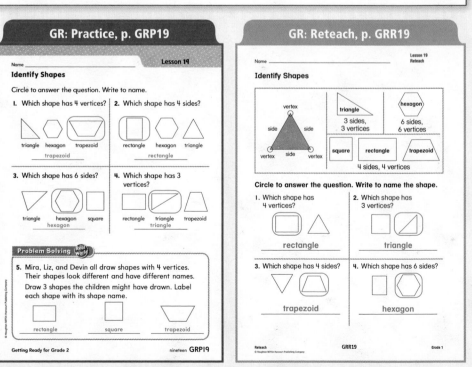

*GR – Getting Ready Lessons and Resources (*www.thinkcentral.com*)

On Your Own

Circle to answer the question. Write to name the shape.

5. Which shape has 3 sides?

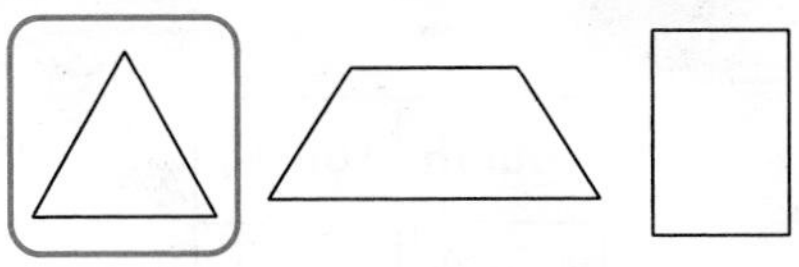

triangle

6. Which shape has 4 vertices?

rectangle

7. Which shape has 4 sides?

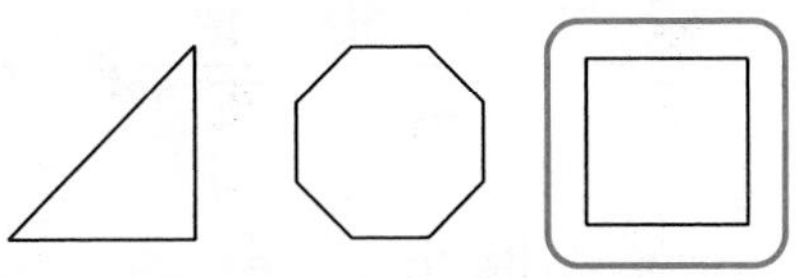

square

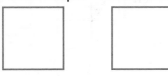

8. Which shape has 6 vertices?

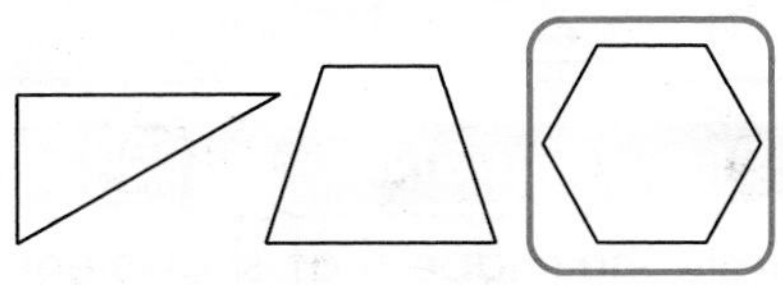

hexagon

Problem Solving (Real World)

9. Jason, Mat, and Carrie each draw a shape with 4 sides. The shapes look different and have different names.

Draw 3 shapes the children might have drawn. Write to name each shape. Possible answers:

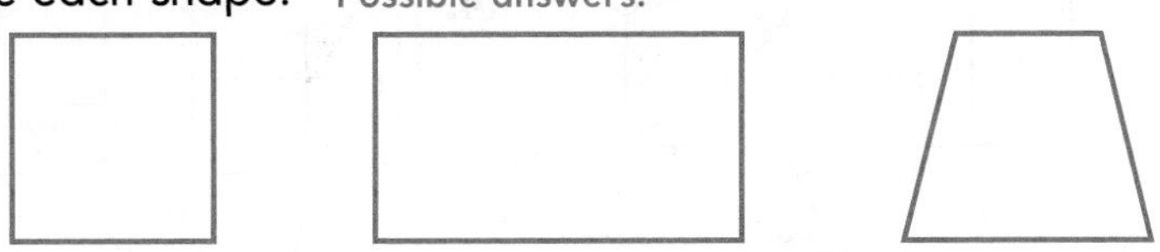

square rectangle trapezoid

TAKE HOME ACTIVITY • Have your child look around the house to find something that looks like a rectangle. Then have your child point to the rectangle and count the vertices. Repeat with the sides.

▶ On Your Own

If children complete Exercises 1–4 correctly, have them continue to use defining attributes to identify the shapes in Exercises 5–8.

- **What is the first shape in Exercise 5?** triangle **What is the first shape in Exercise 6?** triangle **Why do the two triangles look different?** Possible answer: They are turned in different directions.

▶ Problem Solving (Real World)

UNLOCK THE PROBLEM Read aloud the problem in Exercise 9. Then have children draw to show a possible scenario.

- **What do the children's shapes have in common?** They all have 4 sides.
- **How might the shapes be different?** The sides might be different lengths. A shape might have some slanted sides.

3 SUMMARIZE

Common Core MATHEMATICAL PRACTICES

Essential Question

How can attributes help you identify a shape? If I know how many sides or vertices a shape has, it helps me identify what shape it is.

Math Journal (WRITE Math)

Draw a square. Write to describe its attributes.

LESSON 20

Equal Shares

LESSON AT A GLANCE

Common Core Standards
Reason with shapes and their attributes.
1.G.A.3 Partition circles and rectangles into two and four equal shares, describe the shares using the words *halves, fourths,* and *quarters,* and use the phrases *half of, fourth of,* and *quarter of.* Describe the whole as two of, or four of the shares. Understand for these examples that decomposing into more equal shares creates smaller shares.

Reason with shapes and their attributes.
2.G.A.3 Partition circles and rectangles into two, three, or four equal shares, describe the shares using the words *halves, thirds, half of, a third of,* etc., and describe the whole as two halves, three thirds, four fourths. Recognize that equal shares of identical wholes need not have the same shape.

Lesson Objective
Identify halves and fourths in circles and rectangles.

Essential Question
How can you name two or four equal shares?

Materials
MathBoard

GO DIGITAL
Animated Math Models
HMH Mega Math

1 TEACH and TALK
GO DIGITAL • Animated Math Models

Model and Draw
MATHEMATICAL PRACTICES

Use the illustrations at the top of the page to discuss halves and fourths.

- **A whole rectangle has how many halves?** 2 halves **A whole rectangle has how many fourths?** 4 fourths
- **Can one half of a rectangle be larger than the other half? Explain.** No. If one part is larger, the parts are not halves because halves are equal shares.
- **How could you show that the 4 fourths of the rectangle are equal?** Possible answer: I could cut them apart and stack them to show that they match.

This lesson builds on equal shares presented in Chapter 12 and prepares for further work with equal shares taught in Grade 2.

Name ______

Equal Shares
Essential Question How can you name two or four equal shares?

Model and Draw

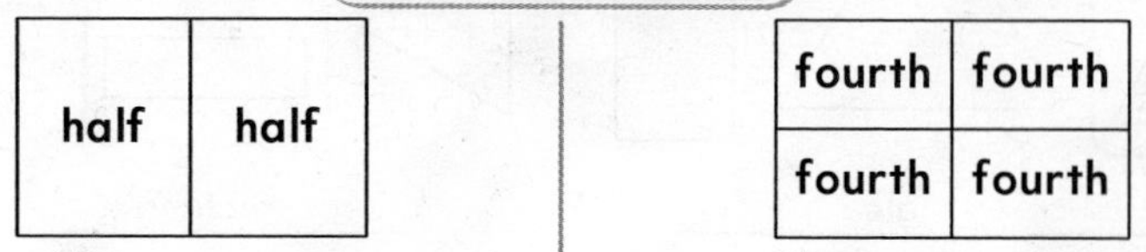

2 equal shares
2 halves

4 equal shares
4 fourths

Share and Show MATH BOARD

Circle the shape that shows equal shares. Write to name the equal shares.

1.
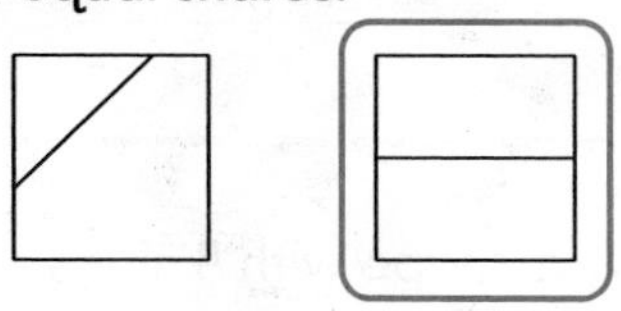
halves

2.
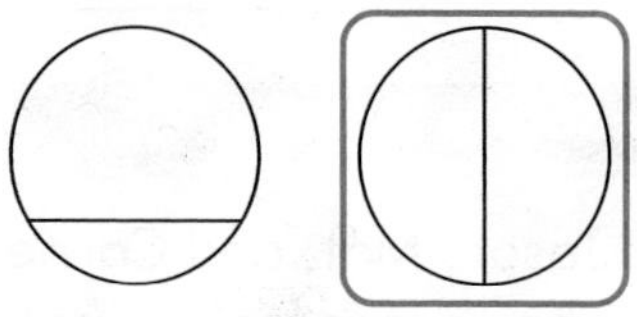
halves

3.
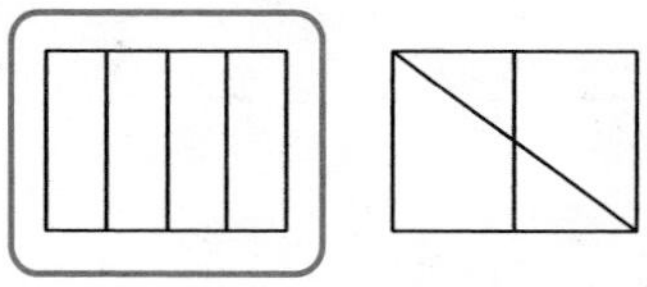
fourths

4.
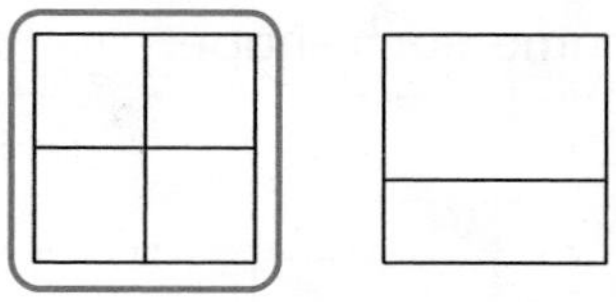
fourths

Possible answer: No, because half of a circle is not the same size and shape as half of a square.

Math Talk Are all equal shares the same size and shape? Explain.

Getting Ready for Grade 2 forty-five GR45

GR: Practice, p. GRP20

Name ______ Lesson 20

Equal Shares

Circle the shape that shows equal shares. Write to name the equal shares.

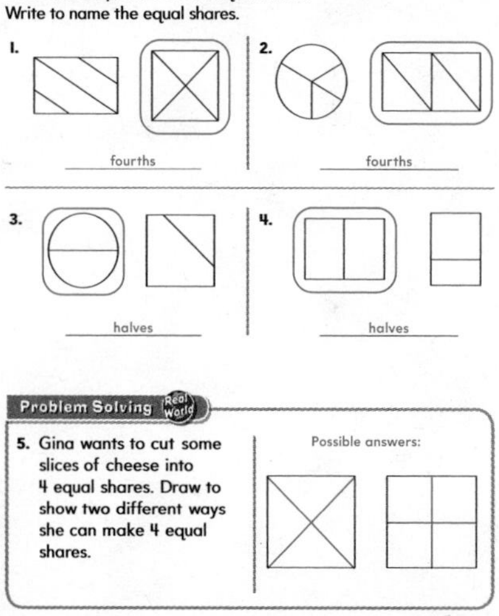

1. fourths
2. fourths
3. halves
4. halves

Problem Solving

5. Gina wants to cut some slices of cheese into 4 equal shares. Draw to show two different ways she can make 4 equal shares.

Possible answers:

Getting Ready for Grade 2 twenty GRP20

GR: Reteach, p. GRR20

Name ______ Lesson 20 Reteach

Equal Shares

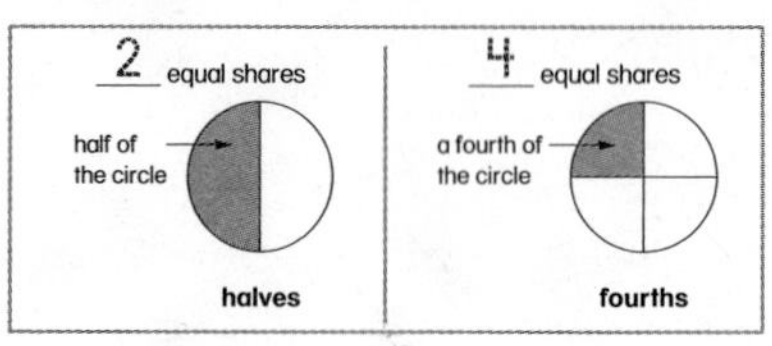

Write to name the equal shares.

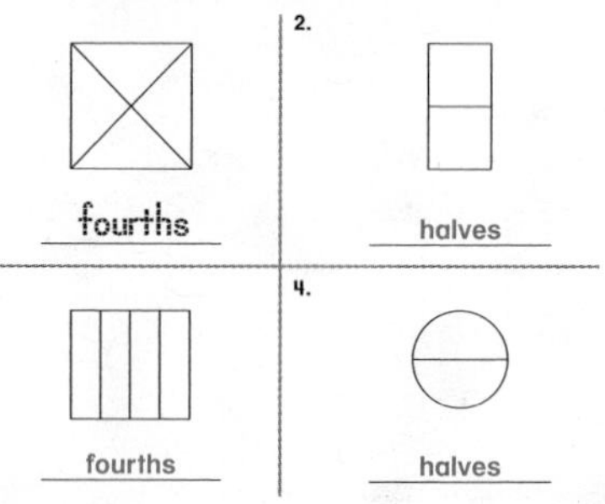

1. fourths
2. halves
3. fourths
4. halves

Reteach GRR20 Grade 1

*GR – Getting Ready Lessons and Resources (*www.thinkcentral.com*)

On Your Own

Circle the shape that shows equal shares. Write to name the equal shares.

5. 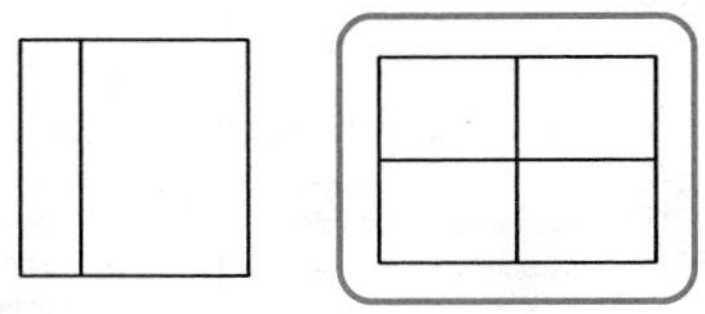

fourths

6. 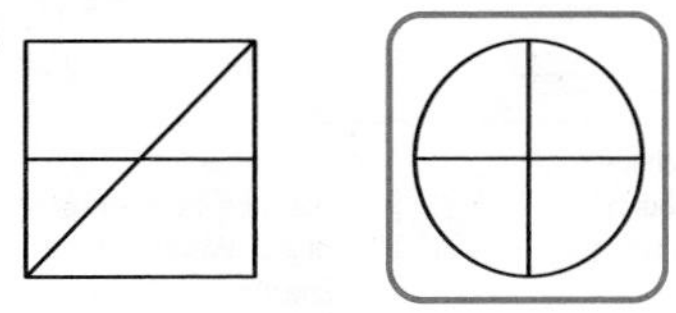

fourths

7. 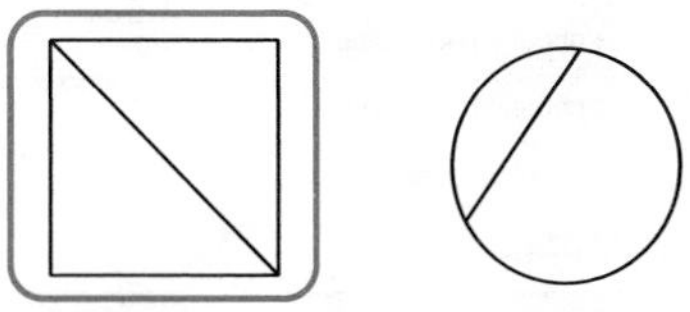

halves

8. 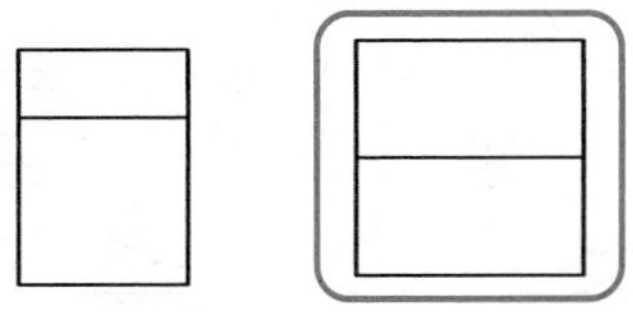

halves

Problem Solving Real World

9. Riley wants to share his cracker with a friend. Draw to show two different ways Riley can cut the cracker into equal shares.

Possible answer:

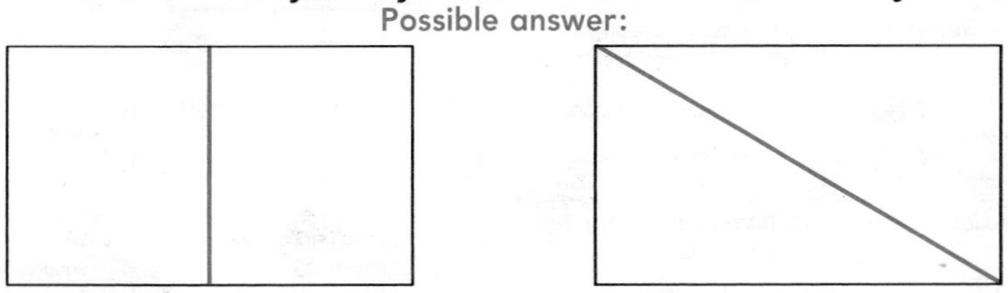

TAKE HOME ACTIVITY • Ask your child to help you cut a piece of toast into fourths.

Getting Ready Lessons and Resources, pp. GR47–GR48 ✓ Checkpoint

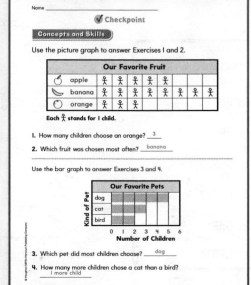

Name ______

✓ Checkpoint

Concepts and Skills

Use the picture graph to answer Exercises 1 and 2.

Our Favorite Fruit								
apple	웃	웃	웃	웃	웃			
banana	웃	웃	웃	웃	웃	웃	웃	웃
orange	웃	웃	웃					

Each 웃 stands for 1 child.

1. How many children choose an orange? 3
2. Which fruit was chosen most often? banana

Use the bar graph to answer Exercises 3 and 4.

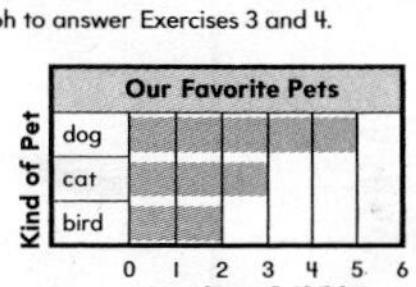

3. Which pet did most children choose? dog
4. How many more children chose a cat than a bird? 1 more child

5. Take a survey. Ask 8 classmates which sport is their favorite. Use tally marks to show their answers.

Check children's answers.

Our Favorite Sport	
Sport	**Tally**
baseball	
football	
soccer	

6. Did more children choose baseball or soccer? ______

Circle to answer the question. Then write the shape name.

7. Which shape has 4 vertices?

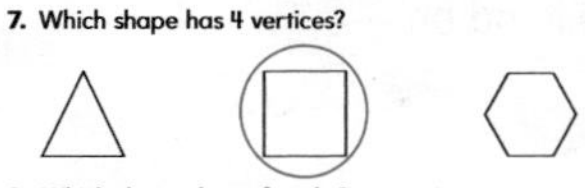

square

8. Which shape shows fourths?

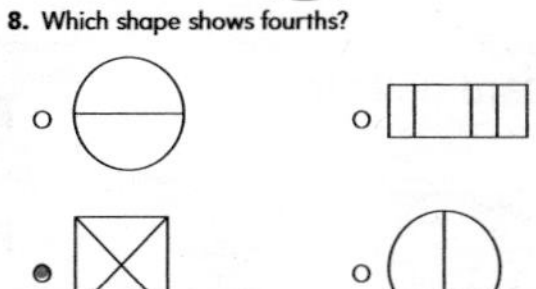

2 PRACTICE MATH BOARD

Share and Show • Guided Practice

- **Explain how you will know what to circle in Exercise 1.** Only one square shows equal shares. I find that square and circle it.

Use **Math Talk** to check children's understanding of the concept of equal shares, halves, and fourths.

On Your Own

If children complete Exercises 1–4 correctly, assign Exercises 5–8.

- **What will you look for when you are trying to identify a shape that shows fourths?** Possible answer: 4 equal-sized parts
- **What will you look for when you are trying to identify a shape that shows halves?** Possible answer: 2 equal-sized parts

Problem Solving Real World

UNLOCK THE PROBLEM Read aloud the problem in Exercise 9. Children can refer to the illustrations in Exercises 5–8 for partitioning ideas.

- **How many equal shares will you cut each cracker into?** Possible answer: 2 equal shares, because I share with one friend.

3 SUMMARIZE

MATHEMATICAL PRACTICES

Essential Question

How can you name two or four equal shares? If a shape shows 2 equal shares, it is halves. If it shows 4 equal shares, it is fourths.

Math Journal WRITE Math

Draw two circles. Draw to show 2 equal shares in one circle. Draw to show 4 equal shares in the other. Write halves or fourths to name the equal shares.

Getting Ready for Grade 2 Test

LESSONS 12 TO 20

Summative Assessment

Use the **Getting Ready Test** to assess children's progress in Getting Ready for Grade 2 Lessons 12–20.

Getting Ready Tests are provided in multiple-choice and mixed-response format in the *Getting Ready Lessons and Resources.*

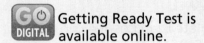

GO DIGITAL Getting Ready Test is available online.

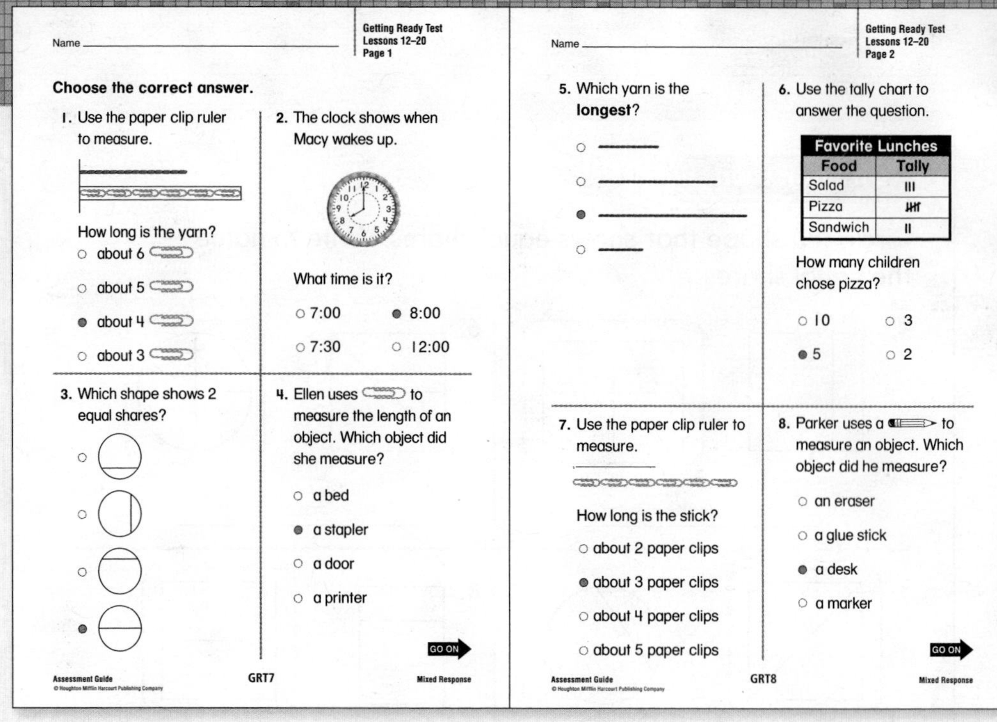

Name ______ Getting Ready Test Lessons 12–20 Page 1

Choose the correct answer.

1. Use the paper clip ruler to measure. How long is the yarn?
   - ○ about 6
   - ○ about 5
   - ● about 4
   - ○ about 3
2. The clock shows when Macy wakes up. What time is it?
   - ○ 7:00
   - ● 8:00
   - ○ 7:30
   - ○ 12:00
3. Which shape shows 2 equal shares?
4. Ellen uses [paper clip] to measure the length of an object. Which object did she measure?
   - ○ a bed
   - ● a stapler
   - ○ a door
   - ○ a printer

GO ON

Assessment Guide © Houghton Mifflin Harcourt Publishing Company GRT7 Mixed Response

Name ______ Getting Ready Test Lessons 12–20 Page 2

5. Which yarn is the **longest**?
6. Use the tally chart to answer the question.

Favorite Lunches	
Food	Tally
Salad	III
Pizza	𝍸
Sandwich	II

How many children chose pizza?
   - ○ 10
   - ○ 3
   - ● 5
   - ○ 2

7. Use the paper clip ruler to measure. How long is the stick?
   - ○ about 2 paper clips
   - ● about 3 paper clips
   - ○ about 4 paper clips
   - ○ about 5 paper clips
8. Parker uses a [crayon] to measure an object. Which object did he measure?
   - ○ an eraser
   - ○ a glue stick
   - ● a desk
   - ○ a marker

GO ON

Assessment Guide © Houghton Mifflin Harcourt Publishing Company GRT8 Mixed Response

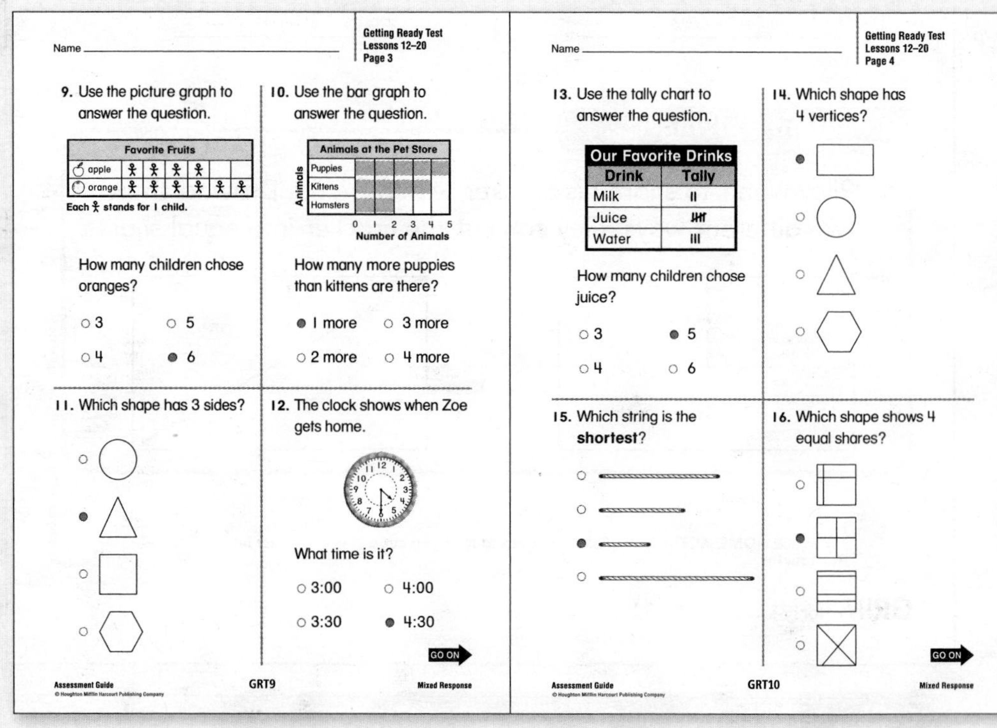

Name ______ Getting Ready Test Lessons 12–20 Page 3

9. Use the picture graph to answer the question.

Favorite Fruits	
apple	4 figures
orange	6 figures

Each [figure] stands for 1 child.

How many children chose oranges?
   - ○ 3
   - ○ 5
   - ○ 4
   - ● 6

10. Use the bar graph to answer the question. (Animals at the Pet Store: Puppies, Kittens, Hamsters; Number of Animals 0–5)

How many more puppies than kittens are there?
   - ● 1 more
   - ○ 3 more
   - ○ 2 more
   - ○ 4 more

11. Which shape has 3 sides?
12. The clock shows when Zoe gets home. What time is it?
   - ○ 3:00
   - ○ 4:00
   - ○ 3:30
   - ● 4:30

GO ON

Assessment Guide © Houghton Mifflin Harcourt Publishing Company GRT9 Mixed Response

Name ______ Getting Ready Test Lessons 12–20 Page 4

13. Use the tally chart to answer the question.

Our Favorite Drinks	
Drink	Tally
Milk	II
Juice	𝍸
Water	III

How many children chose juice?
   - ○ 3
   - ● 5
   - ○ 4
   - ○ 6

14. Which shape has 4 vertices?
15. Which string is the **shortest**?
16. Which shape shows 4 equal shares?

GO ON

Assessment Guide © Houghton Mifflin Harcourt Publishing Company GRT10 Mixed Response

Data-Driven Decision Making RtI

Item	Lesson	Common Error	Intervene With
1, 7, 21	13	May not understand how to use a ruler	**R**—p. GRR13
2, 12, 20	15	May confuse the hour hand and the minute hand on an analog clock	**R**—p. GRR15
3, 16, 23	20	May not recognize 2 or 4 equal shares	**R**—p. GRR20
4, 8, 19	12	May not understand how to choose non-standard units to measure	**R**—p. GRR12
5, 15, 24	14	May confuse the longest and shortest lengths	**R**—p. GRR14
6, 13	18	May not understand how to count tally marks	**R**—p. GRR18

Key: R—Getting Ready Lessons and Resources: Reteach

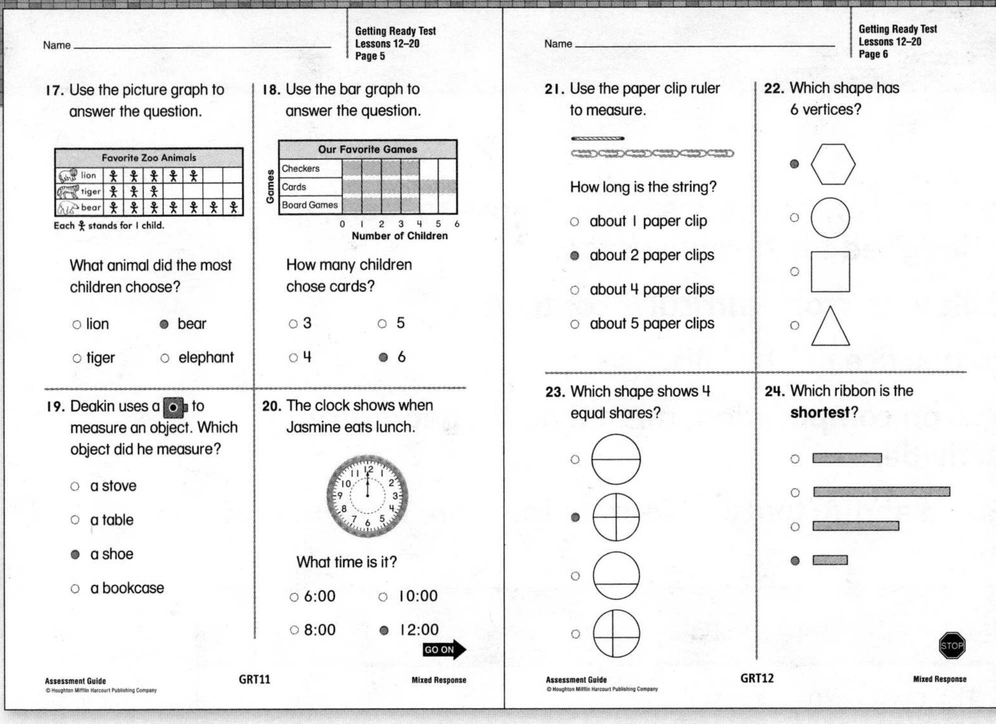
Name

Getting Ready Test
Lessons 12–20
Page 5

17. Use the picture graph to answer the question.

Favorite Zoo Animals
Each stands for 1 child.

What animal did the most children choose?

- lion
- bear
- tiger
- elephant

18. Use the bar graph to answer the question.

Our Favorite Games

How many children chose cards?

- 3
- 5
- 4
- 6

19. Deakin uses a to measure an object. Which object did he measure?

- a stove
- a table
- a shoe
- a bookcase

20. The clock shows when Jasmine eats lunch.

What time is it?

- 6:00
- 10:00
- 8:00
- 12:00

GO ON

Assessment Guide
© Houghton Mifflin Harcourt Publishing Company

GRT11

Mixed Response

Name

Getting Ready Test
Lessons 12–20
Page 6

21. Use the paper clip ruler to measure.

How long is the string?

- about 1 paper clip
- about 2 paper clips
- about 4 paper clips
- about 5 paper clips

22. Which shape has 6 vertices?

23. Which shape shows 4 equal shares?

24. Which ribbon is the **shortest**?

STOP

Assessment Guide
© Houghton Mifflin Harcourt Publishing Company

GRT12

Mixed Response

Portfolio Suggestions The portfolio represents the growth, talents, achievements, and reflections of the mathematics learner. Children might spend a short time selecting work samples for their portfolios.

You may want to have children respond to the following questions:

- Which question was difficult?
- What would you like to learn more about?

For information about how to organize, share, and evaluate portfolios, see the *Chapter Resources*.

Data-Driven Decision Making RtI

Item	Lesson	Common Error	Intervene With
9, 17	16	May not understand how to find information on a picture graph	**R**—p. GRR16
10, 18	17	May look at the wrong bars on the graph for information	**R**—p. GRR17
11, 14, 22	19	May confuse attributes of plane shapes	**R**—p. GRR19

Key: R—Getting Ready Lessons and Resources: Reteach

Grab-and-Go!™

Differentiated Centers Kit

The Grab-and-Go!™ Differentiated Centers Kit contains ready-to-use readers, games, and math center activities that are designed for flexible usage.

- Readers that integrate math skills with cross-curricular content.
- Games that engage students to practice math skills.
- Math Center Activities that focus on computation, mental math, geometry, measurement, and challenge activities.

See the Grab-and-Go!™ Teacher Guide and Activity Resources for more information.

Chapter	Grade 1		
1 Addition Concepts	Reader	The Class Party Math Club Join Us Busy Bugs	
	Game	Addition Bingo	
	Activity	Activity 3	Sum Sentences Put It Together How Many Ways?
		Activity 7	Back and Forth
2 Subtraction Concepts	Reader	The Class Party Milk for Sale	
	Game	Subtraction Slide	
	Activity	Activity 5	Apples Away Runaway Squares
		Activity 9	Subtract! Picture This
3 Addition Strategies	Reader	Join Us Doubles Fun on the Farm Funny Bunny Hats	
	Game	Ducky Sums Neighborhood Sums	
	Activity	Activity 7	Double Trouble Back and Forth
		Activity 16	Make a Ten to Add Add With Ten The Sum Is the Same

Chapter	Grade 1		
4 Subtraction Strategies	Reader	Math Club Miss Bumble's Garden The Class Party	
	Game	Under the Sea	
	Activity	Activity 5	Apples Away Runaway Squares Plus and Minus
		Activity 9	Picture This
5 Addition and Subtraction Relationships	Reader	Picture Puzzles Juggling	
	Game	Ducky Sums Related Fact Race Basic Facts Race	
	Activity	Activity 11	Face Facts Any Way You Cut It Problem Solving
		Activity 16	The Sum Is the Same
		Activity 18	The Missing Piece Number Tales
6 Count and Model Numbers	Reader	Join Us Strawberries	
	Game	Puddle Hopping Tens and Ones Race	
	Activity	Activity 14	Teen Time Groups of Ten Ten and Up

Math Center Activity Cards:

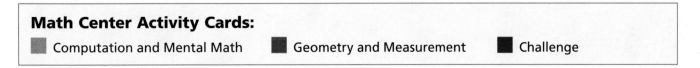

Computation and Mental Math   Geometry and Measurement   Challenge

Chapter	Grade 1		
7 Compare Numbers	Reader	Name That Number Strawberries	
	Game	The Greater Game Rainy Day Fun Puddle Hopping	
	Activity	Activity 4	20 Through 50
8 Two-Digit Addition and Subtraction	Reader	Garden Party It's a Home Run! Party Plans	
	Game	Neighborhood Sums Flying Along Basic Facts Race	
	Activity	Activity 14	Groups of Ten
		Activity 16	Add With Ten
		Activity 20	Regroup Count On Neat Trick
9 Measurement	Reader	The Dog Show Treasure Hunts Time to Play	
	Game	Measure Up! Story Time	
	Activity	Activity 17	Half Past On the Hour

Chapter	Grade 1		
10 Represent Data	Reader	Miss B's Class Makes Tables and Graphs	
	Game	Graph Game	
	Activity	Activity 6	Tally Ho! Graph Math Picture Perfect
		Activity 8	Pass the Bar
11 Three-Dimensional Geometry	Reader	April's First Word Building a Mini-Park	
	Game	On the Water	
	Activity	Activity 10	On the Corner Building Blocks
12 Two-Dimensional Geometry	Reader	Signs Shape Up	
	Game	On the Water	
	Activity	Activity 10	More Alike Than Not On the Corner Building Blocks
		Activity 19	Half Math

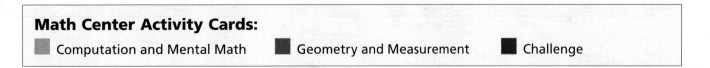

Math Center Activity Cards:
Computation and Mental Math | Geometry and Measurement | Challenge

Sequence Options

GO Math! provides the flexibility to teach the program in a different sequence. If children need background knowledge for the chapter, use the list of prerequisites.

Chapter	Objectives	Prerequisites
1 Addition Concepts COMMON CORE STATE STANDARDS 1.OA.A.1, 1.OA.B.3, 1.OA.C.6	• Use pictures and concrete objects and the strategy make a model to solve "adding to" and "putting together" addition problems. • Understand, apply, and explore the Additive Identity Property for Addition and the Commutative Property of Addition. • Model and record all the ways to put together numbers within 10. • Build fluency for addition within 10.	
2 Subtraction Concepts COMMON CORE STATE STANDARDS 1.OA.A.1, 1.OA.C.6, 1.OA.D.8	• Use pictures and concrete objects and the strategy make a model to solve "taking from" and "taking apart" subtraction problems. • Compare pictorial groups to understand subtraction. • Identify how many are left when subtracting all or 0. • Model and compare groups to show the meaning of subtraction. • Model and record all of the ways to take apart numbers within 10. • Build fluency for subtraction within 10.	Chapter 1
3 Addition Strategies COMMON CORE STATE STANDARDS 1.OA.A.2, 1.OA.B.3, 1.OA.C.5, 1.OA.C.6	• Understand and apply the Commutative Property of Addition for sums within 20. • Use the following strategies to find sums within 20: count on 1, 2, or 3, doubles, doubles plus 1 and doubles minus 1, or make a ten. • Use doubles to create equivalent but easier sums. • Use a ten frame to add 10 and an addend less than 10. • Understand and apply the Associative Property or Commutative Property of Addition to add three addends. • Solve adding to and putting together situations using the strategy draw a picture.	Chapter 1
4 Subtraction Strategies COMMON CORE STATE STANDARDS 1.OA.A.1, 1.OA.B.4, 1.OA.C.5, 1.OA.C.6	• Use the following strategies to find differences within 20: count back 1, 2, or 3, use addition to subtract, or make a ten. • Recall addition facts to subtract numbers within 20. • Subtract by breaking apart to make a ten. • Solve subtraction problem situations using the strategy act it out.	Chapter 2
5 Addition and Subtraction Relationships COMMON CORE STATE STANDARDS 1.OA.A.1, 1.OA.C.6, 1.OA.D.7, 1.OA.D.8	• Solve addition and subtraction problem situations using the strategy make a model. • Identify and record related facts within 20 and use them to subtract. • Apply the inverse relationship of addition and subtraction. • Represent equivalent forms of numbers using sums and differences within 20. • Determine if an equation is true or false. • Add and subtract facts within 20 and demonstrate fluency for addition and subtraction within 10.	Chapters 1–4
6 Count and Model Numbers COMMON CORE STATE STANDARDS 1.NBT.A.1, 1.NBT.B.2, 1.NBT.B.2a, 1.NBT.B.2b, 1.NBT.B.2c, 1.NBT.B.3	• Use models and write to represent equivalent forms of ten and ones through 120. • Use objects, pictures, and numbers to represent numbers (or quantities) to 100. • Solve problems using the strategy make a model. • Count, read, and write numerals to represent a number of 100 to 120 objects.	Chapters 1–5

Chapter	Objectives	Prerequisites
7 Compare Numbers COMMON CORE STATE STANDARDS 1.NBT.B.3, 1.NBT.C.5	• Model and compare two-digit numbers using symbols. • Solve problems using the strategy make a model. • Identify numbers that are 10 less or 10 more than a given number.	Chapter 6
8 Two-Digit Addition and Subtraction COMMON CORE STATE STANDARDS 1.NBT.C.4, 1.NBT.C.6, 1.OA.C.6	• Add and subtract within 20. • Use and draw models and manipulatives to add two-digit numbers. • Solve and explain two-digit addition word problems using the strategy draw a picture.	Chapters 1–6
9 Measurement COMMON CORE STATE STANDARDS 1.MD.A.1, 1.MD.A.2, 1.MD.B.3	• Order objects by length. • Use the Transitivity Principle to measure indirectly. • Make a nonstandard measuring tool to measure length. • Solve measurement problems using the strategy act it out. • Tell times and write times to the hour and half hour.	Chapter 7
10 Represent Data COMMON CORE STATE STANDARDS 1.MD.C.4	• Analyze and compare data shown in a picture graph where each symbol represents one. • Make a picture graph. • Analyze and compare data shown in a bar graph or a tally chart. • Make a bar graph or a tally chart. • Solve problem situations using the strategy make a graph.	Chapter 7
11 Three-Dimensional Geometry COMMON CORE STATE STANDARDS 1.G.A.1, 1.G.A.2	• Identify and describe three-dimensional shapes according to defining attributes. • Compose a new shape by combining three-dimensional shapes. • Use composite three-dimensional shapes to build new shapes. • Identify three-dimensional shapes used to build a composite shape using the strategy act it out. • Identify two-dimensional shapes on three-dimensional shapes.	
12 Two-Dimensional Geometry COMMON CORE STATE STANDARDS 1.G.A.1, 1.G.A.2, 1.G.A.3	• Describe attributes of two-dimensional shapes and use defining attributes to sort shapes. • Compose a new shape by combining two-dimensional shapes. • Make new shapes from composite two-dimensional shapes using the strategy act it out. • Decompose combined shapes into shapes. • Identify equal and unequal parts (or shares) in two-dimensional shapes. • Partition circles and rectangles into two or four equal shares.	Chapter 11

Instructional Path

Lesson	Common Core State Standards for Mathematics		Pacing
Chapter 1 Addition Concepts			
Progress Tracker 1 2 3 4 5 6 7 8 9 10 11 12			
1.1 Algebra • Use Pictures to Add To	**1.OA.A.1**	Use addition and subtraction within 20 to solve word problems involving situations of adding to, taking from, putting together, taking apart, and comparing, with unknowns in all positions, e.g., by using objects, drawings, and equations with a symbol for the unknown number to represent the problem.	1 day
1.2 Hands On • Model Adding To	**1.OA.A.1**	Use addition and subtraction within 20 to solve word problems involving situations of adding to, taking from, putting together, taking apart, and comparing, with unknowns in all positions, e.g., by using objects, drawings, and equations with a symbol for the unknown number to represent the problem.	2 days
1.3 Hands On • Model Putting Together	**1.OA.A.1**	Use addition and subtraction within 20 to solve word problems involving situations of adding to, taking from, putting together, taking apart, and comparing, with unknowns in all positions, e.g., by using objects, drawings, and equations with a symbol for the unknown number to represent the problem.	2 days
1.4 Problem Solving • Model Addition	**1.OA.A.1**	Use addition and subtraction within 20 to solve word problems involving situations of adding to, taking from, putting together, taking apart, and comparing, with unknowns in all positions, e.g., by using objects, drawings, and equations with a symbol for the unknown number to represent the problem.	2 days
1.5 Algebra • Add Zero	**1.OA.B.3**	Apply properties of operations as strategies to add and subtract.	1 day
1.6 Hands On: Algebra • Add in Any Order	**1.OA.B.3**	Apply properties of operations as strategies to add and subtract.	1 day
1.7 Hands On: Algebra • Put Together Numbers to 10	**1.OA.A.1**	Use addition and subtraction within 20 to solve word problems involving situations of adding to, taking from, putting together, taking apart, and comparing, with unknowns in all positions, e.g., by using objects, drawings, and equations with a symbol for the unknown number to represent the problem.	2 days
1.8 Addition to 10	**1.OA.C.6**	Add and subtract within 20, demonstrating fluency for addition and subtraction within 10. Use strategies such as counting on; making ten (e.g., $8 + 6 = 8 + 2 + 4 = 10 + 4 = 14$); decomposing a number leading to a ten (e.g., $13 - 4 = 13 - 3 - 1 = 10 - 1 = 9$); using the relationship between addition and subtraction (e.g., knowing that $8 + 4 = 12$, one knows $12 - 8 = 4$); and creating equivalent but easier or known sums (e.g., adding $6 + 7$ by creating the known equivalent $6 + 6 + 1 = 12 + 1 = 13$).	1 day

Lesson	Common Core State Standards for Mathematics		Pacing
Chapter 2 Subtraction Concepts			
Progress Tracker 1 **2** 3 4 5 6 7 8 9 10 11 12			
2.1 Use Pictures to Show Taking From	■ 1.OA.A.1	Use addition and subtraction within 20 to solve word problems involving situations of adding to, taking from, putting together, taking apart, and comparing, with unknowns in all positions, e.g., by using objects, drawings, and equations with a symbol for the unknown number to represent the problem.	1 day
2.2 Hands On • Model Taking From	■ 1.OA.A.1	Use addition and subtraction within 20 to solve word problems involving situations of adding to, taking from, putting together, taking apart, and comparing, with unknowns in all positions, e.g., by using objects, drawings, and equations with a symbol for the unknown number to represent the problem.	1 day
2.3 Hands On • Model Taking Apart	■ 1.OA.A.1	Use addition and subtraction within 20 to solve word problems involving situations of adding to, taking from, putting together, taking apart, and comparing, with unknowns in all positions, e.g., by using objects, drawings, and equations with a symbol for the unknown number to represent the problem.	2 days
2.4 Problem Solving • Model Subtraction	■ 1.OA.A.1	Use addition and subtraction within 20 to solve word problems involving situations of adding to, taking from, putting together, taking apart, and comparing, with unknowns in all positions, e.g., by using objects, drawings, and equations with a symbol for the unknown number to represent the problem.	2 days
2.5 Use Pictures and Subtraction to Compare	■ 1.OA.A.1	Use addition and subtraction within 20 to solve word problems involving situations of adding to, taking from, putting together, taking apart, and comparing, with unknowns in all positions, e.g., by using objects, drawings, and equations with a symbol for the unknown number to represent the problem.	1 day
	■ 1.OA.D.8	Determine the unknown whole number in an addition or subtraction equation relating three whole numbers.	
2.6 Hands On • Subtract to Compare	■ 1.OA.A.1	Use addition and subtraction within 20 to solve word problems involving situations of adding to, taking from, putting together, taking apart, and comparing, with unknowns in all positions, e.g., by using objects, drawings, and equations with a symbol for the unknown number to represent the problem.	2 days
2.7 Subtract All or Zero	■ 1.OA.D.8	Determine the unknown whole number in an addition or subtraction equation relating three whole numbers.	1 day
2.8 Hands On: Algebra • Take Apart Numbers	■ 1.OA.A.1	Use addition and subtraction within 20 to solve word problems involving situations of adding to, taking from, putting together, taking apart, and comparing, with unknowns in all positions, e.g., by using objects, drawings, and equations with a symbol for the unknown number to represent the problem.	2 days

Chapter continued on next page ▶

■ Major Content □ Supporting Content ○ Additional Content

Lesson		Common Core State Standards for Mathematics	Pacing
Chapter 2 Subtraction Concepts *(continued)*			
2.9 Subtraction from 10 or Less	**1.OA.C.6**	Add and subtract within 20, demonstrating fluency for addition and subtraction within 10. Use strategies such as counting on; making ten (e.g., 8 + 6 = 8 + 2 + 4 = 10 + 4 = 14); decomposing a number leading to a ten (e.g., 13 − 4 = 13 − 3 − 1 = 10 − 1 = 9); using the relationship between addition and subtraction (e.g., knowing that 8 + 4 = 12, one knows 12 − 8 = 4); and creating equivalent but easier or known sums (e.g., adding 6 + 7 by creating the known equivalent 6 + 6 + 1 = 12 + 1 = 13).	1 day

Lesson		Common Core State Standards for Mathematics	Pacing
Chapter 3 Addition Strategies			
Progress Tracker 1 2 3 4 5 6 7 8 9 10 11 12			
3.1 Algebra • Add in Any Order	**1.OA.B.3**	Apply properties of operations as strategies to add and subtract.	1 day
3.2 Count On	**1.OA.C.5**	Relate counting to addition and subtraction (e.g., by counting on 2 to add 2).	1 day
3.3 Hands On • Add Doubles	**1.OA.C.6**	Add and subtract within 20, demonstrating fluency for addition and subtraction within 10. Use strategies such as counting on; making ten (e.g., 8 + 6 = 8 + 2 + 4 = 10 + 4 = 14); decomposing a number leading to a ten (e.g., 13 − 4 = 13 − 3 − 1 = 10 − 1 = 9); using the relationship between addition and subtraction (e.g., knowing that 8 + 4 = 12, one knows 12 − 8 = 4); and creating equivalent but easier or known sums (e.g., adding 6 + 7 by creating the known equivalent 6 + 6 + 1 = 12 + 1 = 13).	1 day
3.4 Hands On • Use Doubles to Add	**1.OA.C.6**	Add and subtract within 20, demonstrating fluency for addition and subtraction within 10. Use strategies such as counting on; making ten (e.g., 8 + 6 = 8 + 2 + 4 = 10 + 4 = 14); decomposing a number leading to a ten (e.g., 13 − 4 = 13 − 3 − 1 = 10 − 1 = 9); using the relationship between addition and subtraction (e.g., knowing that 8 + 4 = 12, one knows 12 − 8 = 4); and creating equivalent but easier or known sums (e.g., adding 6 + 7 by creating the known equivalent 6 + 6 + 1 = 12 + 1 = 13).	1 day
3.5 Hands On • Doubles Plus 1 and Doubles Minus 1	**1.OA.C.6**	Add and subtract within 20, demonstrating fluency for addition and subtraction within 10. Use strategies such as counting on; making ten (e.g., 8 + 6 = 8 + 2 + 4 = 10 + 4 = 14); decomposing a number leading to a ten (e.g., 13 − 4 = 13 − 3 − 1 = 10 − 1 = 9); using the relationship between addition and subtraction (e.g., knowing that 8 + 4 = 12, one knows 12 − 8 = 4); and creating equivalent but easier or known sums (e.g., adding 6 + 7 by creating the known equivalent 6 + 6 + 1 = 12 + 1 = 13).	2 days

Chapter continued on next page ▶

Lesson	Common Core State Standards for Mathematics		Pacing
Chapter 3 Addition Strategies *(continued)*			
3.6 Practice the Strategies	■ **1.OA.C.6**	Add and subtract within 20, demonstrating fluency for addition and subtraction within 10. Use strategies such as counting on; making ten (e.g., $8 + 6 = 8 + 2 + 4 = 10 + 4 = 14$); decomposing a number leading to a ten (e.g., $13 - 4 = 13 - 3 - 1 = 10 - 1 = 9$); using the relationship between addition and subtraction (e.g., knowing that $8 + 4 = 12$, one knows $12 - 8 = 4$); and creating equivalent but easier or known sums (e.g., adding $6 + 7$ by creating the known equivalent $6 + 6 + 1 = 12 + 1 = 13$).	1 day
3.7 Hands On • Add 10 and More	■ **1.OA.C.6**	Add and subtract within 20, demonstrating fluency for addition and subtraction within 10. Use strategies such as counting on; making ten (e.g., $8 + 6 = 8 + 2 + 4 = 10 + 4 = 14$); decomposing a number leading to a ten (e.g., $13 - 4 = 13 - 3 - 1 = 10 - 1 = 9$); using the relationship between addition and subtraction (e.g., knowing that $8 + 4 = 12$, one knows $12 - 8 = 4$); and creating equivalent but easier or known sums (e.g., adding $6 + 7$ by creating the known equivalent $6 + 6 + 1 = 12 + 1 = 13$).	1 day
3.8 Hands On • Make a 10 to Add	■ **1.OA.C.6**	Add and subtract within 20, demonstrating fluency for addition and subtraction within 10. Use strategies such as counting on; making ten (e.g., $8 + 6 = 8 + 2 + 4 = 10 + 4 = 14$); decomposing a number leading to a ten (e.g., $13 - 4 = 13 - 3 - 1 = 10 - 1 = 9$); using the relationship between addition and subtraction (e.g., knowing that $8 + 4 = 12$, one knows $12 - 8 = 4$); and creating equivalent but easier or known sums (e.g., adding $6 + 7$ by creating the known equivalent $6 + 6 + 1 = 12 + 1 = 13$).	2 days
3.9 Use Make a 10 to Add	■ **1.OA.C.6**	Add and subtract within 20, demonstrating fluency for addition and subtraction within 10. Use strategies such as counting on; making ten (e.g., $8 + 6 = 8 + 2 + 4 = 10 + 4 = 14$); decomposing a number leading to a ten (e.g., $13 - 4 = 13 - 3 - 1 = 10 - 1 = 9$); using the relationship between addition and subtraction (e.g., knowing that $8 + 4 = 12$, one knows $12 - 8 = 4$); and creating equivalent but easier or known sums (e.g., adding $6 + 7$ by creating the known equivalent $6 + 6 + 1 = 12 + 1 = 13$).	1 day
3.10 Hands On: Algebra • Add 3 Numbers	■ **1.OA.B.3**	Apply properties of operations as strategies to add and subtract.	2 days
3.11 Algebra • Add 3 Numbers	■ **1.OA.B.3**	Apply properties of operations as strategies to add and subtract.	1 day
3.12 Problem Solving • Use Addition Strategies	■ **1.OA.A.2**	Solve word problems that call for addition of three whole numbers whose sum is less than or equal to 20, e.g., by using objects, drawings, and equations with a symbol for the unknown number to represent the problem.	2 days

■ Major Content ☐ Supporting Content ○ Additional Content

Lesson	Common Core State Standards for Mathematics		Pacing
Chapter 4 Subtraction Strategies			
Progress Tracker 1 2 3 **4** 5 6 7 8 9 10 11 12			
4.1 Count Back	**1.OA.C.5**	Relate counting to addition and subtraction (e.g., by counting on 2 to add 2).	1 day
4.2 Hands On • Think Addition to Subtract	**1.OA.B.4**	Understand subtraction as an unknown-addend problem.	2 days
4.3 Use Think Addition to Subtract	**1.OA.B.4**	Understand subtraction as an unknown-addend problem.	1 day
4.4 Hands On • Use 10 to Subtract	**1.OA.C.6**	Add and subtract within 20, demonstrating fluency for addition and subtraction within 10. Use strategies such as counting on; making ten (e.g., 8 + 6 = 8 + 2 + 4 = 10 + 4 = 14); decomposing a number leading to a ten (e.g., 13 − 4 = 13 − 3 − 1 = 10 − 1 = 9); using the relationship between addition and subtraction (e.g., knowing that 8 + 4 = 12, one knows 12 − 8 = 4); and creating equivalent but easier or known sums (e.g., adding 6 + 7 by creating the known equivalent 6 + 6 + 1 = 12 + 1 = 13).	2 days
4.5 Break Apart to Subtract	**1.OA.C.6**	Add and subtract within 20, demonstrating fluency for addition and subtraction within 10. Use strategies such as counting on; making ten (e.g., 8 + 6 = 8 + 2 + 4 = 10 + 4 = 14); decomposing a number leading to a ten (e.g., 13 – 4 = 13 – 3 – 1 = 10 – 1 = 9); using the relationship between addition and subtraction (e.g., knowing that 8 + 4 = 12, one knows 12 – 8 = 4); and creating equivalent but easier or known sums (e.g., adding 6 + 7 by creating the known equivalent 6 + 6 + 1 = 12 + 1 = 13).	2 days
4.6 Problem Solving • Use Subtraction Strategies	**1.OA.A.1**	Use addition and subtraction within 20 to solve word problems involving situations of adding to, taking from, putting together, taking apart, and comparing, with unknowns in all positions, e.g., by using objects, drawings, and equations with a symbol for the unknown number to represent the problem.	2 days

Chapter 5 Addition and Subtraction Relationships			
Progress Tracker 1 2 3 4 **5** 6 7 8 9 10 11 12			
5.1 Problem Solving • Add or Subtract	**1.OA.A.1**	Use addition and subtraction within 20 to solve word problems involving situations of adding to, taking from, putting together, taking apart, and comparing, with unknowns in all positions, e.g., by using objects, drawings, and equations with a symbol for the unknown number to represent the problem.	2 days

Chapter continued on next page ▶

Lesson	Common Core State Standards for Mathematics		Pacing
Chapter 5 Addition and Subtraction Relationships *(continued)*			
5.2 Hands on • Record Related Facts	■ **1.OA.C.6**	Add and subtract within 20, demonstrating fluency for addition and subtraction within 10. Use strategies such as counting on; making ten (e.g., 8 + 6 = 8 + 2 + 4 = 10 + 4 = 14); decomposing a number leading to a ten (e.g., 13 – 4 = 13 – 3 – 1 = 10 – 1 = 9); using the relationship between addition and subtraction (e.g., knowing that 8 + 4 = 12, one knows 12 – 8 = 4); and creating equivalent but easier or known sums (e.g., adding 6 + 7 by creating the known equivalent 6 + 6 + 1 = 12 + 1 = 13).	2 days
5.3 Identify Related Facts	■ **1.OA.C.6**	Add and subtract within 20, demonstrating fluency for addition and subtraction within 10. Use strategies such as counting on; making ten (e.g., 8 + 6 = 8 + 2 + 4 = 10 + 4 = 14); decomposing a number leading to a ten (e.g., 13 – 4 = 13 – 3 – 1 = 10 – 1 = 9); using the relationship between addition and subtraction (e.g., knowing that 8 + 4 = 12, one knows 12 – 8 = 4); and creating equivalent but easier or known sums (e.g., adding 6 + 7 by creating the known equivalent 6 + 6 + 1 = 12 + 1 = 13).	1 day
5.4 Use Addition to Check Subtraction	■ **1.OA.C.6**	Add and subtract within 20, demonstrating fluency for addition and subtraction within 10. Use strategies such as counting on; making ten (e.g., 8 + 6 = 8 + 2 + 4 = 10 + 4 = 14); decomposing a number leading to a ten (e.g., 13 – 4 = 13 – 3 – 1 = 10 – 1 = 9); using the relationship between addition and subtraction (e.g., knowing that 8 + 4 = 12, one knows 12 – 8 = 4); and creating equivalent but easier or known sums (e.g., adding 6 + 7 by creating the known equivalent 6 + 6 + 1 = 12 + 1 = 13).	1 day
5.5 Hands on: Algebra • Unknown Numbers	■ **1.OA.D.8**	Determine the unknown whole number in an addition or subtraction equation relating three whole numbers.	2 days
5.6 Algebra • Use Related Facts	■ **1.OA.D.8**	Determine the unknown whole number in an addition or subtraction equation relating three whole numbers.	1 day
5.7 Choose an Operation	■ **1.OA.A.1**	Use addition and subtraction within 20 to solve word problems involving situations of adding to, taking from, putting together, taking apart, and comparing, with unknowns in all positions, e.g., by using objects, drawings, and equations with a symbol for the unknown number to represent the problem.	1 day
5.8 Hands On: Algebra • Ways to Make Numbers to 20	■ **1.OA.C.6**	Add and subtract within 20, demonstrating fluency for addition and subtraction within 10. Use strategies such as counting on; making ten (e.g., 8 + 6 = 8 + 2 + 4 = 10 + 4 = 14); decomposing a number leading to a ten (e.g., 13 – 4 = 13 – 3 – 1 = 10 – 1 = 9); using the relationship between addition and subtraction (e.g., knowing that 8 + 4 = 12, one knows 12 – 8 = 4); and creating equivalent but easier or known sums (e.g., adding 6 + 7 by creating the known equivalent 6 + 6 + 1 = 12 + 1 = 13).	2 days

Chapter continued on next page ▶

■ Major Content ☐ Supporting Content ◯ Additional Content

Lesson	Common Core State Standards for Mathematics		Pacing
Chapter 5 Addition and Subtraction Relationships *(continued)*			
5.9 Algebra • Equal and Not Equal	**1.OA.D.7**	Understand the meaning of the equal sign, and determine if equations involving addition and subtraction are true or false.	1 day
5.10 Facts Practice to 20	**1.OA.C.6**	Add and subtract within 20, demonstrating fluency for addition and subtraction within 10. Use strategies such as counting on; making ten (e.g., 8 + 6 = 8 + 2 + 4 = 10 + 4 = 14); decomposing a number leading to a ten (e.g., 13 – 4 = 13 – 3 – 1 = 10 – 1 = 9); using the relationship between addition and subtraction (e.g., knowing that 8 + 4 = 12, one knows 12 – 8 = 4); and creating equivalent but easier or known sums (e.g., adding 6 + 7 by creating the known equivalent 6 + 6 + 1 = 12 + 1 = 13).	1 day

Chapter 6 Count and Model Numbers

Progress Tracker 1 2 3 4 5 **6** 7 8 9 10 11 12

Lesson	Standard	Description	Pacing
6.1 Count by Ones to 120	**1.NBT.A.1**	Count to 120, starting at any number less than 120. In this range, read and write numerals and represent a number of objects with a written numeral.	1 day
6.2 Count by Tens to 120	**1.NBT.A.1**	Count to 120, starting at any number less than 120. In this range, read and write numerals and represent a number of objects with a written numeral.	1 day
6.3 Understand Ten and Ones	**1.NBT.B.2b**	The numbers from 11 to 19 are composed of a ten and one, two, three, four, five, six, seven, eight, or nine ones.	1 day
6.4 Hands On • Make Ten and Ones	**1.NBT.B.2b**	The numbers from 11 to 19 are composed of a ten and one, two, three, four, five, six, seven, eight, or nine ones.	2 days
6.5 Hands On • Tens	**1.NBT.B.2a** **1.NBT.B.2c**	10 can be thought of as a bundle of ten ones — called a "ten." The numbers 10, 20, 30, 40, 50, 60, 70, 80, 90 refer to one, two, three, four, five, six, seven, eight, or nine tens (and 0 ones).	1 day
6.6 Hands On • Tens and Ones to 50	**1.NBT.B.2**	Understand that the two digits of a two-digit number represent amounts of tens and ones.	1 day
6.7 Hands On • Tens and Ones to 100	**1.NBT.B.2**	Understand that the two digits of a two-digit number represent amounts of tens and ones.	2 days
6.8 Problem Solving • Show Numbers in Different Ways	**1.NBT.B.2a** **1.NBT.B.3**	10 can be thought of as a bundle of ten ones — called a "ten." Compare two two-digit numbers based on meanings of the tens and ones digits, recording the results of comparisons with the symbols >, =, and <.	2 days

Chapter continued on next page ▶

Lesson	Common Core State Standards for Mathematics		Pacing
Chapter 6 Count and Model Numbers *(continued)*			
6.9 Hands On • Model, Read, and Write Numbers from 100 to 110	■ **1.NBT.A.1**	Count to 120, starting at any number less than 120. In this range, read and write numerals and represent a number of objects with a written numeral.	1 day
6.10 Hands On • Model, Read, and Write Numbers from 110 to 120	■ **1.NBT.A.1**	Count to 120, starting at any number less than 120. In this range, read and write numerals and represent a number of objects with a written numeral.	2 days

Chapter 7 Compare Numbers			
Progress Tracker 1 2 3 4 5 6 **7** 8 9 10 11 12			
7.1 Hands On: Algebra • Greater Than	■ **1.NBT.B.3**	Compare two two-digit numbers based on meanings of the tens and ones digits, recording the results of comparisons with the symbols $>$, $=$, and $<$.	1 day
7.2 Hands On: Algebra • Less Than	■ **1.NBT.B.3**	Compare two two-digit numbers based on meanings of the tens and ones digits, recording the results of comparisons with the symbols $>$, $=$, and $<$.	2 days
7.3 Hands On: Algebra • Use Symbols to Compare	■ **1.NBT.B.3**	Compare two two-digit numbers based on meanings of the tens and ones digits, recording the results of comparisons with the symbols $>$, $=$, and $<$.	2 days
7.4 Problem Solving • Compare Numbers	■ **1.NBT.B.3**	Compare two two-digit numbers based on meanings of the tens and ones digits, recording the results of comparisons with the symbols $>$, $=$, and $<$.	2 days
7.5 Hands On • 10 Less, 10 More	■ **1.NBT.C.5**	Given a two-digit number, mentally find 10 more or 10 less than the number, without having to count; explain the reasoning used.	2 days

Chapter 8 Two-Digit Addition and Subtraction			
Progress Tracker 1 2 3 4 5 6 7 **8** 9 10 11 12			
8.1 Add and Subtract Within 20	■ **1.OA.C.6**	Add and subtract within 20, demonstrating fluency for addition and subtraction within 10. Use strategies such as counting on; making ten (e.g., $8 + 6 = 8 + 2 + 4 = 10 + 4 = 14$); decomposing a number leading to a ten (e.g., $13 - 4 = 13 - 3 - 1 = 10 - 1 = 9$); using the relationship between addition and subtraction (e.g., knowing that $8 + 4 = 12$, one knows $12 - 8 = 4$); and creating equivalent but easier or known sums (e.g., adding $6 + 7$ by creating the known equivalent $6 + 6 + 1 = 12 + 1 = 13$).	1 day

Chapter continued on next page ▶

■ Major Content □ Supporting Content ○ Additional Content

Lesson	Common Core State Standards for Mathematics		Pacing
Chapter 8 Two-Digit Addition and Subtraction *(continued)*			
8.2 Hands On • Add Tens	**1.NBT.C.4**	Add within 100, including adding a two-digit number and a one-digit number, and adding a two-digit number and a multiple of 10, using concrete models or drawings and strategies based on place value, properties of operations, and/or the relationship between addition and subtraction; relate the strategy to a written method and explain the reasoning used. Understand that in adding two-digit numbers, one adds tens and tens, ones and ones; and sometimes it is necessary to compose a ten.	1 day
8.3 Hands On • Subtract Tens	**1.NBT.C.6**	Subtract multiples of 10 in the range 10-90 from multiples of 10 in the range 10-90 (positive or zero differences), using concrete models or drawings and strategies based on place value, properties of operations, and/or the relationship between addition and subtraction; relate the strategy to a written method and explain the reasoning used.	1 day
8.4 Use a Hundred Chart to Add	**1.NBT.C.4**	Add within 100, including adding a two-digit number and a one-digit number, and adding a two-digit number and a multiple of 10, using concrete models or drawings and strategies based on place value, properties of operations, and/or the relationship between addition and subtraction; relate the strategy to a written method and explain the reasoning used. Understand that in adding two-digit numbers, one adds tens and tens, ones and ones; and sometimes it is necessary to compose a ten.	1 day
8.5 Hands On • Use Models to Add	**1.NBT.C.4**	Add within 100, including adding a two-digit number and a one-digit number, and adding a two-digit number and a multiple of 10, using concrete models or drawings and strategies based on place value, properties of operations, and/or the relationship between addition and subtraction; relate the strategy to a written method and explain the reasoning used. Understand that in adding two-digit numbers, one adds tens and tens, ones and ones; and sometimes it is necessary to compose a ten.	1 day
8.6 Hands On • Make Ten to Add	**1.NBT.C.4**	Add within 100, including adding a two-digit number and a one-digit number, and adding a two-digit number and a multiple of 10, using concrete models or drawings and strategies based on place value, properties of operations, and/or the relationship between addition and subtraction; relate the strategy to a written method and explain the reasoning used. Understand that in adding two-digit numbers, one adds tens and tens, ones and ones; and sometimes it is necessary to compose a ten.	2 days
8.7 Hands On • Use Place Value to Add	**1.NBT.C.4**	Add within 100, including adding a two-digit number and a one-digit number, and adding a two-digit number and a multiple of 10, using concrete models or drawings and strategies based on place value, properties of operations, and/or the relationship between addition and subtraction; relate the strategy to a written method and explain the reasoning used. Understand that in adding two-digit numbers, one adds tens and tens, ones and ones; and sometimes it is necessary to compose a ten.	2 days

Chapter continued on next page ▶

Lesson	Common Core State Standards for Mathematics		Pacing
Chapter 8 Two-Digit Addition and Subtraction *(continued)*			
8.8 Problem Solving • Addition Word Problems	**1.NBT.C.4**	Add within 100, including adding a two-digit number and a one-digit number, and adding a two-digit number and a multiple of 10, using concrete models or drawings and strategies based on place value, properties of operations, and/or the relationship between addition and subtraction; relate the strategy to a written method and explain the reasoning used. Understand that in adding two-digit numbers, one adds tens and tens, ones and ones; and sometimes it is necessary to compose a ten.	2 days
8.9 Related Addition and Subtraction	**1.NBT.C.4**	Add within 100, including adding a two-digit number and a one-digit number, and adding a two-digit number and a multiple of 10, using concrete models or drawings and strategies based on place value, properties of operations, and/or the relationship between addition and subtraction; relate the strategy to a written method and explain the reasoning used. Understand that in adding two-digit numbers, one adds tens and tens, ones and ones; and sometimes it is necessary to compose a ten.	2 days
8.10 Practice Addition and Subtraction	**1.NBT.C.4**	Add within 100, including adding a two-digit number and a one-digit number, and adding a two-digit number and a multiple of 10, using concrete models or drawings and strategies based on place value, properties of operations, and/or the relationship between addition and subtraction; relate the strategy to a written method and explain the reasoning used. Understand that in adding two-digit numbers, one adds tens and tens, ones and ones; and sometimes it is necessary to compose a ten.	1 day
	1.NBT.C.6	Subtract multiples of 10 in the range 10-90 from multiples of 10 in the range 10-90 (positive or zero differences), using concrete models or drawings and strategies based on place value, properties of operations, and/or the relationship between addition and subtraction; relate the strategy to a written method and explain the reasoning used.	

Major Content | Supporting Content | Additional Content

Lesson	Common Core State Standards for Mathematics		Pacing
Chapter 9 Measurement			
Progress Tracker 1 2 3 4 5 6 7 8 **9** 10 11 12			
9.1 Hands On • Order Length	**1.MD.A.1**	Order three objects by length; compare the lengths of two objects indirectly by using a third object.	2 days
9.2 Indirect Measurement	**1.MD.A.1**	Order three objects by length; compare the lengths of two objects indirectly by using a third object.	1 day
9.3 Hands On • Use Nonstandard Units to Measure Length	**1.MD.A.2**	Express the length of an object as a whole number of length units, by laying multiple copies of a shorter object (the length unit) end to end; understand that the length measurement of an object is the number of same-size length units that span it with no gaps or overlaps.	2 days
9.4 Hands On • Make a Nonstandard Measuring Tool	**1.MD.A.2**	Express the length of an object as a whole number of length units, by laying multiple copies of a shorter object (the length unit) end to end; understand that the length measurement of an object is the number of same-size length units that span it with no gaps or overlaps.	2 days
9.5 Problem Solving • Measure and Compare	**1.MD.A.2**	Express the length of an object as a whole number of length units, by laying multiple copies of a shorter object (the length unit) end to end; understand that the length measurement of an object is the number of same-size length units that span it with no gaps or overlaps.	2 days
9.6 Time to the Hour	**1.MD.B.3**	Tell and write time in hours and half-hours using analog and digital clocks.	1 day
9.7 Time to the Half Hour	**1.MD.B.3**	Tell and write time in hours and half-hours using analog and digital clocks.	1 day
9.8 Tell Time to the Hour and Half Hour	**1.MD.B.3**	Tell and write time in hours and half-hours using analog and digital clocks.	1 day
9.9 Practice Time to the Hour and Half Hour	**1.MD.B.3**	Tell and write time in hours and half-hours using analog and digital clocks.	1 day

Chapter 10 Represent Data			
Progress Tracker 1 2 3 4 5 6 7 8 9 **10** 11 12			
10.1 Read Picture Graphs	**1.MD.C.4**	Organize, represent, and interpret data with up to three categories; ask and answer questions about the total number of data points, how many in each category, and how many more or less are in one category than in another.	1 day
10.2 Hands On • Make Picture Graphs	**1.MD.C.4**	Organize, represent, and interpret data with up to three categories; ask and answer questions about the total number of data points, how many in each category, and how many more or less are in one category than in another.	1 day

Chapter continued on next page ▶

Lesson	Common Core State Standards for Mathematics		Pacing
Chapter 10 Represent Data *(continued)*			
10.3 Read Bar Graphs	1.MD.C.4	Organize, represent, and interpret data with up to three categories; ask and answer questions about the total number of data points, how many in each category, and how many more or less are in one category than in another.	1 day
10.4 Hands On • Make Bar Graphs	1.MD.C.4	Organize, represent, and interpret data with up to three categories; ask and answer questions about the total number of data points, how many in each category, and how many more or less are in one category than in another.	1 day
10.5 Read Tally Charts	1.MD.C.4	Organize, represent, and interpret data with up to three categories; ask and answer questions about the total number of data points, how many in each category, and how many more or less are in one category than in another.	1 day
10.6 Hands On • Make Tally Charts	1.MD.C.4	Organize, represent, and interpret data with up to three categories; ask and answer questions about the total number of data points, how many in each category, and how many more or less are in one category than in another.	1 day
10.7 Problem Solving • Represent Data	1.MD.C.4	Organize, represent, and interpret data with up to three categories; ask and answer questions about the total number of data points, how many in each category, and how many more or less are in one category than in another.	1 day

Chapter 11 Three-Dimensional Geometry			
Progress Tracker 1 2 3 4 5 6 7 8 9 10 **11** 12			
11.1 Hands On • Three-Dimensional Shapes	1.G.A.1	Distinguish between defining attributes (e.g., triangles are closed and three-sided) versus non-defining attributes (e.g., color, orientation, overall size); build and draw shapes to possess defining attributes.	1 day
11.2 Hands On • Combine Three-Dimensional Shapes	1.G.A.2	Compose two-dimensional shapes (rectangles, squares, trapezoids, triangles, half-circles, and quarter-circles) or three-dimensional shapes (cubes, right rectangular prisms, right circular cones, and right circular cylinders) to create a composite shape, and compose new shapes from the composite shape.	1 day
11.3 Hands On • Make New Three-Dimensional Shapes	1.G.A.2	Compose two-dimensional shapes (rectangles, squares, trapezoids, triangles, half-circles, and quarter-circles) or three-dimensional shapes (cubes, right rectangular prisms, right circular cones, and right circular cylinders) to create a composite shape, and compose new shapes from the composite shape.	1 day
11.4 Problem Solving • Take Apart Three-Dimensional Shapes	1.G.A.2	Compose two-dimensional shapes (rectangles, squares, trapezoids, triangles, half-circles, and quarter-circles) or three-dimensional shapes (cubes, right rectangular prisms, right circular cones, and right circular cylinders) to create a composite shape, and compose new shapes from the composite shape.	1 day

Chapter continued on next page ▶

Major Content | Supporting Content | Additional Content

Lesson	Common Core State Standards for Mathematics		Pacing
Chapter 11 Three-Dimensional Geometry *(continued)*			
11.5 Hands On • Two-Dimensional Shapes on Three-Dimensional Shapes	**1.G.A.1**	Distinguish between defining attributes (e.g., triangles are closed and three-sided) versus non-defining attributes (e.g., color, orientation, overall size); build and draw shapes to possess defining attributes.	1 day

Chapter 12 Two-Dimensional Geometry			
Progress Tracker 1 2 3 4 5 6 7 8 9 10 11 12			
12.1 Sort Two-Dimensional Shapes	**1.G.A.1**	Distinguish between defining attributes (e.g., triangles are closed and three-sided) versus non-defining attributes (e.g., color, orientation, overall size); build and draw shapes to possess defining attributes.	1 day
12.2 Hands On • Describe Two-Dimensional Shapes	**1.G.A.1**	Distinguish between defining attributes (e.g., triangles are closed and three-sided) versus non-defining attributes (e.g., color, orientation, overall size); build and draw shapes to possess defining attributes.	1 day
12.3 Hands On • Combine Two-Dimensional Shapes	**1.G.A.2**	Compose two-dimensional shapes (rectangles, squares, trapezoids, triangles, half-circles, and quarter-circles) or three-dimensional shapes (cubes, right rectangular prisms, right circular cones, and right circular cylinders) to create a composite shape, and compose new shapes from the composite shape.	1 day
12.4 Combine More Shapes	**1.G.A.2**	Compose two-dimensional shapes (rectangles, squares, trapezoids, triangles, half-circles, and quarter-circles) or three-dimensional shapes (cubes, right rectangular prisms, right circular cones, and right circular cylinders) to create a composite shape, and compose new shapes from the composite shape.	1 day
12.5 Problem Solving • Make New Two-Dimensional Shapes	**1.G.A.2**	Compose two-dimensional shapes (rectangles, squares, trapezoids, triangles, half-circles, and quarter-circles) or three-dimensional shapes (cubes, right rectangular prisms, right circular cones, and right circular cylinders) to create a composite shape, and compose new shapes from the composite shape.	1 day
12.6 Hands On • Find Shapes in Shapes	**1.G.A.2**	Compose two-dimensional shapes (rectangles, squares, trapezoids, triangles, half-circles, and quarter-circles) or three-dimensional shapes (cubes, right rectangular prisms, right circular cones, and right circular cylinders) to create a composite shape, and compose new shapes from the composite shape.	1 day
12.7 Take Apart Two-Dimensional Shapes	**1.G.A.2**	Compose two-dimensional shapes (rectangles, squares, trapezoids, triangles, half-circles, and quarter-circles) or three-dimensional shapes (cubes, right rectangular prisms, right circular cones, and right circular cylinders) to create a composite shape, and compose new shapes from the composite shape.	1 day

Chapter continued on next page ▶

Lesson	Common Core State Standards for Mathematics		Pacing
Chapter 12 Two-Dimensional Geometry *(continued)*			
12.8 Equal or Unequal Parts	**1.G.A.3**	Partition circles and rectangles into two and four equal shares, describe the shares using the words *halves, fourths,* and *quarters*, and use the phrases *half of, fourth of,* and *quarter of.* Describe the whole as two of, or four of the shares. Understand for these examples that decomposing into more equal shares creates smaller shares.	1 day
12.9 Halves	**1.G.A.3**	Partition circles and rectangles into two and four equal shares, describe the shares using the words *halves, fourths,* and *quarters*, and use the phrases *half of, fourth of,* and *quarter of.* Describe the whole as two of, or four of the shares. Understand for these examples that decomposing into more equal shares creates smaller shares.	1 day
12.10 Fourths	**1.G.A.3**	Partition circles and rectangles into two and four equal shares, describe the shares using the words *halves, fourths,* and *quarters*, and use the phrases *half of, fourth of,* and *quarter of.* Describe the whole as two of, or four of the shares. Understand for these examples that decomposing into more equal shares creates smaller shares.	1 day

Major Content | Supporting Content | Additional Content

Path to Fluency: Kindergarten through Grade 6

GO Math! includes a plan for helping students achieve fluency with the Common Core State Standards that are suggested for each grade. This plan provides targeted instruction and practice in the Student Edition, Teacher Edition, Teacher Resource Book, Strategies and Practice for Skills and Facts Fluency, Personal Math Trainer, and Animated Math Models. Individual components will aid students in building proficiency. Together, they offer a unique suite of materials to help all students achieve mastery.

Fluency and Memorization for Basic Facts

Grade	Standards	Resources
Kindergarten Fluency	**K.OA.A.5** Fluently add and subtract within 5.	• Games (Student Edition) • Fluency Standard Lessons (Student Edition) • Fluency Builder (Teacher Edition) • Strategies and Practice for Skills and Facts Fluency—Primary, GK–3 • Teacher Resource Book • HMH Mega Math • Personal Math Trainer: Standards Quizzes • Animated Math Models
Grade 1 Fluency	**1.OA.C.6** Add and subtract within 20, demonstrating fluency for addition and subtraction within 10. Use strategies such as counting on; making ten; decomposing a number leading to a ten; using the relationship between addition and subtraction; and creating equivalent but easier or known sums.	• Games (Student Edition) • Fluency Standard Lessons (Student Edition) • Fluency Builder (Teacher Edition) • Strategies and Practice for Skills and Facts Fluency—Primary, GK–3 • Teacher Resource Book • HMH Mega Math • Personal Math Trainer: Standards Quizzes • Animated Math Models
Grade 2 Memorization	**2.OA.B.2** Fluently add and subtract within 20 using mental strategies.	• Games (Student Edition) • Fluency Standard Lessons (Student Edition) • Fluency Builder (Teacher Edition) • Strategies and Practice for Skills and Facts Fluency—Primary, GK–3 • Teacher Resource Book • HMH Mega Math • Personal Math Trainer: Standards Quizzes • Animated Math Models
Grade 3 Memorization	**3.OA.C.7** Fluently multiply and divide within 100, using strategies such as the relationship between multiplication and division or properties of operations. By the end of Grade 3, know from memory all products of two one-digit numbers.	• Fluency Standard Lessons (Student Edition) • Fluency Builder (Teacher Edition) • Strategies and Practice for Skills and Facts Fluency—Primary, GK–3 • Strategies and Practice for Skills and Facts Fluency—Intermediate, G3–6 • Teacher Resource Book • HMH Mega Math • Personal Math Trainer: Standards Quizzes • Animated Math Models
Grades 3, 4, 5, and 6 Intervention	For those students who still need additional time for memorizing basic facts.	• Fluency Builder (Teacher Edition) • Strategies and Practice for Skills and Facts Fluency—Intermediate, G3–6 • Teacher Resource Book • HMH Mega Math • Personal Math Trainer: Standards Quizzes • Animated Math Models

Fluency for Operations with Multi-digit Numbers

Grade	Standards	Resources
Grade 2 Fluency	**2.NBT.B.5** Fluently add and subtract within 100 using strategies based on place value, properties of operations, and/or the relationship between addition and subtraction.	• Games (Student Edition) • Fluency Standard Lessons (Student Edition) • Fluency Builder (Teacher Edition) • HMH Mega Math • Personal Math Trainer: Standards Quizzes • Animated Math Models
Grade 3 Fluency	**3.NBT.A.2** Fluently add and subtract within 1000 using strategies and algorithms based on place value, properties of operations, and/or the relationship between addition and subtraction.	• Fluency Standard Lessons (Student Edition) • Fluency Builder (Teacher Edition) • Strategies and Practice for Skills and Facts Fluency—Intermediate, G3–6 • HMH Mega Math • Personal Math Trainer: Standards Quizzes • Animated Math Models
Grade 4 Fluency	**4.NBT.B.4** Fluently add and subtract multi-digit whole numbers using the standard algorithm.	• Fluency Standard Lessons (Student Edition) • Fluency Builder (Teacher Edition) • Strategies and Practice for Skills and Facts Fluency—Intermediate, G3–6 • HMH Mega Math • Personal Math Trainer: Standards Quizzes • Animated Math Models
Grade 5 Fluency	**5.NBT.B.5** Fluently multiply multi-digit whole numbers using the standard algorithm.	• Fluency Standard Lessons (Student Edition) • Fluency Builder (Teacher Edition) • Strategies and Practice for Skills and Facts Fluency—Intermediate, G3–6 • HMH Mega Math • Personal Math Trainer: Standards Quizzes • Animated Math Models
Grade 6 Fluency	**6.NS.B.2** Fluently divide multi-digit numbers using the standard algorithm. **6.NS.B.3** Fluently add, subtract, multiply, and divide multi-digit decimals using the standard algorithm for each operation.	• Fluency Standard Lessons (Student Edition) • Fluency Builder (Teacher Edition) • Strategies and Practice for Skills and Facts Fluency—Intermediate, G3–6 • Fluency Builders (Teacher Resource Book) • HMH Mega Math Personal Math Trainer: Standards Quizzes • Animated Math Models

Correlations

Standards for Mathematical Practices		Teacher Edition and Student Edition Pages
MP1	Make sense of problems and persevere in solving them.	In most Teacher Edition lessons. Some examples are: *25, 46, 52, 57, 71, 83, 89, 139, 237, 449A, 645* In most Student Edition lessons. Some examples are: 32, 78, 131, 137, 223, 279, 473, 605, 645, 657
MP2	Reason abstractly and quantitatively.	In most Teacher Edition lessons. Some examples are: *45, 75, 211, 223A, 237, 367, 419, 457, 463, 475* In most Student Edition lessons. Some examples are: 75, 167, 169, 198, 211, 288, 367, 385, 443, 525, 549
MP3	Construct viable arguments and critique the reasoning of others.	In most Teacher Edition lessons. Some examples are: *71, 106, 185, 187, 191, 194, 291A, 405, 475, 513, 515, 587, 595* In most Student Edition lessons. Some examples are: 93, 111, 185, 349, 405, 437, 485, 581, 587, 639
MP4	Model with mathematics.	In most Teacher Edition lessons. Some examples are: *37, 49A, 89, 113, 180, 255A, 461, 563, 691, 703* In most Student Edition lessons. Some examples are: 33, 88, 199, 256, 418, 519, 589, 691, 696, 727
MP5	Use appropriate tools strategically.	In most Teacher Edition lessons. Some examples are: *75A, 146, 150, 169, 170, 173, 261, 399, 532, 555, 701* In most Student Edition lessons. Some examples are: 81, 299, 339, 399, 407, 457, 467, 531, 612, 683, 685, 703
MP6	Attend to precision.	In most Teacher Edition lessons. Some examples are: *19, 133, 139, 179A, 213, 363, 461, 527, 611A, 634, 673* In most Student Edition lessons. Some examples are: 49, 99, 155, 291, 351, 374, 455, 480, 557, 613, 680
MP7	Look for and make use of structure.	In most Teacher Edition lessons. Some examples are: *45, 113, 217, 237, 263, 401, 463, 475, 672, 673, 677, 679, 707A, 709* In most Student Edition lessons. Some examples are: 45, 113, 145, 217, 267, 273, 331, 355, 379, 487, 543, 707
MP8	Look for and express regularity in repeated reasoning.	In most Teacher Edition lessons. Some examples are: *263, 407, 423A, 527, 563, 595, 633, 673, 679, 709* In most Student Edition lessons. Some examples are: 40, 51, 105, 107, 140, 193, 264, 357, 493, 595, 633, 674

Domain: Operations and Algebraic Thinking

		Teacher Edition and Student Edition Pages
Cluster A: Represent and solve problems involving addition and subtraction.		
1.OA.A.1	Use addition and subtraction within 20 to solve word problems involving situations of adding to, taking from, putting together, taking apart, and comparing, with unknowns in all positions, e.g., by using objects, drawings, and equations with a symbol for the unknown number to represent the problem.	*13A–13B*, 13–16, *19A–19B*, 19–22, *25A–25B*, 25–28, *31A–31B*, 31–33, *49A–49B*, 49–52, *69A–69B*, 69–72, *75A–75B*, 75–78, *81A–81B*, 81–84, *87A–87B*, 87–90, *93A–93B*, 93–96, *99A–99B*, 99–101, *111A–111B*, 111–114, *241A–241B*, 241–244, *255A–255B*, 255–258, *291A–291B*, 291–294
1.OA.A.2	Solve word problems that call for addition of three whole numbers whose sum is less than or equal to 20, e.g., by using objects, drawings, and equations with a symbol for the unknown number to represent the problem.	*197A–197B*, 197–200
Cluster B: Understand and apply properties of operations and the relationship between addition and subtraction.		
1.OA.B.3	Apply properties of operations as strategies to add and subtract.	*37A–37B*, 37–40, *43A–43B*, 43–46, *131A–131B*, 131–134, *185A–185B*, 185–188, *191A–191B*, 191–194
1.OA.B.4	Understand subtraction as an unknown-addend problem.	*217A–217B*, 217–220, *223A–223B*, 223–225

Pages only in Teacher Edition are shown in italics.

Domain continued on next page ►

Domain: Operations and Algebraic Thinking *(continued)*

Standard	Description	Teacher Edition and Student Edition Pages
Cluster C: Add and subtract within 20.		
1.OA.C.5	Relate counting to addition and subtraction (e.g., by counting on 2 to add 2).	***137A–137B*, 137–140, *211A–211B*, 211–214**
1.OA.C.6	Add and subtract within 20, demonstrating fluency for addition and subtraction within 10. Use strategies such as counting on; making ten (e.g., 8 + 6 = 8 + 2 + 4 = 10 + 4 = 14); decomposing a number leading to a ten (e.g., 13 − 4 = 13 − 3 − 1 = 10 − 1 = 9); using the relationship between addition and subtraction (e.g., knowing that 8 + 4 = 12, one knows 12 − 8 = 4); and creating equivalent but easier or known sums (e.g., adding 6 + 7 by creating the known equivalent 6 + 6 + 1 = 12 + 1 = 13).	***55A–55B*, 55–58, *117A–117B*, 117–120, *143A–143B*, 143–146, *149A–149B*, 149–152, *155A–155B*, 155–158, *161A–161B*, 161–163, *167A–167B*, 167–170, *173A–173B*, 173–176, *179A–179B*, 179–182, *229A–229B*, 229–232, *235A–235B*, 235–238, *261A–261B*, 261–264, *267A–267B*, 267–270, *273A–273B*, 273–275, *297A–297B*, 297–300, *309A–309B*, 309–312, *437A–437B*, 437–440** See Also: *49A–49B*, 49–52, *111A–111B*, 111–114, *137A–137B*, 137–140, *185A–185B*, 185–188, *191A–191B*, 191–194, *197A–197B*, 197–200, *211A–211B*, 211–214, *279A–279B*, 279–282, *285A–285B*, 285–288, *291A–291B*, 291–294, *303A–303B*, 303–306, *491A–491B*, 491–494
Cluster D: Work with addition and subtraction equations.		
1.OA.D.7	Understand the meaning of the equal sign, and determine if equations involving addition and subtraction are true or false.	***303A–303B*, 303–306** See Also: *13A–13B*, 13–16, *19A–19B*, 19–22, *411A–411B*, 411–413
1.OA.D.8	Determine the unknown whole number in an addition or subtraction equation relating three whole numbers.	***93A–93B*, 93–96, *105A–105B*, 105–108, *279A–279B*, 279–282, *285A–285B*, 285–288** See Also: *99A–99B*, 99–101, *137A–137B*, 137–140, *143A–143B*, 143–146, *149A–149B*, 149–152, *155A–155B*, 155–158, *161A–161B*, 161–163, *167A–167B*, 167–170, *173A–173B*, 173–176, *179A–179B*, 179–182, *211A–211B*, 211–214, *223A–223B*, 223–225, *229A–229B*, 229–232, *235A–235B*, 235–238, *261A–261B*, 261–264, *267A–267B*, 267–270, *273A–273B*, 273–275

Pages only in Teacher Edition are shown in italics.

Domain: Number and Operations in Base Ten

		Teacher Edition and Student Edition Pages
Cluster A: Extend the counting sequence.		
1.NBT.A.1	Count to 120, starting at any number less than 120. In this range, read and write numerals and represent a number of objects with a written numeral.	***331A–331B***, **331–334**, ***337A–337B***, **337–340**, ***379A–379B***, **379–382**, ***385A–385B***, **385–388**
Cluster B: Understand place value.		
1.NBT.B.2	Understand that the two digits of a two-digit number represent amounts of tens and ones. Understand the following as special cases:	***361A–361B***, **361–364**, ***367A–367B***, **367–370**
	a. 10 can be thought of as a bundle of ten ones — called a "ten."	***355A–355B***, **355–357**, ***373A–373B***, **373–376**
	b. The numbers from 11 to 19 are composed of a ten and one, two, three, four, five, six, seven, eight, or nine ones.	***343A–343B***, **343–346**, ***349A–349B***, **349–352**
	c. The numbers 10, 20, 30, 40, 50, 60, 70, 80, 90 refer to one, two, three, four, five, six, seven, eight, or nine tens (and 0 ones).	***355A–355B***, **355–357**
1.NBT.B.3	Compare two two-digit numbers based on meanings of the tens and ones digits, recording the results of comparisons with the symbols $>$, $=$, and $<$.	***373A–373B***, **373–376**, ***399A–399B***, **399–402**, ***405A–405B***, **405–408**, ***411A–411B***, **411–413**, ***417A–417B***, **417–420**
Cluster C: Use place value understanding and properties of operations to add and subtract.		
1.NBT.C.4	Add within 100, including adding a two-digit number and a one-digit number, and adding a two-digit number and a multiple of 10, using concrete models or drawings and strategies based on place value, properties of operations, and/or the relationship between addition and subtraction; relate the strategy to a written method and explain the reasoning used. Understand that in adding two-digit numbers, one adds tens and tens, ones and ones; and sometimes it is necessary to compose a ten.	***443A–443B***, **443–446**, ***455A–455B***, **455–458**, ***461A–461B***, **461–464**, ***467A–467B***, **467–470**, ***473A–473B***, **473–476**, ***479A–479B***, **479–482**, ***485A–485B***, **485–488**, ***491A–491B***, **491–494**
1.NBT.C.5	Given a two-digit number, mentally find 10 more or 10 less than the number, without having to count; explain the reasoning used.	***423A–423B***, **423–426**
1.NBT.C.6	Subtract multiples of 10 in the range 10–90 from multiples of 10 in the range 10-90 (positive or zero differences), using concrete models or drawings and strategies based on place value, properties of operations, and/or the relationship between addition and subtraction; relate the strategy to a written method and explain the reasoning used.	***449A–449B***, **449–451**, ***491A–491B***, **491–494**

Pages only in Teacher Edition are shown in italics.

Domain: Measurement and Data

		Teacher Edition and Student Edition Pages
Cluster A: Measure lengths indirectly and by iterating length units.		
1.MD.A.1	Order three objects by length; compare the lengths of two objects indirectly by using a third object.	***513A–513B***, **513–516,** ***519A–519B***, **519–522**
1.MD.A.2	Express the length of an object as a whole number of length units, by laying multiple copies of a shorter object (the length unit) end to end; understand that the length measurement of an object is the number of same-size length units that span it with no gaps or overlaps. *Limit to contexts where the object being measured is spanned by a whole number of length units with no gaps or overlaps.*	***525A–525B***, **525–528,** ***531A–531B***, **531–534,** ***537A–537B***, **537–539**
Cluster B: Tell and write time.		
1.MD.B.3	Tell and write time in hours and half-hours using analog and digital clocks.	***543A–543B***, **543–546,** ***549A–549B***, **549–552,** ***555A–555B***, **555–558,** ***561A–561B***, **561–564**
Cluster C: Represent and interpret data.		
1.MD.C.4	Organize, represent, and interpret data with up to three categories; ask and answer questions about the total number of data points, how many in each category, and how many more or less are in one category than in another.	***575A–575B***, **575–578,** ***581A–581B***, **581–584,** ***587A–587B***, **587–590,** ***593A–593B***, **593–595,** ***599A–599B***, **599–602,** ***605A–605B***, **605–608,** ***611A–611B***, **611–614**

Pages only in Teacher Edition are shown in italics.

Domain: Geometry

Cluster A: Reason with shapes and their attributes.		Teacher Edition and Student Edition Pages
1.G.A.1	Distinguish between defining attributes (e.g., triangles are closed and three-sided) versus non-defining attributes (e.g., color, orientation, overall size); build and draw shapes to possess defining attributes.	*633A–633B*, 633–636, *657A–657B*, 657–660, *671A–671B*, 671–674, *677A–677B*, 677–680
1.G.A.2	Compose two-dimensional shapes (rectangles, squares, trapezoids, triangles, half-circles, and quarter-circles) or three-dimensional shapes (cubes, right rectangular prisms, right circular cones, and right circular cylinders) to create a composite shape, and compose new shapes from the composite shape.	*639A–639B*, 639–642, *645A–645B*, 645–647, *651A–651B*, 651–654, *683A–683B*, 683–686, *689A–689B*, 689–692, *695A–695B*, 695–697, *701A–701B*, 701–704, *707A–707B*, 707–710
1.G.A.3	Partition circles and rectangles into two and four equal shares, describe the shares using the words *halves, fourths,* and *quarters,* and use the phrases *half of, fourth of,* and *quarter of.* Describe the whole as two of, or four of the shares. Understand for these examples that decomposing into more equal shares creates smaller shares.	*713A–713B*, 713–716, *719A–719B*, 719–722, *725A–725B*, 725–728

Pages only in Teacher Edition are shown in italics.

Student Edition Glossary

Picture Glossary

add sumar

3 + 2 = 5

addend sumando

1 + 3 = 4

addend

addition sentence enunciado de suma

2 + 1 = 3 is an **addition sentence.**

bar graph gráfica de barras

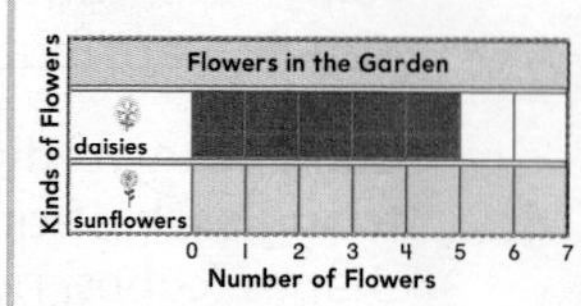

circle círculo

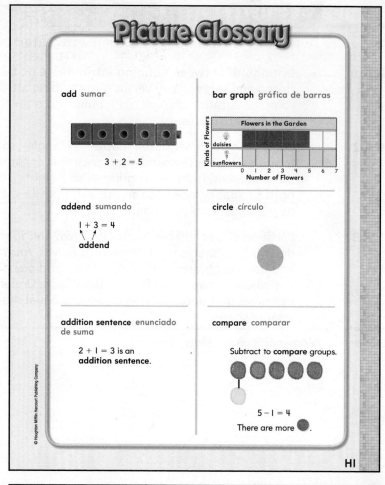

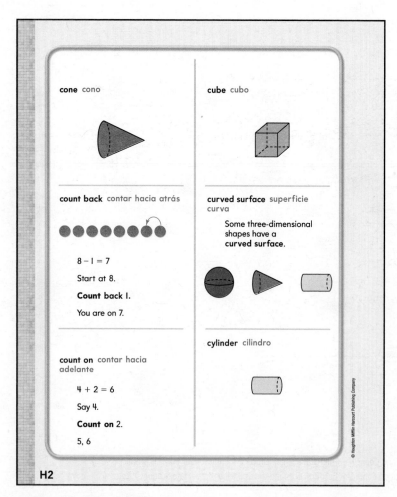

compare comparar

Subtract to **compare** groups.

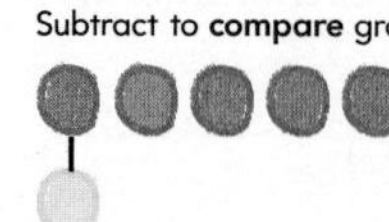

5 − 1 = 4

There are more ●.

cone cono

count back contar hacia atrás

8 − 1 = 7

Start at 8.

Count back 1.

You are on 7.

count on contar hacia adelante

4 + 2 = 6

Say 4.

Count on 2.

5, 6

cube cubo

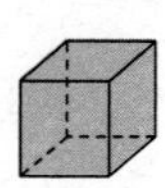

curved surface superficie curva

Some three-dimensional shapes have a **curved surface.**

cylinder cilindro

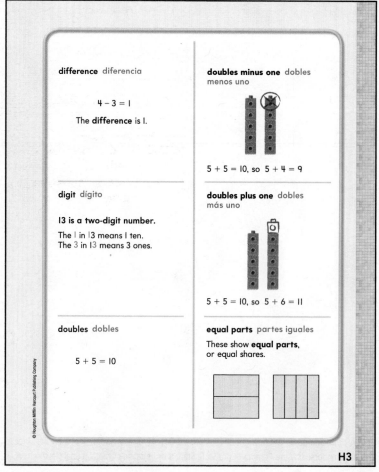

difference diferencia

4 − 3 = 1

The **difference** is 1.

digit dígito

13 is a two-digit number.

The 1 in 13 means 1 ten.
The 3 in 13 means 3 ones.

doubles dobles

5 + 5 = 10

doubles minus one dobles menos uno

5 + 5 = 10, so 5 + 4 = 9

doubles plus one dobles más uno

5 + 5 = 10, so 5 + 6 = 11

equal parts partes iguales

These show **equal parts,** or equal shares.

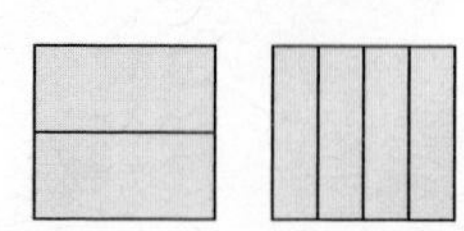

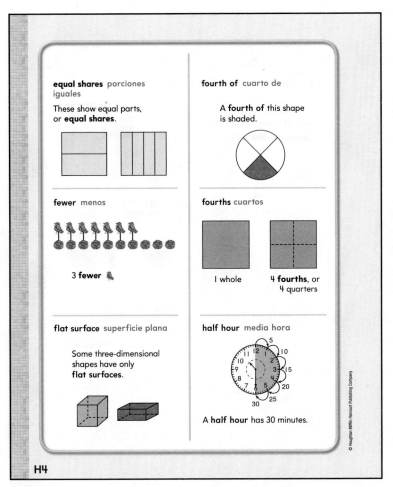

equal shares porciones iguales

These show equal parts, or **equal shares**.

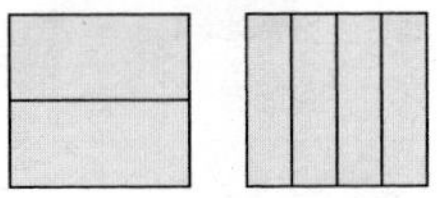

fewer menos

3 **fewer**

flat surface superficie plana

Some three-dimensional shapes have only **flat surfaces**.

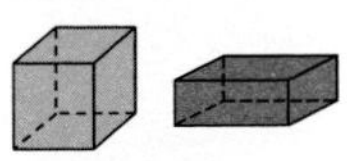

fourth of cuarto de

A **fourth of** this shape is shaded.

fourths cuartos

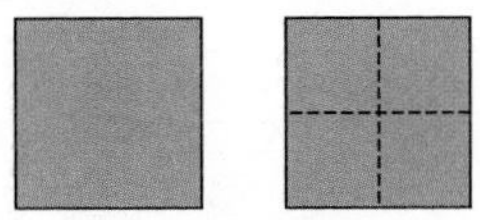

1 whole — 4 **fourths**, or 4 quarters

half hour media hora

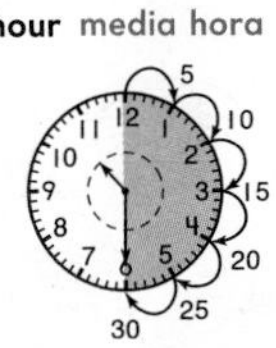

A **half hour** has 30 minutes.

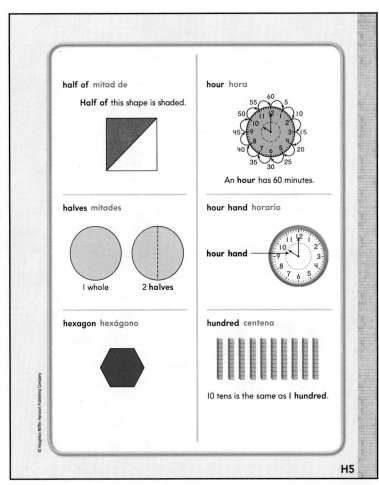

half of mitad de

Half of this shape is shaded.

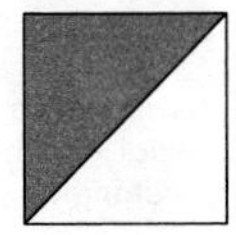

halves mitades

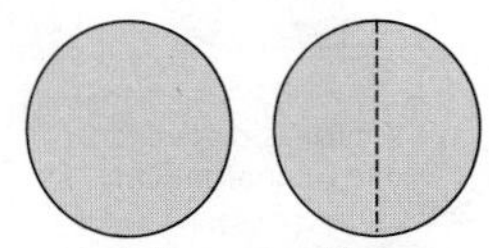

1 whole — 2 **halves**

hexagon hexágono

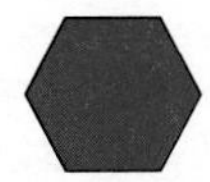

hour hora

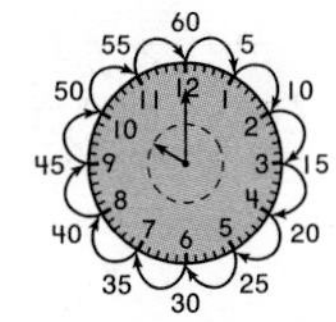

An **hour** has 60 minutes.

hour hand horario

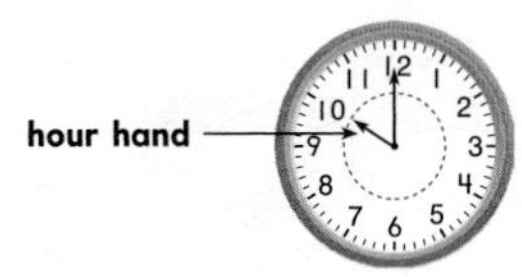

hundred centena

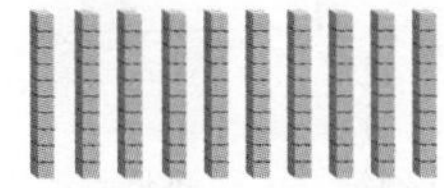

10 tens is the same as 1 **hundred**.

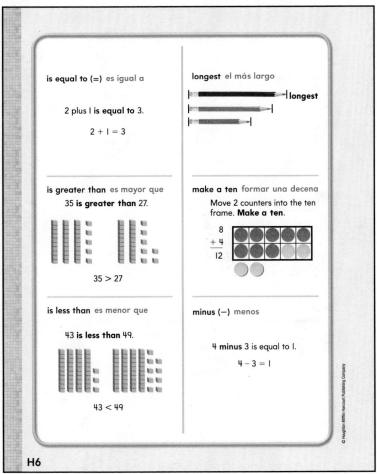

is equal to (=) es igual a

2 plus 1 **is equal to** 3.

2 + 1 = 3

is greater than es mayor que

35 **is greater than** 27.

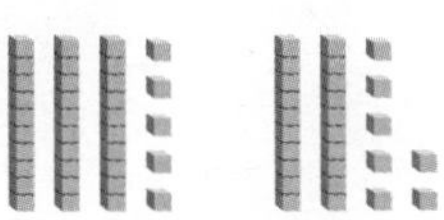

35 > 27

is less than es menor que

43 **is less than** 49.

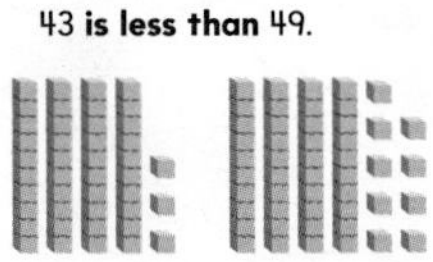

43 < 49

longest el más largo

make a ten formar una decena

Move 2 counters into the ten frame. **Make a ten.**

8
+ 4
12

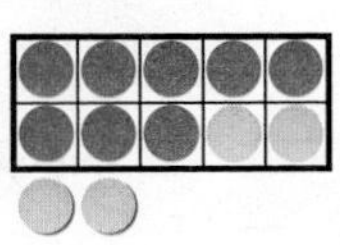

minus (−) menos

4 **minus** 3 is equal to 1.

4 − 3 = 1

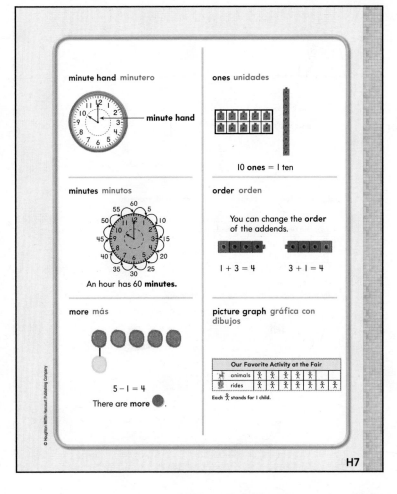

minute hand minutero

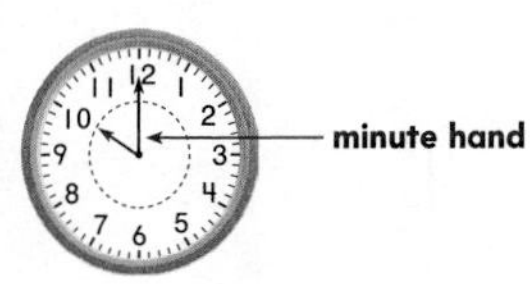

minutes minutos

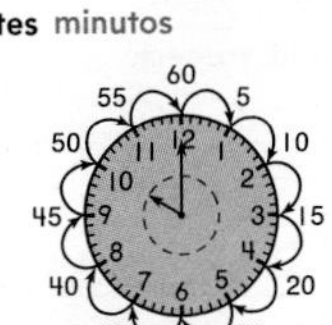

An hour has 60 **minutes.**

more más

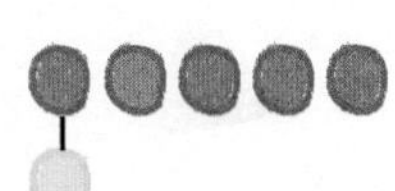

5 − 1 = 4

There are **more** ●.

ones unidades

10 **ones** = 1 ten

order orden

You can change the **order** of the addends.

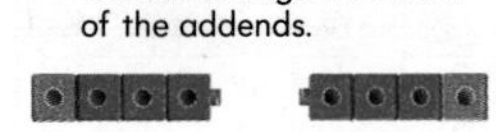

1 + 3 = 4 — 3 + 1 = 4

picture graph gráfica con dibujos

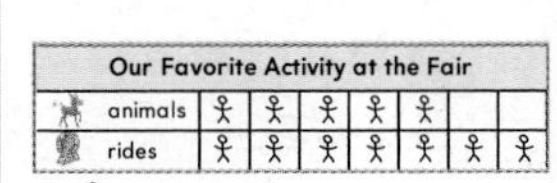

Our Favorite Activity at the Fair
animals
rides
Each stands for 1 child.

Student Edition Glossary continued

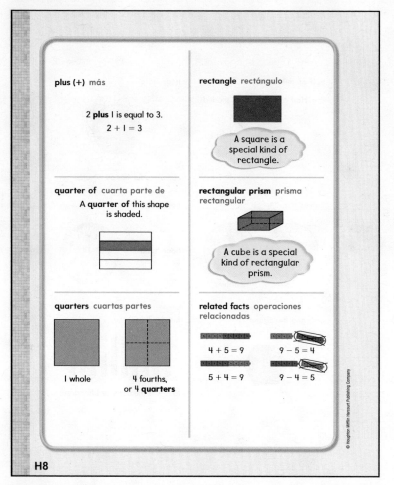

plus (+) más

2 **plus** 1 is equal to 3.
2 + 1 = 3

quarter of cuarta parte de

A **quarter of** this shape is shaded.

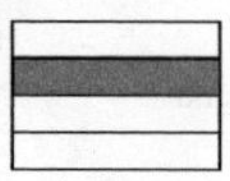

quarters cuartas partes

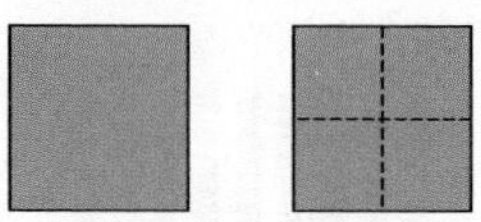

1 whole — 4 fourths, or 4 **quarters**

rectangle rectángulo

A square is a special kind of rectangle.

rectangular prism prisma rectangular

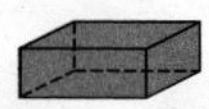

A cube is a special kind of rectangular prism.

related facts operaciones relacionadas

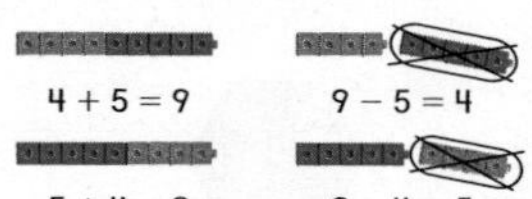

4 + 5 = 9 — 9 − 5 = 4
5 + 4 = 9 — 9 − 4 = 5

shortest el más corto

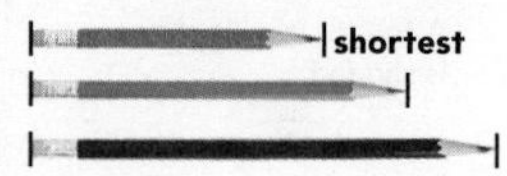

side lado

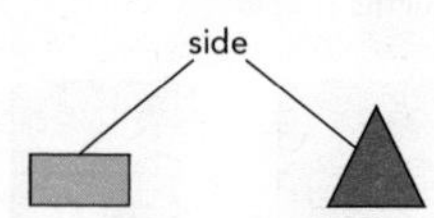

sphere esfera

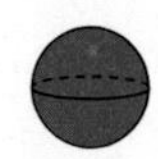

square cuadrado

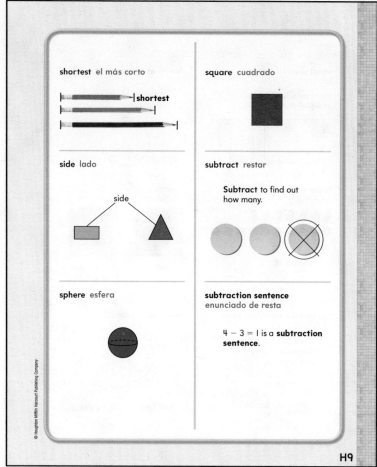

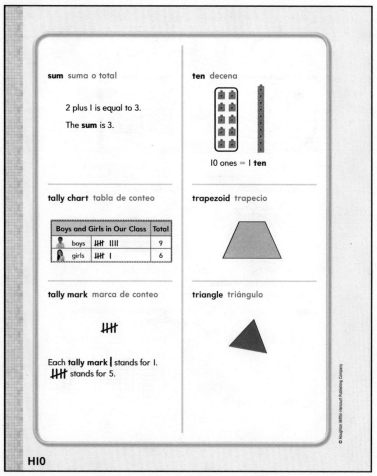

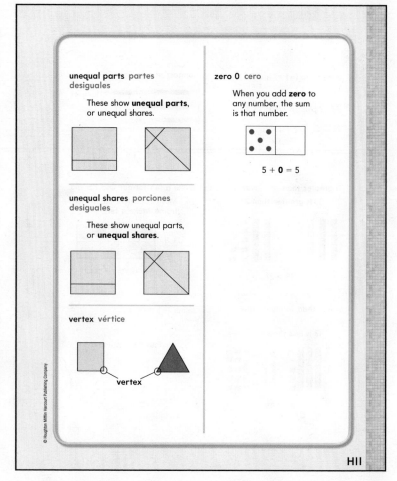

subtract restar

Subtract to find out how many.

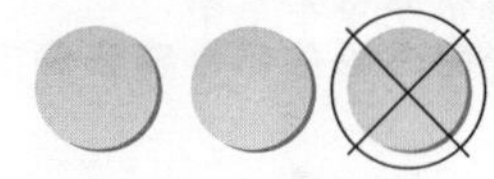

subtraction sentence enunciado de resta

4 − 3 = 1 is a **subtraction sentence**.

sum suma o total

2 plus 1 is equal to 3.

The **sum** is 3.

tally chart tabla de conteo

Boys and Girls in Our Class		Total
boys	𝍸 IIII	9
girls	𝍸 I	6

tally mark marca de conteo

Each **tally mark** | stands for 1.
𝍸 stands for 5.

ten decena

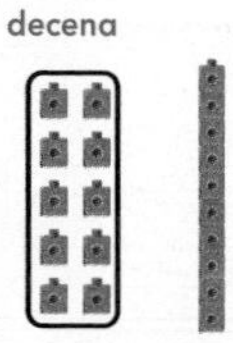

10 ones = 1 **ten**

trapezoid trapecio

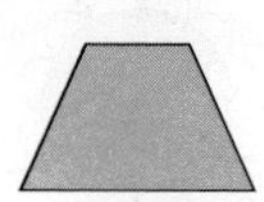

triangle triángulo

unequal parts partes desiguales

These show **unequal parts**, or unequal shares.

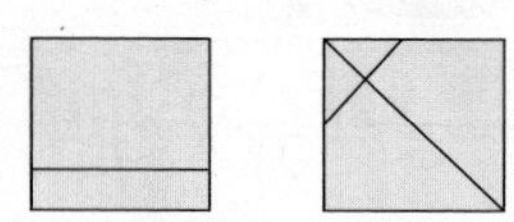

unequal shares porciones desiguales

These show unequal parts, or **unequal shares**.

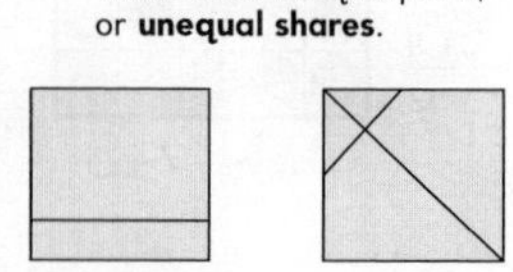

vertex vértice

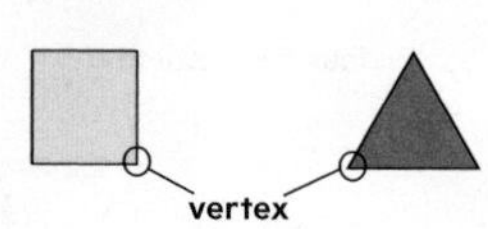

zero 0 cero

When you add **zero** to any number, the sum is that number.

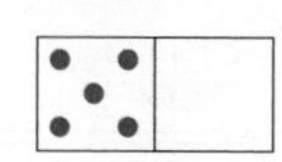

5 + **0** = 5

Teacher Notes

Professional Development References

Bahr, D. L., & de Garcia, L. A. (2010). *Elementary mathematics is anything but elementary.* Belmont, CA: Wadsworth.

Baldi, S., Jin, Y., Skemer, M., Green, P. J., & Herget, D. (2007). *Highlights from PISA 2006: Performance of U.S. 15-year-old students in science and mathematics literacy in an international context* (NCES-2008-016). National Center for Education Statistics, Institute of Education Sciences. Washington, DC: U.S. Department of Education.

Carpenter, T. P., Franke, M. L., & Levi, L. (2003). *Thinking mathematically: Integrating arithmetic and algebra in elementary school.* Portsmouth, NH: Heinemann.

Furhman, S. H., Resnick, L., & Shepard, L. (2009). Standards aren't enough. *Education Week, 29*(7), 28.

Gonzales, P., Williams, T., Jocelyn, L., Roey, S., Katsberg, D., & Brenwald, S. (2008). *Highlights from TIMSS 2007: Mathematics and science achievement of U.S. fourth- and eighth-grade students in an international context* (NCES 2009-001 Revised). National Center for Education Statistics, Institute of Education Sciences. Washington, DC: U.S. Department of Education.

Kennedy, L., Tipps, S., & Johnson, A. (2004). *Guiding children's learning of mathematics* (10th ed.). Belmont, CA: Wadsworth/Thomson Learning.

National Council of Teachers of Mathematics. (2000). *Principles and standards for school mathematics.* Reston, VA: Author.

National Council of Teachers of Mathematics. (2005). *Standards and Curriculum: A view from the nation, a joint report by the National Council of Teachers of Mathematics (NCTM) and the Association of State Supervisors of Mathematics (ASSM).* J. W. Lott & K. Nishimura (Eds.). Reston, VA: Author.

National Governors Association Center/ Council of Chief State School Officers (2010). Common Core State Standards for Mathematics. Retrieved from http://www.corestandards.org/the-standards/mathematics.

National Mathematics Advisory Panel. (2008). *Foundations for success: The final report of the National Mathematics Advisory Panel.* Washington, DC: U. S. Department of Education.

National Research Council. (2001). *Adding it up: Helping children learn mathematics.* J. Kilpatrick, J. Swafford, & B. Findell (Eds.). Washington, DC: National Academy Press.

Reed, D. S. (2009). Is there an expectations gap? Educational federalism and the demographic distribution of proficiency cut scores. *American Educational Research Journal, 46*(3), 718-742.

Reys, B. J., Chval, K., Dingman, S., McNaught, M., Regis, T. P., & Togashi, J. (2007). Grade-level learning expectations: A new challenge for elementary mathematics teachers. *Teaching Children Mathematics, 14*(1), 6-11.

Schneider, M. (2007). *National Assessment of Education Progress: Mapping 2005 state proficiency standards onto the NAEP scales.* Washington, DC: IES National Center for Education Statistics.

Schwartz, J. E. (2008). *Elementary mathematics pedagogical content knowledge: Powerful ideas for teachers*. Boston, MA: Pearson.

Van de Walle, J. A. (2004). *Elementary and middle school mathematics: Teaching developmentally* (5th ed.). Boston, MA: Pearson.

Van de Walle, J. A. (2007). *Elementary and middle school mathematics: Teaching developmentally* (6th ed.). Boston, MA: Pearson.

Wall, E., & Posamentier, A. (2007). *What successful math teachers do, Grades PreK–5 : 47 research-based strategies for the standards-based classroom*. Thousand Oaks, CA: Corwin Press.

Teacher Notes

Index

Teacher Edition and Planning Guide references in *italics*; Planning Guide references begin with PG

D

Teacher Edition and Planning Guide references in *italics*; Planning Guide references begin with PG

E

F

Teacher Edition and Planning Guide references in *italics*; Planning Guide references begin with PG

Teacher Edition and Planning Guide references in *italics*; Planning Guide references begin with PG

M

Teacher Edition and Planning Guide references in *italics*; Planning Guide references begin with PG

Q

R

S

T

Teacher Edition and Planning Guide references in *italics*; Planning Guide references begin with PG

Teacher Edition and Planning Guide references in *italics*; Planning Guide references begin with PG